LETTERS FROM EDWARD THOMAS
TO GORDON BOTTOMLEY

Letters from Edward Thomas to Gordon Bottomley

Edited and introduced by
R. George Thomas

London
OXFORD UNIVERSITY PRESS
NEW YORK   TORONTO
1968

Oxford University Press, Ely House, London W. 1

GLASGOW NEW YORK TORONTO MELBOURNE WELLINGTON
CAPE TOWN SALISBURY IBADAN NAIROBI LUSAKA ADDIS ABABA
BOMBAY CALCUTTA MADRAS KARACHI LAHORE DACCA
KUALA LUMPUR HONG KONG TOKYO

Printed in Great Britain

CONTENTS

PLATES

INTRODUCTION

More than thirty years ago the poet and dramatist, Gordon Bottomley, paid a visit to the English Society at the University College of South Wales and Monmouthshire and pleaded eloquently for a revival of interest in poetic drama if the outworn commercial theatre was to be replaced by a 'theatre unborn'. He was a bearded, patriarchal figure and a packed student audience in the Women's Junior Common Room heard him with sympathetic understanding and, to his unconcealed surprise and delight, plied him with questions and flocked around him afterwards—and even planned to perform some of his plays. It was the gala evening of a very flourishing society and my only meeting with the friend of Edward Thomas about whom he spoke briefly, with restrained feeling. He was delighted to learn that Thomas's friend, Gwili, had been a librarian and wartime teacher, in the University, but expressed some surprise that the College Library did not possess a complete set of Thomas's published works. On 8 June 1940, after a brief correspondence with Sir Frederick Rees, Principal of the College, Gordon Bottomley presented to the Cardiff University College Library the manuscript of Thomas's *Beautiful Wales*, with the following words: 'After treasuring it for 35 years (sent 8.iv.05) I grow old; and private possessions are in danger of destruction by enemy action. I am happy in transferring it to the greater safety of the University College of Cardiff, where I myself in the past have received a welcoming hospitality, to represent a great Welshman in his own ancestral quarter of Wales.' At the same time he announced the hope that the letters of Edward Thomas written to him 'shall pass into your Library's ownership' after his time. On 24 June 1940 he deposited them in the Library strongroom 'on temporary loan, until our present dangers are past' and added, in a covering note, 'if, however, it is in their custody at the time of my death, it is then to become the property of the College, for preservation among the Mss. in the College Library'. After Bottomley's death on 25 August 1948 it was agreed by the Senate and Library Committee of the College that I should, with the approval of the poet's widow, prepare an edition of the letters for future publication, preferably after the fiftieth anniversary of Thomas's death at Arras on Easter Monday 1917.

The box deposited by Bottomley contains 238 letters or postcards from Thomas, as well as some verses and music used in *Beautiful Wales*, an early review cutting, four explanatory notes by Bottomley, a letter from Helen Thomas (12 April 1917) announcing Edward's death, and a letter from Eleanor Farjeon (18 April 1917) written on behalf of Mrs. Thomas. Some of the later letters are in pencil and a few have faded, but the College Library has a photographic copy of all the letters. The present edition contains 181 of them in their entirety except for a few short references of a personal nature that might give offence to close relatives of Thomas's friends. The omitted letters are of three kinds: brief notes and postcards about the transmission and receipt of proofs and books, postcards or telegrams arranging meetings or visits, and working material about *Wales* and *The Pocket Book of Songs for the Open Air*. All omissions are recorded in the footnotes to subsequent letters.

II

Bottomley's kindness and attractive personality are well preserved for us by his friend and literary executor, Professor Claude Colleer Abbott, in an introduction to Gordon Bottomley's *Poems and Plays* and in *Poet and Painter: Being the correspondence between Gordon Bottomley and Paul Nash 1910–1946*.[1] Born in 1874, incapacitated by crippling ill health for most of his early life until 1920, and confined to comparative isolation at Cartmel and Silverdale, his gift for friendship and for ready sponsorship of young artists found a natural outlet in correspondence. His own and his wife's letters to Paul Nash indicate the kindliness and genuine interest in the aspirations of his friends that must have nourished and sustained Edward Thomas during the long

---

[1] Gordon Bottomley, *Poems and Plays*, compiled with an Introduction by Claude Colleer Abbott, 1953. *Poet and Painter: Being the correspondence between Gordon Bottomley and Paul Nash 1900–1946*. Edited by C. C. Abbott and Anthony Bertram, 1953.

intervals between their infrequent meetings. Their natures and experiences interlocked with complementary exactitude. Throughout their friendship Bottomley was in constant danger from haemorrhages and spent long periods confined either to his room or to his bed. Supported by warm parental affection and the devoted care of his wife, Emily, he faced all his difficulties with a calm serenity, accepting his ill health as a fine opportunity to live 'a life of passionate, intense meditation and contemplation' of 'that part of the spiritual world where beauty is law'. For him the imagination worked by 'still and inward symmetries':

> Imagination is acceptance wrought
> When things beyond ourselves with faint sounds press
> Upon the limits of the consciousness.

Thomas entered this closed world like some 'Gipsy-Scholar' or

> Some tall hero still unknown
> Out of the Mabinogion,

bringing news from the literary world of London and the South. Quickly the two men forged a bond of friendship based on their common love of poetry, songs, and the life of ordinary country people. Such interests found expression in Thomas's essays and topographical works and in the plays that Bottomley had begun to write and which later established his name as a verse-dramatist in England, Scotland, and America. At first they disagreed about the premisses and nature of poetry; in public reviews, and in private discourse, Thomas was critical of Bottomley's achievement as a poet, though he shared and fostered his aspirations. But their liking for each other survived all technical disagreements and when, years later, Thomas had met Robert Frost and had expounded Frost's 'theory of verse' to Bottomley, the latter found the idea 'convincing as Thomas expressed it'. As Bottomley recalled in 1945, 'his thought has remained with me ever since, never long dormant in my own practice of verse; and has led me, for many years now, to believe that poetry is only complete when the voice makes it audible, and that THE SOUND OF POETRY IS PART OF ITS MEANING'.[1]

Only Bottomley's last letter to Thomas has survived, but the

[1] Gordon Bottomley, 'A Note on Edward Thomas', *The Welsh Review*, Vol. IV, No. 3, September 1945, p. 175 and pp. 177–8.

slippered ease with which Thomas writes to him, moving so naturally from critical comment to gossip, or turning aside from intense introspection to convey wry self-disparagement, is sufficient testimony to the firmness and depth of their understanding. Inordinately shy with strangers, Edward Thomas had the precious gift of friendship and a great deal of his unpublished correspondence still remains in private hands. The tone and content of the letters I have seen suggest that, apart from his lifelong friendships with Harry Hooton, Ian MacAlister, and Jesse Berridge, Edward Thomas's most intimate friends were James Guthrie and Gordon Bottomley. Until he met Frost in 1913, it was with these two fellow-craftsmen that he discussed his secret aspirations as an artist and writer. Can there be any significance in the fact that it was Guthrie who published *Six Poems By Edward Eastaway* and that the first substantial body of Eastaway's poems appeared in *An Annual of New Poetry*, sponsored by Bottomley and his friends, Lascelles Abercrombie and R. C. Trevelyan? Guthrie and Bottomley were firm friends and Bottomley made much of his own Highland heritage on his mother's side. These are intangible speculations, but I believe that this shared sense of a Celtic heritage—which was such an influential current in literary opinion during the two decades before 1914—partially explains Thomas's willingness to open his heart to these two men, as much as he ever dared to anyone else except Frost. In 1919, in a dedicatory poem to *Gruach* (the first of his plays on Scottish themes), Bottomley restates his creed as a writer. He found assurance that 'romance is wisdom and truth', and desired from art

> not the mean content
> Or discontent of average helpless souls
> But unmatched moments and exceptional deeds.

In the same spirit ten years earlier, he had introduced his play, *Riding to Lithend*, with a poem to Edward Thomas:

> Because your heart could understand
> The hopes of their primeval land,
> The hearts of dim heroic forms
> Made clear by tenderness and storms.

The enveloping irony of their mature relationship is never mentioned by either man: Bottomley, the invalid who believed that 'art is a distillation of life and nature,' continued to support Thomas, the great walker who was a sorry victim of overwork and melancholy, with practical aid and sage advice. The links of their friendship held and, as Helen Thomas told me, Thomas was determined to spend part of his final embarkation leave at Silverdale. In *A Note on Edward Thomas* Bottomley recalled his last visit:

We had him for half a week in, I think, the first days of December, 1916; a month, that year, of clear skies, some sun, and flurries of snow. Those days are still vividly memorable. He was a happy, tranquillizing presence, with a steadfast, gentle outlook on new dangers and old troubles; newly and finely tempered, no longer moody, or distracted about the future. He still spoke of joining Robert Frost in the United States after the war: we still spoke of books and pictures and friends and old songs, as we had always done: and he walked the near-by fells again, reminding himself of those farther off which he could not reach for lack of time.

It was too equable and quiet a time for salient episodes to stand out—a time to be remembered and cherished as a whole, by reason of his grave happiness, and of his tender thoughtfulness that stilled the inevitable wild surmise in us until he had gone. One moment I do remember again on account of his comment. The room in which I write of him is the one in which we spent those days, an upper chamber with a wide outlook on sea, river, and mountain. As we talked, I looked up, then drew his attention to an epic turbulence of storm sweeping towards us from the mountains of the Kirkstone Pass on the northern horizon. He watched for an appreciable time, then said 'You are a fortunate fellow. . . .' I indicated that quite a number of people would not be willing to pay my price of ill-health for such fortune, and that I might be said to deserve the compensation in the circumstances. But he would not agree that so much *could* be deserved. That storm finds a place in a poem called 'The Sheiling', to be found in his *Collected Poems*: a poem that contains the whole essence of those farewell days. He left us before dawn on a December morning: his husky mellow voice called up to me for the last time as he passed under my open window.

III

With little qualification the letters to Gordon Bottomley constitute a marginal comment on Edward Thomas's writing life; they illuminate and interpret his attitude to the work which, until he became a soldier, was the central activity of his life. For a knowledge of his books is essential if the full flavour of the letters—and their writer—is to be understood. Those of his friends who, in the immediate postwar years, expressed disappointment with his letters, because they dealt exclusively with technical literary topics, were reading them for the wrong things. They were searching for letters that would convey to others the rare quality of a man they had known through conversation and who had suddenly surprised them with his verse. As most of his published letters make clear, this quest was doomed to failure. Except in the letters written to his wife, during his frequent absences from her, and in these to Bottomley—whom he met so infrequently during their fifteen years of correspondence—the, letters to his English friends were mere notes about practical matters that gave no echo of his conversation. He never indulged in writing as a way of trying out a *persona* or exploiting a 'character'. He valued his craft as a writer because it offered him a unique, if dissatisfying opportunity for faithful self expression. His failure to match his style to the clamant demands of journalism, with its consequent disastrous effect on his income and way of life—especially in the three years before the War—is proof enough of the value he attached to honesty in writing of any sort.

Frequently he apologizes to Bottomley because his letters offer the fag-end of a tired brain but, although he never says as much, these late-night letters are substitutes for conversation after a long day's work spent in solitude and isolation with his books. This is their value. They provide an intimate and candid journal of a working writer's life, without posturing and certainly without any thought of posterity. Like any other gloss, they should ideally be read alongside the text they embellish; read in isolation from his books, they can be quite misleading. (For this reason I have tried to give frequent references to his books in my notes.) This is particularly true of the comments he makes on his later books: fatigue, dissatisfaction with proofs, and a growing realization of missed opportunities are the natural reactions of any busy writer and, at all times, Thomas's energies were intolerably tried by the double stress of his professionally-developed critical faculty and his own physical temperament. Read in conjunction with his books, these letters cast serious doubt on the use of the description 'hack-writing' that has slipped increasingly into much uninformed posthumous comment on his prose writings. Used as a short cut—an inadequate substitute for his voluminous working notebooks—the letters at least demonstrate the patient care, the intensive scholarship, and the fastidious honesty with which he prepared himself for each successive publisher's assignment.

IV

Edward Thomas must have been a critic of rhymes in his nursery. How much generous help and encouragement many living poets owe to his counsel only themselves could say. To his candour, too. For the true cause, he believed, is better served by an uncompromising 'Trespassers will be prosecuted' than by an amiable 'All are welcome'.

Walter de la Mare, Westminster Gazette, 28 April 1917

His knowledge of poetry soon took me out of my depth. To the younger men he was a Rhadamanthus and a Cerberus in one. He was the man with the Keys to the Paradise of English poetry, and probably reviewed more modern verse than any critic of his time. . . . The quality of his prose was apt to be too costly for the modern market, and the result was often Love and Literature, with its precarious awards, literally in a cottage. There is such a thing as Welsh influence, no doubt: but there is also a Welsh pride, and Thomas would be beholden to no man for a penny that he had not earned. His pride in the dignity of letters was intense. . . . His system of writing was almost too intensive, if that be possible.

Thomas Seccombe, Times Literary Supplement, 16 April 1917

Obituary notices are rarely precise repositories of literal truth and yet these two judgements can still be verified by anyone who takes the trouble to read the reviews that Thomas wrote between 1902 and 1915. They are so numerous, so widely scattered and so often unsigned, that this is no easy task; consequently one is not surprised that the posthumous judgement of Thomas has been directed towards interpreting his poetry, dipping disdainfully into his prose works (when they were available), with a consequent neglect of all but a handful of his more accessible reviews. To neglect the truth about Thomas's life as a writer between 1902 and 1914 is to misunderstand his poetry and to throw away a useful key to the changing critical audience brought

7

about by the Harmsworthian revolution in newspaper publication. He was himself clearly aware of the changing nature of public critical practice and, in March 1914, he contributed to Harold Monro's journal, *Poetry and Drama*, a clear, sharply-worded and thoughtful article on 'Reviewing: An unskilled labour'. By that time he had ceased to earn a competent, if modest, living as a regular reviewer for an influential daily newspaper. His pulpit in the *Daily Chronicle*—whose daily literary page, twenty years earlier, had been one of the revolutionary features in modern daily journalism effected by the editors (Fletcher, Massingham, and Nevinson)—had disappeared under the impact of James Milne's determination to modernize the paper with an emphasis on 'honest, human writing in this modern age of realism, yet grace'![1] Milne continued to use Thomas as an occasional reviewer of modern poetry and nature books, but with much reduced allocation of space; the rest of his criticism found a place in the mushroom growth of weeklies, monthlies, and short-lived quarterlies that proliferated between 1910 and 1914.

The sheer amount of Thomas's reviews is forbidding and in the notes to these letters I have tried, without any attempt at completeness, to indicate its range and bulk as well as drawing attention to significant single reviews. Ideally the footnotes should have contained ample quotation from the reviews. There is an abundance of apposite, quotable material, but to use it would have upset the balance of the story that the letters themselves unfold. One special quality of this correspondence is that Bottomley was Thomas's ideal reader. He was a writer of (enforced) leisure with an enormous appetite for books and an informed interest in music, painting, literature, and drama; he seemed to represent the kind of reader for whom Massingham and Nevinson devised their literary columns—the kind of man who, after the War, supported *Criterion*, *Adelphi*, *Life and Letters*, and *The English Review*. The notes to the letters are designed merely to suggest the shared interests of the two friends; they are in no way exhaustive and fall far short of providing a complete picture of the range, depth, and consistent insight of Thomas's criticism.

Aided by these letters, and the bibliographical work of Mr.

[1] James Milne, *A Window in Fleet Street*, 1931, pp. 294–311.

R. P. Eckert, I had been able to trace and read most of Thomas's identifiable (and clearly recognizable) reviews between 1900 and 1909. And, then, Mrs. Helen Thomas kindly made available to me the most invaluable of aids: six volumes of newspaper cuttings of the poet's longer reviews and a bound index to them which I learned to call, in true Mabinogion style, the 'Red Book of Steep'. The first volume begins with the *Daily Chronicle* articles dating from 1902—probably after Thomas succeeded Lionel Johnson—and the sixth volume ends with various weekly, daily, and monthly reviews that are not clearly dated but belong to the spring and summer of 1914. Many of the earlier volumes have been 'placed' by Thomas, with occasional indications of sub-editorial alterations to his work; the later volumes have mostly been identified by Mrs. Thomas.

Not all the articles are signed. Many of the earlier ones were written for weeklies before the practice of signed reviews had come in, and, moreover, we have James Milne's word for the fact that Thomas, unlike most critics, was never fussy about having his name attached to his work. However, as these letters to Bottomley make quite clear, Thomas carefully collected his reviews in the *Chronicle* when away from home, and since these volumes, which are uniform in binding, were not destroyed in the bonfires of 1916 when Thomas moved from Steep to High Beech, it must be assumed that he knew their value and wished to preserve them. My own follow-up of the clues supplied in these letters has uncovered many more shorter notices and a few longer ones. At a conservative estimate I think that these pre-served reviews represent about two-thirds of Thomas's total output as a reviewer.

A minimum count, based on the entries in the 'Red Book', will best show the implication of his frequent remarks to Bottomley that he has been busy and can write only a short letter after a long day in his study. The index begins in November 1900 and ends in July(?) 1914. It contains 102 pages, representing a minimum of 1,122 reviews—just over a million words about 1,200 books. During the first four years he averaged 80 reviews a year and in 1913–14—when his daily reviewing slackened off and he was writing 4 or 5 books annually—he wrote only 60 full-length reviews. So that between the Christmasses of 1905 and 1912 he was contributing 100 signed (or full-length) reviews annually to the *Daily Chronicle* or the *Daily Post* (or to both), to *The Nation*, *The Athenæum*, *The Academy*, or *The English Review*, besides at least 50 shorter notices to weeklies and, after 1907, a monthly article or two-column unsigned review to *The Bookman*. The output is staggering because, as these letters imply, none of the preparation for these reviews was skimped and, when the same book was reviewed in two, three, or four different places, each additional review extended and amplified the original judgement. As a walker and countryman, Thomas may have traversed the length and breadth of southern England by ordnance map and compass; as a critic of books, desperately in need of money, he seemed incapable of taking even an allowable short-cut.

The quality of all this writing, which admittedly suited his temperamental desire to write continuously for about 1,200 to 1,500 words, is well sustained; and a random check of the footnotes to the letters written between 1908 and 1910 will illustrate the range of topics covered. He was competent in French, German, Latin and, as befitted a scholar in the Eighth at St. Paul's, in Greek. Throughout his life, even as an Oxford undergraduate, he was employed as a specialist reviewer of nature and country books of all kinds and he remained the premier interpreter of modern poetry until June 1915, when he wrote the obituary notice on Rupert Brooke for *The English Review*. The list of his 'first mentions' of new writers of quality, a long tally, included Synge, Masefield, Conrad, Galsworthy, and Lawrence. Not once has his judgement on a significant writer been revised by later critics, for even his enthusiasm for T. Sturge Moore, W. H. Davies, and C. M. Doughty was qualified from the outset in the direction of our present-day assessment. To my mind he was the ideal reviewer for a serious writer—thorough, detached, honest and critically aware, ready at all times to reread a book and then to record his altered opinions. In contrast with most of his fellow-columnists, both in the dailies and the weeklies, he allowed sustained quotation to form part of his interpretation and, although his severities were sharply turned, they were directed towards the work under review and never used as a pyrotechnical exhibition of the reviewer's 'personality'.

Smooth, vague verbiage was anathema to him and when, on rare occasions, it has crept editorially into the cuttings that are preserved in the bound volumes, Thomas's pencil has silently deleted it. His heyday as a reviewer coincided with the golden days of the cheap reprints of the standard English writers and the rapid development of the scholarly industry that has grown up around 'Eng. Lit.'. Even ignoring all other evidence, and relying solely on the evidence supplied in his series of *Daily Chronicle* reviews of the successive volumes of the *Cambridge History of English Literature*, Thomas emerges as a thoroughly competent scholar in this particular field.

His closest friends, men like Bottomley, Jesse Berridge, de la Mare, and (to a lesser extent) W. H. Davies, valued the honest tenacity with which Thomas expressed in public his objections to failures in their work. Perceptive editors, like Nevinson, Belloc, Ford Madox Hueffer, H. Monro, and R. A. Scott-James continued to employ him as a critic when his native candour might conceivably have justified their dropping him because, in some influential quarters, his opinions had given offence. In a generous review of the posthumous volume of Thomas's *Poems*, 1917, T. Sturge Moore twice refers to the 'opinionated savage youngster'[1] that Thomas had been before he had 'saddened and mellowed' and Ezra Pound continued a feud against him long after his death. And yet Edward Thomas's four reviews of Pound's work between 1909 and 1914 constitute the best testimony to his honest consistency as a critic. He backed his judgement—it was never fancy. He refused to clap a label on a writer and then to exploit that label in order to save himself the trouble of further effort and hard reassessment. Thomas was much ridiculed by his literary-luncheon London friends for his enthusiastic reception of the unknown Pound's *Personae* and, a little later, he expressed in print his own reasoned disappointment with *Lustra*; but his long review of *The Spirit of Romance* and his shorter comment on Pound's contribution to *Des Imagistes* were a favourable and perceptive underwriting of his original re-reading of *Personae*. Because of his scrupulous dedication to the truth of interpretation he failed to make a living as a literary journalist, while less perceptive reviewers flourished. This same quality, which endeared him to his friends, has been strangely neglected by historians of the first twenty years of poetry in this century. 'We turn from his clear, abstemious, unemphatic prose to the

[1] T. Sturge Moore, *Some Soldier Poets*, 1939, pp. 77–85.

11

verses of the *Poems*. Thomas had been criticizing other men's poetry for twenty years, and all these years had been steadily storing up his own,' wrote Walter de la Mare in the *Times Literary Supplement* of 18 October 1917. The validity of this accurate assessment is borne out by the evidence of these letters to Bottomley.

V

Edward Thomas possessed a beautiful speaking voice; its distinctive soft quality was undoubtedly part of the Welsh heritage that he treasured so much. 'He read in an almost unaccentuated monotone, slowly, clearly, so that not one word, not one shade of meaning was lost.' He was particularly sensitive to words and to songs: language, place-names, even the notes of individual birds retained a special interest for him throughout his life. When he came to the borders of sleep, it was silence that he heard and obeyed

> That I may lose my way
> And myself.

The dream land, that he had never seen before, would exact from him a song that could not be whispered even to his soul and demanded for its expression the use of 'a language not to be betrayed'—a language used by 'the trees and birds'. As he listened to the mill-water,

> Often the silentness
> Has but this one
> Companion: wherever one creeps in the other is:
> Sometimes a thought is drowned
> By it, sometimes
> Out of it climbs;
> All thoughts begin or end upon this sound.

The most cursory reading of his thirteen years of comment upon the verse of his contemporaries makes clear his hypersensitiveness to the charged and mysterious quality of words that are used by poets to reveal and communicate the hidden springs of a man's inner life. In March 1914, when he cast up the account of his life as 'an unskilled labourer' who worked at reviewing—'the only thing to be said for it is that it produces money, which produces food and clothing for aged parents, fair wives, innocent children'—Thomas lodged two specific bills of complaint against the unprofitable craft: 'It is nothing, masquerading as something' and the reviewer 'has no idea whom he is addressing. He is writing in an indifferent vacuum.' Even so he believed that a careful answer to the following questions 'might help to turn reviewing from unskilled to skilled labour: Is he to address the author? Or readers who know the book, or who do not? Is he to hold forth simply to his equals who happen not to write for a living?' Shy reticence and ironic humour were an essential part of Thomas's personality and it would be perilous to discount their part in any of his published comments on himself or his craft. Allowing for this, I believe that this article on reviewing, like the one on 'How I Began',[1] expresses a desire that his written words should say something meaningful because they were addressed directly to someone he could recognize. For him, ideally, the art of talking was inseparable from the art of writing: both should be conversation, not for its own sake, but as an earnest of the deep-seated need of one human being to communicate fully with another. The letters to Bottomley succeed triumphantly in passing this test.

Having known these letters for over twenty years and having re-read them frequently since 1960, I have been most impressed by the uniform tone that pervades the correspondence. True writing for him was not a mere act of self-expression or a necessary social act of communication: it was literally an extension of his innermost thought. The period of gestation was always long and arduous but, once pen was set to paper, he wrote effortlessly until he was done—and then he came to a full stop. These letters—like the few preserved manuscripts of his prose—bear few marks of correction and, by the graded spacings between phrases and sentences, they seem to convey the slow deliberation of his speech and—if it is not too fanciful a phrase—the captured echo of his thought. Thomas re-drafted and altered a few of his poems drastically and, according to the little evidence we have, he constantly altered minutiae in the typescript of others until he embarked for France in January 1917. The dates

[1] 'Reviewing: An unskilled Labour', *Poetry and Drama*, vol. II, No. 1, March 1914, pp. 37–41; 'How I Began', reprinted in Edward Thomas, *The Last Sheaf*, 1928, pp. 15–20.

attached to individual poems in the two extant manuscript books of his poems indicate the speed at which they were composed: 141 poems between December 1914 and Christmas 1916, most of them while he was a soldier under training but with considerable freedom of movement. Once he had decided to write verse his poetry began 'to run' freely. In this respect his first letter to Bottomley was prophetic: *his* lyrics, like his letters were supplied by the Muse (not a favourite word of his).

Could one but discover it precisely, there exists a close relationship between the total effect of reading these letters and of reading through his collected poems: the transition from the one voice to the other is smooth and unbroken. For I find that, read in their entirety, these letters conform to Thomas's own praise of Frost's achievement in *North of Boston*:[1] 'a unique one, as perfectly Mr. Frost's own as his vocabulary, the ordinary English speech of a man accustomed to poetry and philosophy . . . possessing a kind of healthy, natural delicacy like Wordsworth's, or at least Shelley's rather than that of Keats.' This is not the flourish of a peroration. Thomas's opinion of the language of Wordsworth, Shelley, and Keats was based on careful scholarship and sustained re-reading. So the preference for Shelley— his adolescent and undergraduate favourite—curiously underlines the constancy of his taste when he came to pronounce on Frost's poetry that confirmed (and also released) his own inner vision of what writing poetry in the twentieth century should mean for him. Because of this consistency of purpose, it is no surprise that he should shy from revealing the citadel of his most personal utterances under his own much-publicized name. He was clearly aware, and distrustful, of the uneasy relationship that could exist between a writer's character and his personality; reticence was part of his character and, for his intimates, it was an essential ingredient of his humour. The letters, like the poems, are direct and personal, without gush, parade of irrelevant information, or unnecessary assertion: their silences, like the generous margin that usually surrounds the careful script of each page, also add significantly to their total statement.

The reader may judge for himself how well these letters measure up to the standard of Thomas's own review of E. V.

1 See Letter 153, note 1.

Lucas's *The Gentlest Art, a Choice of Letters by Entertaining Hands*:

The best letters, or most of them, are literature addressed to one instead of to the world, while literature is addressed to the world and has to be given its particular application by each for himself. For the letter writer, like the child, is for the time being a genius singularly moved to say what has been hitherto hidden from the world. And the order of literature which they most resemble is the essay. . . . De Quincey, I believe, it was who pointed to the letters of women as examples of English unsurpassed in its directness, idiom, and purity, and it might be maintained that letters have at many periods been a strong influence against the tendency of literature to stiffen itself by conformity to a once good fashion, that they have been an undercurrent of homeliness and truth second in importance to nothing except the influence of nature.[1]

Here, in one paragraph are gathered so many of Edward Thomas's chief preoccupations and insights as a writer: the desire to find an appropriate listener, the wish to uncover the hidden places of the spirit, the concern to lead literature back to homeliness and truth, and the ever-present reminder that man is irrevocably at one with the natural world that surrounds him. As Letter 150—and so many others—can show, he was, in truth, all of a piece. To this correspondent, if not to some others, his pen was as flexible and responsive as an extra limb and Bottomley protested, with justice, against the one-sided picture of his friend that the official biography provoked from some critics in 1937:

It was a cruelly untrue valuation of a patient, suffering man who had his own steadfast, unspectacular heroism; a continually thwarted delight in life lived naturally, which nevertheless remained a delight— a man of pride in his blood, a spiritual insight that was most nourished by the aspects of uncivilized nature; of a very touching humility about his own abilities and powers, which made him woundable to wincing, and put him at the mercy of hard-headed business men when his living depended on them.[2]

We should be grateful to Gordon Bottomley for preserving intact the letters that substantiate such a gracious epitaph.

[1] The *Daily Chronicle*, 10 February 1908.
[2] 'A Note on Edward Thomas', p. 166.

VI

Thomas was a practised letter writer who liked to set his text neatly within the page and, although he often varied this handwriting, his script is quite clear and it has been possible to follow him faithfully. The letters are printed exactly as they were written with the following exceptions:

1. It has not been practicable to reproduce the significant gaps between phrases and sentences which seem to be a special feature of Thomas's writing both in these letters and elsewhere in the manuscript material I have examined. Otherwise his punctuation has been followed precisely, except for the occasional insertion of an omitted comma after the introduction 'My dear Gordon'.

2. Most of these letters were hurriedly written and obvious slips of the pen have been silently corrected. Where a word or letter has been omitted, it has been supplied in square brackets.

3. Every address from which he writes is given in full in the first instance, but thereafter abbreviated. The forms of dates have been standardized, except where they occur within the text of a letter. Other additions (*Sunday, Wednesday morning* etc.) are reproduced as they occur.

4. Letters and postcards here printed are numbered for convenient cross-reference; omitted letters and cards, all of which are indicated in the notes, are not numbered.

5. All titles are standardized. Those of short poems and articles are printed in Roman type between single quotation marks; those of long poems, books, plays, journals, newspapers, in italics. All foreign words and phrases are printed in italics, as are the rare medical terms and the occasional sub-headings that indicate that a letter has been resumed after an interval. Words underlined by Thomas to give special emphasis, or to indicate tone, are in italics.

6. Usually, words or phrases struck out by the writer have been silently omitted; they are rare and only one such sentence has been retained.

7. There are a few deliberate omissions, all unimportant, to avoid hurting the feelings of living people, or in obedience to the

written request of Gordon Bottomley. Such omissions are clearly indicated and the total number of words involved is 319.

8. At six points in these letters Gordon Bottomley inserted explanatory notes, which serve to link the correspondence. Whenever these occur they are printed in italics and followed by the initials 'GB'. Occasionally, too, he has annotated the text of the letters with names or short comments; such annotations are included in the footnotes to the relevant letters, followed by the initials 'GB' in square brackets.

My own annotations are of three sorts. Some are necessary for the ready identification of people, events, and objects. Others, forming the bulk of the notes, indicate the scope of Thomas's activity as a reviewer; in these notes his reviews are traced to their source and, occasionally, quotations are given from significant reviews. Finally, cross-references are made to extant letters, already in print or in private hands, when it has seemed necessary to fill in some longish gaps in the letters to Bottomley, particularly during the last four years of Thomas's life.

The following abbreviations are used in the Biographical Table and in the annotations to the text, after the first reference, which is given in full:

A	*The Academy*
AIW	Helen Thomas, *As It Was*, Heinemann, 1926. All page references are to the combined edition of *As It Was* and *World Without End*, Faber and Faber, 1946
B	*The Bookman*
COET	*The Childhood of Edward Thomas*, a fragment of autobiography, Faber and Faber, 1938
CP	Edward Thomas, *Collected Poems*, with a foreword by Walter de la Mare, Faber and Faber, 1936
DC	The *Daily Chronicle*
DN	The *Daily News*
EF	Eleanor Farjeon, *Edward Thomas: The Last Four Years*, Oxford University Press, 1958
ER	*The English Review*
ET	Edward Thomas
GB	Gordon Bottomley

JB   Unpublished letters from Edward Thomas to Canon
          Jesse Berridge
JM   John Moore, *The Life and Letters of Edward
          Thomas*, Heinemann, 1939
MP   The *Morning Post*
N   *The Nation*
Poems and Plays   Gordon Bottomley, *Poems and Plays*, com-
          piled with an Introduction by Claude Colleer
          Abbott, The Bodley Head, 1953
Poems of Thirty Years   Gordon Bottomley, *Poems of Thirty
          Years*, Constable, 1925
Red Book Six bound volumes of Edward Thomas's longer
          reviews. Now in the Library, University College,
          Cardiff
RPE   Robert P. Eckert, *Edward Thomas/A Biography
          And A Bibliography*, Dent, 1937
S   *The Speaker*
SR   *The Saturday Review*
W   *The World*
WS   *The Week's Survey*
WWE   Helen Thomas, *World Without End*, Heinemann,
          1931. All page references are to the combined
          edition of *As It Was* and *World Without End*, Faber
          and Faber, 1946

Both in the Biographical Table and in the footnotes, books
written by Thomas are referred to by their titles, without bibliographical elaboration. The Appendix lists all works by him
published in book form in Great Britain; it is essentially a booklist and not a complete bibliographical study. Unless otherwise
stated, the place of publication was London; for American editions the reader is referred to *RPE*, pp. 185–277. The question
of reprints and subsequent editions of Thomas's books is extremely complicated and I have merely tried to indicate significant reprints, the inclusion of some books in new series, and any
subsequent changes of publishers.

I owe debts of gratitude to so many people that it would be
impossible to name them all. My chief debt is to the late Helen
Thomas and her daughters, Bronwen and Myfanwy, who have
generously placed at my disposal their time as well as the source

material and photographs in their possession. My second debt is to the Senate, Library Committee, and Librarian of my own College who first invited me to edit these letters and then made it possible for me to complete the task by encouragement and material assistance. I am also indebted to the Oxford University Press, particularly to Mr. John Bell and Mr. Jon Stallworthy for their advice and wise counsel during the various stages of seeing this book through the press. My special debt to Professor Gwyn Jones cannot be adequately expressed here; his special knowledge, his timely encouragement, and the private material in his possession have at all times been at my back.

I am also greatly indebted to Professor C. C. Abbott for permission to print Gordon Bottomley's last letter to Edward Thomas; again to Professor Abbott and Professor Gwyn Jones for permission to quote from Bottomley's article in *The Welsh Review* (1945); to the late Helen Thomas and Faber and Faber for permission to include short extracts from *As It Was, World Without End*, and *The Childhood of Edward Thomas*; to her daughters, Bronwen and Myfanwy, for the loan and use of photographs and sketches; to Mr. Christian Berridge for permission to quote from Edward Thomas's letters to his father; to Mr. Gervase Farjeon and the Oxford University Press for permission to quote from *Edward Thomas: The Last Four Years*; to Mr. Alun I. John for permission to read his unpublished dissertation, *The Life and Works of Edward Thomas* (1953), deposited in the library of University College, Cardiff; to Mr. Stanley Smith for many kindnesses while we both used the *Red Book*; to Mr. Rowland Watson, Secretary of the Edward Thomas Memorial Committee, who, with unfailing courtesy and devotion, has placed so much information and material at my disposal; to Mr. D. H. Davies of my College Library, and to Mrs. Celia Coward and Mrs. H. I. Fawcett for accurate and cheerful assistance.

My wife and two sons know best of all my overwhelming debt to their forbearance and unobtrusive assistance which it is now my pleasure to record.

R.G.T.

November 1967

BIOGRAPHICAL TABLE

1878	3 March	Philip Edward Thomas born at Lambeth, the eldest son of Philip Henry and Elizabeth Thomas. Parents and grandparents came from South Wales and/or Monmouthshire. His father was a staff clerk for light railways and tramways at the Board of Trade. As the family grew—there were six sons—the family moved successively to Wandsworth, Clapham, and Balham.
1883–90		Attended various Board-schools and private schools. 'I exchanged the Board-school when I was ten for a private school. . . . When I was about twelve I entered my fourth school [Battersea Grammar School].' [*COET*, pp. 64 and 99]
1892		Makes the acquaintance of Dad Uzzell near Swindon, the home of his grandparents. 'I read books of travel, sport and natural history . . . but above all Richard Jefferies.' [*COET*, p. 134]
1893		'I had begun to write accounts of my walks in an approach as near as possible to the style of Jefferies. . . . My father wanted me to go to a Public School and I received special lessons in Latin verse and in Greek.' [*COET*, pp. 135–6]
1894	January	'I had gone to the Public School [St. Paul's]. . . . I had failed to win a scholarship; only in English did I make any show at all: and I entered a form consisting of a few boys who had won or were going to compete for history scholarships at Oxford and Cambridge. . . . I now had a faint ambition, both definite and indefinite, to do something in connection with literature or learning. . . . Still

		everything at school was an aimless task performed to the letter only.' [*COET*, pp. 141–4]
1894		A frequent visitor to the Wandsworth home of the critic and writer, James Ashcroft Noble. 'My father helped him a great deal with advice about writing and reading. . . . My father got several of them [his descriptions of nature] accepted by a weekly paper.' [*AIW*, pp. 16–17]
1895	Easter	Left St. Paul's at the end of term. In accord with his father's wishes, begins desultory reading for a Civil Service Examination. Essays published in *Globe, Academy, Speaker, New Age*. Friendship with Noble's second daughter, Helen. James Noble 'began to show signs of tuberculosis of the throat': Mrs. Noble forbids Helen to write to, or visit, ET [*AIW*, p. 25]. He walks from London to Swindon
	1 April	Begins 'A Diary in English Fields and Woods'
1896	30 March	Completes his 'Diary'
	3 April	J. A. Noble dies and Helen leaves home to become a child's governess. Work for Civil Service Examination abandoned. ET allowed to enter Oxford
	September	ET and Helen spend a 'honeymoon' at Swindon, 'and put up in the cottage of his old game-keeper friend'. [*AIW*, p. 43]
1897		*The Woodland Life*, by ET, published
	October	Matriculates as a non-collegiate student at Oxford. Helen becomes 'an intimate of a circle of people living in Hammersmith . . . artistic Bohemian people, young mostly'. [*AIW*, p. 51]
1898	March	Wins a history scholarship to Lincoln College. Frequent visits to Helen at Hammersmith and 'gradually got on better with the circle'. Continues his journalism. 'He

		was earning about £80 a year by writing. He became a more or less regular contributor to *The Speaker*, *The Academy*, and *The Literary World*.' [*AIW*, pp. 53–54]
1899	20 June	Edward and Helen married at Fulham Registry. Helen receives a legacy of £250 and continues her work as a governess until December when she lives with ET's parents
1900	15 January	Mervyn [Merfyn] born. Gordon Bottomley writes to Helen and Edward, who returns to Oxford. Helen and Mervyn live with Mrs. Thomas
	Summer	'It was no surprise to Edward, though a bitter disappointment to his father, when he got only a second-class degree.' [*WWE*, p. 80]. ET refuses to consider entering the Civil Service
	August	Moved for a few months to a small house in Atheldene Road, Earlsfield, and then to 7 Nightingale Parade, Balham. Occasional journalism; unsuccessful at various jobs as a sub-editor; works briefly with a Charity Organization
1901	June	Had earned £52 by his pen since leaving Oxford; had sold many of his Oxford books; and had begun occasional reviewing for the *Daily Chronicle*, whose literary editor was H. W. Nevinson
	September	Moves to Rose Acre Cottage (1 mile outside Bearsted), near Maidstone. Reviewing and 'practice essays' [*JB*]; sold books to realize £70. [*JB*]
1902	January	Sends manuscript of essays to various publishers
	May	More reviewing and reading proofs of his essays. [*JB*]
	June	*Horae Solitariae*, by ET, published. 'The title is the one unread book in my shelves— unopened in fact. . . . I keep it for its title and for its faintly shining old calf.' [*JB*]

	September	'The reviewers make me out a very fine chap.' [*JB*]
	30 September	First letter to Gordon Bottomley, who had probably written about *Horae*
	29 October	A daughter, Rachel Mary Bronwen, born
	November	On the death of Lionel Johnson, ET becomes a regular reviewer for the *Daily Chronicle*; earning less than £2 a week. Begins work on *The Poems of John Dyer*
	December	Busy with reviews
1903	11 February	Stays with his parents in London while looking for work. 'I have come to live in town for an indefinite length of time, because I am in debt, and am not earning much nor likely to, for some months.' [*JB*]
	16 February	Commissioned to write *Oxford* for £100, with a £20 advance
	May	ET and GB meet in London. *The Poems of John Dyer*, edited by ET, published
	14 June	'The book *Oxford* is practically finished.' [*JB*]
	Early July	Moves to cottage on Bearsted Green
	September	Consults a London specialist about ill health, irritation, and exhaustion
	October–December	Less work; exaggerated fears about editorial changes on the *Daily Chronicle*. Visits to Swindon and Warminster. ET contemplates emigrating to Canada with his school and college friend, Ian Mac-Alister. *Oxford*, painted by John Fulleylove, R.I., described by ET, published
1904	January	Returns to London and finds adequate reviewing. Meets Arthur Ransome
	February	At Bearsted Green. Helen falls ill and spends a holiday at Walmer
	May	ET's first visit to GB at Cartmel. Bronwen severely ill. ET moves to Elses Farm, The Weald, near Sevenoaks

	Summer	Busy with reviews and articles. Friendship with Edward Garnett begins
	September	Increased money worries. 'I am sick of books and am selling many old possessions now (prose; never poetry, I hope). Ruskin is the first to go. I want to begin again and this is my frantic and vain protest.' [*JB*]. Stays in London with Ransome
	October	Commissioned to write *Beautiful Wales*. Spends a short holiday with Helen at Ammanford, followed by a long, solitary tramp across the middle of Wales. Continues reviewing: works from 9 a.m. to 1 a.m. in his small study cottage, earning £5 a week. *Rose Acre Papers*, by ET, published
1905	1 March	*Beautiful Wales* finished
	Summer	Physically and mentally exhausted
	September	Experiments with 'ejaculations in prose'. [*JB*]. Visits London fortnightly and attends Edward Garnett's literary gatherings at St. George's Restaurant in St. Martin's Lane
	October	Meets W. H. Davies; invites him to share his small study cottage. *Beautiful Wales*, painted by Robert Fowler, R.I., described by ET, with a note on Mr. Fowler's Landscapes by Alex. J. Finberg, published
1906		W. H. Davies still sharing the study cottage. Reviewing discontinued by *World* and *Academy*. Collaborates with Frank Podmore in a series on 'Apparitions, Thought Transference' for the *Grand Magazine*; contracts to edit a 'Popular Natural History' in 12 monthly instalments. Meets W. H. Hudson and de la Mare
	March	Visits GB at Cartmel for 10 days
	April–July	Walking tours and work on *The Heart of England*

	August	Contract to produce an anthology of songs. Collects £7 from his friends to replace Davies's broken (wooden) leg and finds a publisher for Davies's autobiography
	October	Notice to quit Elses Farm. Stays with parents and relations
	November	Begins regular reviewing for the *Morning Post* under Belloc's literary editorship
	December	Moves to Berryfield Cottage, Ashford, Petersfield, close to Bedales School. *The Heart of England*, by ET, with coloured illustrations by H. L. Richardson, published. *The Bible in Spain*, with an Introduction by ET, published
1907	February	First visit to James Guthrie at Harting
	March	Completing 'Anthology of Songs' and the final proofs of his *Book of the Open Air*. A short walking tour in Wiltshire
	April	Visits a specialist about his 'melancholia'
	May	Commissioned to write a book on Richard Jefferies
	June	A fortnight at Cartmel with GB. *The Book of the Open Air*, edited by ET, published
	July	*The Pocket Book of Poems and Songs for the Open Air*, compiled by ET, published
	August	Walking tour with Helen in Jefferies country. Obliged to continue reviewing
	September	Meets Muirhead Bone at a literary dinner in London
	October– November	Slow progress on the 'Jefferies' and constant reviewing for the *Daily Chronicle* and the *Morning Post*. Visits to Wiltshire and the British Museum
	27 December	Leaves for Minsmere, near Dunwich, to write *Richard Jefferies*. 'My own soul remains a blasted heath: perhaps when I come to look at Jefferies more intently I shall be the better for it.' [*JB*]

25

1908	January–February	First draft of *Richard Jefferies* completed at Minsmere
	March–Early June	Completes *Richard Jefferies*, reviewing at home, and walking about Sussex, Surrey, and Kent in preparation for a book to be entitled *The South Country*. Simultaneously preparing for a book on George Borrow
	August	Appointed Assistant Secretary to a Royal Commission on Welsh Monuments. Continues with reviewing and with his reading in the B.M.
	September	Decides to live in London and not to travel daily to his new post
	October	Advises W. H. Davies on his autobiography; completes *The South Country*; continues work on *George Borrow* at the B.M. Herbert's *The Temple*, with an Introduction by ET, published
	November	Visits Swansea but learns that most of his work with the Royal Commission will be in the London office. Meets Dixon Scott
	December	Indifferent health, resigns Assistant Secretaryship. Plans for a new house, close to Bedales, to be built by Geoffrey Lupton. *British Butterflies and other Insects* and *Some British Birds*, both edited by ET, published
1909	January	Returns to Ashford and follows the advice of a new doctor who recommends complete freedom of diet. Works regularly in the garden of his new house
	February	Continues to find extraordinary energy for writing short sketches. *Richard Jefferies*, by ET, published
	March	Less reviewing; continues to write sketches, some of which are accepted by editors. Ransome marries and comes to live near ET
	April	Enters new study at the top of Ashford

	Hanger. Work begun on the new house, Wick Green. ET visits Wales for 10 days
June	Spends 8 days in Cornwall with E. S. P. Haynes
Summer	Helen takes in pupils from Bedales as boarders. Reviewing slackens off; essays accepted for publication as a book; articles and reviews in *The English Review*; de la Mare and family visit Ashford
Autumn	Merfyn and Bronwen attend Bedales; Helen teaches there in the kindergarten. *Marlowe's Plays*, with an Introduction by ET, published. Richard Jefferies' *The Hills and the Vales*, with an Introduction by ET, published
November– December	Regular work in new garden, constant reviewing, writing short stories based on old legends; commission to write a book about 'the influence of women on English poets'. *The South Country*, by ET, published
Before Christmas	Moves into new house, Wick Green, Petersfield
1910 January	*Windsor Castle*, described by ET, pictured by E. W. Haslehurst, published
February	*Rest and Unrest*, by ET, published
March	Undertakes to produce books on 'Maeterlinck' and 'Women and Poets' during the year. Reads widely on 'mysticism'
July	*Feminine Influence on the Poets* completed. His new garden planned and worked over
August	Visited by de la Mare and his family. Continues to write sketches and to review regularly for the *Daily Chronicle*, the *Morning Post*, *Saturday Review*, and *The Bookman*. Daughter born, Helen Elizabeth Myfanwy
September	Cycling tour with Merfyn. Visits Conrad, Belloc, Ralph Hodgson, and Rupert Brooke (who had visited him earlier in the

		year). Spends a fortnight in the wilds of Cardiganshire
	October	*Feminine Influence on the Poets*, by ET, published; 'killed by its price [10/6] and the Election.' [*JB*]
	November	Writing *Maurice Maeterlinck* and undertakes to write on the Icknield Way. *Rose Acre Papers*, including essays from *Horae Solitariae*, by ET, published
1911	January	*Maurice Maeterlinck* completed. Collecting a volume of essays and reviewing. Follows a strict vegetarian diet
	February	Agrees to write two short books (Celtic Tales and a brief biography of Lafcadio Hearn). Assists Edward Garnett with a petition for a Civil List Pension for W. H. Davies. His own reviewing for the *Morning Post* stops
	March	Visited by Guthrie. Low in health and spirits
	April–July	Various trips in preparation for *The Icknield Way*. *Light and Twilight* and *Isaac Taylor's Words and Places*, with an Introduction by ET, published
	Autumn	Four books published: *The Tenth Muse* [Slightly adapted from Chapter VIII of *Femine Influence*]; *Celtic Stories*; *Maurice Maeterlinck*; *The Isle of Wight*, pictured by Ernest Haslehurst, described by ET
	September	Severe breakdown caused by overwork and financial worry. Sent to West Wales to recover and to finish writing *The Icknield Way*. Visits his friend 'Gwili'
	October	After a period of indecision, returns to West Wales for 7 weeks and writes *George Borrow*. Second edition of *Richard Jefferies* published
	Christmas	Returns to Wick Green and agrees to write books on Swinburne and Pater. Borrow's *The Zincali* etc., with an Introduction by ET, published

1912	January	Begins to write for H. Monro's *Poetry Review*. Continues his fortnightly visits to London. *Lafcadio Hearn*, by ET, published
	March	Book on Pater 'roughly finished'. Sets off on a walking tour of Warwickshire and Gloucestershire to think about his book on Swinburne
	April	Stays with Clifford Bax in Somerset and is treated by Godwin Baynes
	May–June	Near Bath writing *Algernon Charles Swinburne*
	July	Begins to review for *The English Review* and *The Nation* as well as the *Daily Chronicle*. *Norse Tales*, by ET, published
	August	Cycles with Merfyn through Somerset and Kent; plays cricket with Bax, visits de la Mare, W. H. Davies, and Vivian Locke Ellis
	September	Writes a series of articles on the country for the Underground Railway. More reviewing, but his earnings are less. *Cobbett's Rural Rides*, with an Introduction by ET, and *The Pocket George Borrow* [Passages chosen by ET), published
	October	Gordon Bottomley lives at the house of R. C. Trevelyan on Leith Hill, Surrey. ET begins *The Happy-Go-Lucky Morgans*. *Algernon Charles Swinburne: A Critical Study*, and *George Borrow: The Man and his Books*, both by ET, published
	November	Leaves Wick Green and stays with Locke Ellis at East Grinstead to complete *Walter Pater* and to find extra work. Decides to give up the house at Wick Green. ET is one of the panel of judges who award a *Poetry Review* prize to Rupert Brooke
1913	January–February	His health much worse—'not mere depression'. Travels a great deal through

	Wiltshire and Somerset, filling his note-books for 'In Pursuit of Spring'
March–May	Preparing *The Icknield Way* for the press; finishing *The Happy-Go-Lucky Morgans*; reviewing for monthlies, quarterlies and, less frequently, the *Daily Chronicle*. Meets Robert Frost at East Grinstead
April	Gordon Bottomley returns to the North
Easter	Helen and the children in Norfolk; ET cycling in the Quantocks. Herbert and Eleanor Farjeon at Wick Green. *The Country*, by ET, published
July	Selling books prior to moving into a smaller, new, semi-detached cottage (Yew-tree Cottage) in Steep
August	Move to new cottage; ET retains his hill-top study. Helen leaves for Switzerland with her sister and invalid brother-in-law. ET and Merfyn join a boat-party on the Norfolk Broads and then visit Guthrie at Flansham. *The Icknield Way*, by ET, with illustrations by A. L. Collins, published
September	Preparing a book about proverbs and a short study of Keats. Abandons a book in the Batsford Fellowship Book Series on 'Ecstasy'
November–February 1914	GB winters again on Leith Hill
December	He begins to write his autobiography at Selsfield House, East Grinstead. Writes occasional weekly reviews and frequent monthly reviews. *The Happy-Go-Lucky Morgans*, a novel by ET, published
Christmas	Helen and children join ET at Selsfield House. *Walter Pater: A Critical Study*, by ET, published
1914 January–February	Chiefly in London with his parents or at Clifford Bax's home in Hammersmith. Working on his autobiography

	March	In Steep, reviewing, proof-reading, writing articles
	April	First visits Wales (with Merfyn and Bronwen) and then stays with Robert Frost in Herefordshire. Meets Lascelles Abercrombie. Reviewing modern poetry and preparing 'Homes and Haunts' of English writers. *In Pursuit of Spring*, by ET, with illustrations from drawings by Ernest Haselhurst, published
	June	Spends a week at Cartmel with GB and then visits Frost
	July	Reviews Frost's *North of Boston* in *Daily News*. Preparing an anthology. Helen and ET spend a few days at Ledington and Coventry. Preparing articles for *The English Review*
	August	Thomases on holiday with the Frosts at Ledington, near Ledbury
	September	Cycling in the Midlands and the north of England, with occasional visits to Frost. Uncertain of the future, plans to leave for U.S.A. with Frost
	October	Continues monthly and quarterly reviewing of poetry. Decides to leave Bedales district. Cycling tour in Wales and then back to Robert Frost
	November	At Steep, writing early poems
	December	Still talking of emigration to U.S.A.; tries to find a useful job of 'national importance', and agrees to compile an anthology of verse and prose
1915	January	Sprains his ankle; prepares the anthology and writes poetry
	February	Still unable to walk. Helen accompanies Merfyn and the Frosts to Liverpool for their voyage to New Hampshire. ET attempts to publish his verse under the pseudonym of 'Edward Eastaway'. Sends

poems to his closest friends and, un-successfully, to some editors

March	H. Monro turns down the offer to publish the verse in book form. ET includes 2 poems by 'Eastaway' in his own anthology. Visits Guthrie. Decides to accept a commission to write, at speed, a life of the Duke of Marlborough
April	*In Pursuit of Spring*, by ET, published
June	Finishing *The Life of the Duke of Marlborough*. Cycles with Jesse Berridge and then to Coventry in search of a teaching post
July	Enlists in the Artists' Rifles. Sends poems to GB for inclusion in *An Annual of New Poetry*
August–September	Billeted with his parents during his initial period of training in London
October	In camp at High Beech, near Loughton, Essex. Continues to write poetry
November	Moved to Hare Hall Camp, Gidea Park, Romford, Essex. Guthrie decides to print some of the 'Eastaway' poems in *Root and Branch*. Promoted L/Cpl. *Four-and-Twenty Blackbirds* and *The Life of the Duke of Marlborough*, both by ET, published; also *This England, An Anthology from her writers*, compiled by ET, and a reprint of *Maurice Maeterlinck*
December	Writing poems, some reviewing; planning another anthology of verse; Merfyn returns from U.S.A.
1916 January	Still at Hare Hall Camp as a map-reading instructor. Two poems accepted for *Form*. Merfyn attends a school in Coventry
February	Guthrie plans to print some poems by 'EE'. A convalescent leave spent at Steep
March	Sends 40 poems to GB to be considered for *An Annual of New Poetry*. Promoted Cpl. *Keats*, by ET, published

	June	Awarded a £300 grant instead of a Civil List Pension. Applies for a commission in the artillery. Mrs. Lupton turns him out of his study at Steep
	July	He and Helen spend a leave with various friends. Allowed a further £1 a week by the Civil Liability Commission (to cease if he became an officer). Declines an offer to stay on the permanent staff of his unit
	August	Roger Ingpen considers the publication of a volume of his poetry by Selwyn and Blount
	September	Training as an officer cadet with the R.A. at St. John's Wood and at the Royal Artillery School, Handel St., W.C.
	October	Moves to firing camp in Wiltshire. Asks GB to see proofs of *An Annual of New Poetry* through the press *The Flowers I Love*, compiled by ET, with colour drawings by Katherine Cameron, published
	November	Commissioned 2/Lt.; posted to 244 Siege Battery, R.G.A., Lydd, Kent. Granted leave; visits GB at Cartmel and J. W. Haines at Gloucester before returning to High Beech. *Six Poems*, by Edward Eastaway, published
	December	Volunteers for service overseas. Selwyn and Blount decide to publish a volume of his poetry. Unexpected leave on Christmas Eve
1917	6–12 January	Embarkation leave. Then, final firing practice at Codford, near Warminster. Arranges for John Freeman and Eleanor Farjeon to supervise the proofs of his volume of verse
	29 January	Embarkation
	Mid-February	In action near Arras. Then a spell at Group H.Q. as temporary adjutant. Learns that his proofs are going well
	Mid-March	Returns to his battery in preparation for

	the Easter 'Arras Offensive'. America interested in his verses and *Poetry* has accepted some. Still awaits *An Annual of New Poetry*
4 April	Reads *T.L.S.* review of *An Annual of New Poetry*
9 April Easter Day	On duty at the O.P., killed by the blast of a shell in the first hour of the Battle of Arras, 7.36 a.m.

LETTERS FROM EDWARD THOMAS
TO GORDON BOTTOMLEY

In 1896 I was 22 years of age.[1] *It was a few years earlier that Verlaine had signalized the firm of Mathews and Lane as the publisher of 'les jeunes'. Everything which that firm published seemed to be better than other publishers' books to the young men of that generation.*

One of their books was James Ashcroft Noble's Sonnet In England and Other Essays.[2] *It had a strong attraction for me, and my respect for its author's opinion induced me to copy out most of my verses and send them for his opinion.*

At that moment an Unitarian minister (I think his name was Horder[3]*) had asked Mr. Noble for his opinion of some nature writings by the son of a friend: these were ET's first attempts, and when as a boy of 18 he called on Mr. Noble, the latter put my M.S. into his hands as having come to him at the same time.*

Mr. Noble died that year; but a contact had been made with his widow, and when she visited her relatives in Lancashire she visited my parents too—so that when her second daughter married ET it came about naturally that I began writing to them both. In due course ET's first letter followed, as you find it here.   *G B*

1

30 September 1902   *Rose Acre, Bearsted, nr Maidstone*

Dear Gordon Bottomley,

Nearly seven years ago I glanced at a manuscript of yours in Mr. Noble's house,[4] and now I wish that I had written to you straight-way. For I have been staring at this paper half an hour, trying to get a take-off for a leap to Well Knowe House.[5] The

1 Gordon Bottomley (1874–1948), poet and dramatist.
2 James Ashcroft Noble (1844–96), journalist, editor, and author of a number of books, among them *The Sonnet in England and Other Essays*, 1893, was the father of Edward Thomas's wife, Helen. Noble moved from his birthplace, Liverpool, to London in 1888.
3 Helen Thomas stated that the minister's name was Tarrant.
4 6 Patten Road, Wandsworth Common.
5 Bottomley's address until early 1914 was Well Knowe, Cartmel, nr. Carnforth, Westmorland; thereafter, until his death, it was The Shieling, Silverdale, nr. Carnforth.

North Western Railway could not have been much slower than my unimaginative mind. But seven years ago I could have made the leap with the same confidence as the idiot who dropped a letter 'to heaven' into a scarlet pillar-box. You, I know, think little of such strides—mere carasolings of the fancy—and your letters come here not in the least out of breath. So perhaps you will some day write a letter specially to me. Then, I think, the swiftness of your fancy will carry mine back to you—which I devoutly wish.

No, I can't make the leap. A letter is the only kind of writing which in these dark ages can still be called inspired. Even lyrical poetry—look at Shelley's manuscripts, or read the *Ars Poetica*— is largely an exhausting muscular labour. But in a letter the Muse supplies everything but pen, paper & ink. It should be (not, as this appears to be, the tortuous labour of a spider newly risen from the ink horn) the inwoven shadow of immortal things. . . . (*multa desunt*)

Yours sincerely Edward Thomas

2

17 October 1902   *Rose Acre*

Dear Gordon Bottomley,

I have just got your letter: I cannot thank you for it more plainly than by saying that I can write back as easily as a wall makes an echo. But I am in the midst of a heavy piece of work (reviewing) and must not spend any *time* on your letter & your book, though my *thoughts* are there. I opened the play[1] and saw

> . . . Past where the imaged moon shakes like a soul
> Pausing in death between two unknown worlds.

So I am sure I can thank you for the gift as well as the giving, very heartily. In a week's time I shall be free, I hope, and shall write again. But I will not promise you any criticism. For though I have to live by reviewing,[2] I am by nature most uncritical. I

---

[1] *The Crier by Night.*
[2] Between January and September 1902, 40 reviews by ET appeared in *DC*, 2 reviews in *A*, 7 in *WS*.

read very much as I eat, & all I know is that a book feeds me or it does not. In my daily work I blame the books that do not feed me, though I have no more right to than to blame claret because it leaves an unpleasant taste in my mouth.

Still, perhaps I know something about technique.

Helen sends her love & her thanks with mine. So would Mervyn[1] if he could.

Edward Thomas

P.S. Do you know *Kentucky Poems* by Madison Cawain.[2] If you don't I shall give you a copy.

3

31 October 1902   *Rose Acre*

My dear Gordon Bottomley,

You have got my postcard[3] now, I expect, & will understand why this is only a postcard in disguise. Helen & the girl are very well, & Helen at least is cheerful, but I am still excited & can hardly read. Work pours in more often than it used to do, & of a difficult kind sometimes. So the only peaceful task I can joy now is reading letters and going over the Christian names of women. I think we shall choose Rachel Mary, especially as both are names which have some call upon me. I should have liked Maudlin but must give it up.

I have not read your book. Since I wrote to you I have read nothing for pleasure, except in the half hour before sleep when I always read, in bed, either *Elia*, or *The Anatomy of Melancholy*, or *Paradise Lost*. But, unless I get more work at once, I shall read it tomorrow, when I shall walk sixteen miles along the Pilgrim's Road towards Canterbury.

Here is the Kentucky poet. I have a guilty feeling that it is partly meant to stifle your reproaches for this postcard letter.

Helen sends her love. Merfyn is in London, absorbed in five

[1] ET's eldest child, Philip Mervyn (1900–65). (ET frequently adopts the Welsh form, *Merfyn*, in these letters.)
[2] Reviewed *WS*, 4 October.
[3] Dated 29 October 1902, announcing the birth of a daughter, Rachel Mary Bronwen.

uncles and a grandfather & grandmother.[1] He sometimes writes
to us and our dog, but I doubt if he could be persuaded to write
to you.

Goodbye Gordon Bottomley,

Edward Thomas

4

10 November 1902   *Rose Acre*

To the writer of *The Crier by Night*
Greetings and congratulations—

I read the play as I said I would, on the Saturday before last at
an inn on the Pilgrim's Road,[2] and I have just read it again, not
so much to look for beauties or faults as to renew the unbroken
wave of pleasure which it gave me at first. For me, at any rate,
the play is a delicate experience and I don't want to criticize it. I
said it gave an *unbroken* wave etc, because it seemed to me to
have perfect unity; that is a great thing. As to the nature of the
impression it made, I find it hard to speak. There are a few books
or passages in books—in W. B. Yeats, in Keats, in *The Roadmender*,[3] in *The Opium Eater* & *Religio Medici* & one or two
more—which quite overcome my intelligence, because (I
think) I am so much in sympathy with them that they seem to
belong to my own experience; in some cases, I even feel, I hope
not impudently, 'I ought to have written that myself!' That is
how I felt when I put down your book. The story, the air of the
thing, above all the rhythm, made an atmosphere that I lived in
more freely than I can often do. It is magical; your Muse is the
one that visits Yeats. In two places only I think the Muse was
ungenerous to you (or you did not listen to Her). I mean in the
lyrics. The first one[4] contains several lines that are exquisite in
sound, but I cannot justify your use of 'hear' in this line—

[1] ET was the eldest of six sons; the uncles were Ernest, Oscar, Theodore, Reginald,
Julian.

[2] Throughout his life ET was an indefatigable walker, most frequently alone. (See
the dedication to his friend, Harry Hooton, of *The Icknield Way*: 'For I have
walked more miles with you than with anyone else except myself . . . from
Winchester to Canterbury on the Pilgrim's Way, many times.')

[3] W. B. Yeats, *The Celtic Twilight*, new ed., reviewed *DC*, 12 July; Michael
Fairless, *The Roadmender*, reviewed *DC*, 25 March.

[4] 'Blainid's Song' in Gordon Bottomley, *Poems of Thirty Years*, p. 101.

'The scent of the mead at the harping I shall not hear again.'

The three verses don't seem to me clear enough. You are as fantastic in other places, but in these lyrics I think I see an effort at being fantastic which is invisible elsewhere. Thus in the line—

'My bare cry shivers along the shiny rushes of the drowned lake.'

I know exactly what you mean, but I think the expression does not properly clothe the fancy. Still it is a terribly difficult thing to express; it is a fancy that would come to anybody else almost as elusively & untranslateably as for example a scent. That is your danger; you hover continually on the verge of what is probably inexpressible. Your success is all the more brilliant. I have one quibble: you use the word 'imaged' too often, & where you use the word twice in successive lines you are obscure. . . . Where did you get the cry 'Ohohey' from? I quite frightened myself by repeating it on a dark road.

You know I spoke about certain books as *feeding* me? Yours is one. It sets my brain on fire. I could write an essay on it or 'after' it, & someday I hope I shall; but I am still busy reviewing, & there are many things I have to postpone. So this note is merely a greeting & congratulation. Have you a copy of *White Nights*[1] I could see? I think Helen has a letter for you. She sends her love with mine.

Edward Thomas

5

16 December 1902   *Rose Acre*

My Dear Gordon Bottomley,

Your letter is dated November 19, and with it came *White Nights*. It was delayed by 'a spell of work, a damaged wrist & original sin'.[2] But I have only the worst of these excuses—a spell of work—I was very glad to get your letter but I only looked into *White Nights* (finding something to like and, in the diction, a good deal to regret). I was in London at the time, preparing an edition of John Dyer.[3] Do you know him & his

[1] GB's second volume of verse, *Poems at White-Nights*, 1899.

[2] I am unable to trace this quotation.

[3] In *The Welsh Library Series*, edited by Owen M. Edwards, ET's tutor at Lincoln College, Oxford.

'Grongar Hill' & 'Ruins of Rome'? Long ago I found him a
pleasant oasis in the midst of the 18th century and its coffee-
houses and its rhymes as like one another as Windsor chairs or
policemen. But he is little else & it was not easy to avoid showing that I thought so in my introduction—And now when my
work is finished, the publisher seems disinclined to have a
written agreement about my profits.

Since I came back, I have been busy reading a fine complete
edition of John Lyly, by a very able English scholar of Saintsbury's type.[1] I suppose I dislike all moles that are not velvety;
anyhow, such editors bore me completely, and I have spent ten
days & nights in earning 26/- by reviewing the fellow. Lyly
himself is another matter. Don't you think he made some
beautiful sentences?

No sooner had I done with Lyly than I received *Nova
Solyma*.[2] You have heard of it?—the Latin romance that is
attributed (I think quite justly) to Milton. I suspect you won't
like it in translation. I was very disappointed to find that the
youthful Milton could do nothing more romantic; for it is more
like Harrington than Spenser.

You asked me about the author of *The Roadmender*. All I
know I learned from the *Pilot* review of the book. She was a
woman who had seen much of life in such different places as East
End slums and German countrysides. She died before her book
was published. The book tempts one to try to re-construct her
experiences, but is it very vague. In fact I think the vagueness is
obscure and, from a literary point of view, entirely bad—her
own fault.

Many thanks for the history of 'Ohohey'. And I am glad you
are getting good notices. I fear my review in the *Chronicle*
betrayed my haste and fatigue.[3] For I assure you it is not a
pastime to consider 26 volumes of verse, to discard the very bad,
and then to review the few that have survived. I have to conceal
my own preferences & to keep my mind open to all different &
apparently inconsistent kinds of excellences. I sometimes wonder
if I have illtreated anyone who is to be a poet. Do you know any

[1] *The Complete Works of John Lyly*, collected and edited by R. Warwick Bond,
reviewed *DC*, 2 January 1903.
[2] *Nova Solyma*. An anonymous romance. With introduction, translation and a
bibliography, by the Rev. Walter Begley, reviewed *DC*, 18 December 1902.
[3] *The Crier by Night*, reviewed *DC*, 5 December.

1 Edward Thomas in 1899

2 Edward Thomas
and Merfyn
outside Rose Acre

of these books which are among the best that have appeared since
Autumn 1900?

Polyphemus by R. C. Trevelyan.
The Unknown Way by S. R. Lysaght.
Gísli Súrsson by Beatrice Barmby.
The Wild Knight by G. K. Chesterton.[1]

Gísli Súrsson is a fine Icelandic play, but Miss Barmby died before
it was printed. I thought 'Polyphemus' was as promising as
Keats's earliest works—nearly.

I envy you your folio Burton. I had one too, but had to sell it
in my penniless month last Summer, along with folios of Beaumont & Fletcher, Sidney's *Arcadia* & Fuller's *Worthies*. I have
read it through about three times in this life, mainly at Oxford
or in bed, or both. Someday I shall write a book without a point
& perhaps my digressive skill may make it good. I can't construct
anything worth constructing—look at my 'November'.[2]

Helen seems to be busier than I am. Luckily she is very well,
& walks as usual. The girl, by the way, has been given three
names—Rachel, Mary, & Bronwen.

I think I must stop this letter. For I have planned & in fact
written the opening sentence of a paper 'On lighting the First
Fire in Autumn'.

Just one question. Do you know any house inscriptions or
mottoes (I remember your 'beam-verses') which you could write
down for me? I have a very bad book on the subject, to review.[3]
But I want to make the review an essay pure & simple.

Helen sends her love with mine.

Edward Thomas

I had quite forgotten to say how much I hope that you will come
to Rose Acre. We have, as you know, an ugly little house here,
which we are trying to leave & shall certainly leave before next
October.[4]

[1] *Polyphemus and Other Poems,* reviewed *DC,* 23 March; *Gísli Súrsson,* reviewed
DC, 20 December 1900.
[2] 'Recollections of November' in *Horae Solitariae.*
[3] S. F. A. Caulfield, *House Mottoes and Inscriptions, Old and New,* reviewed *DC,*
8 January 1903, where ET quotes 'Beam-verses at Well Knowe' by GB: see *Poems
of Thirty Years,* p. 131.
[4] Cf. Helen Thomas's description, *AIW,* p. 87.

6

22 December 1902   *Rose Acre*

My dear Gordon Bottomley,

I am so pressed for time that I don't know if I shall be able
to finish thanking you for your letter, your beam-verses, your
copy of William Morris's bed-verses, & for revealing to us
your dear scribe. I haven't time or leisure (and unhappily I know
very well the distinction between the two) to send you a letter.
So I am sending you a *book of sonnets* which you may like.[1] They
are too windy & Rossettyish, I think: but there are lines that
raise them above mediocrity; and they seem to me very well
constructed. They perhaps suggest that the author meant far
more than he expresses. He is, by the way, a poor, bookish bank-
clerk, & the most perverse Complete 'idealist' I ever met, & if
he is apt to mistake the first faint thrills of indigestion for an
understanding of Plotinus, who is there among truthful men that
would refuse Dyspepsia a place among the Muses?

As for John Dyer, let me make a few quotations which are the
best form of criticism unless one is a University Extension
lecturer:—

'No pridely brambles, white with woolly theft.'

'Rolling by ruins hoar of antient towns'.

'Nor what the peasant, nor some lucid wave,
Pactolus, Simois, or Meander slow,
Renown'd in story with his plough up-turns'.

'The pilgrim oft, 'mid his oraison hears,
Aghast, the voice of June disparting towers.'

'Be full ye Courts! be great who will;
Search for Peace with all your skill:
Open wide the lofty door,
Seek her on the marble floor:
In vain you search, she is not there;
In vain ye search the domes of Care:
Grass & flowers Quiet treads,

[1] By Jesse Berridge: he afterwards became a clergyman. [*GB*]

> On the meads & mountain-heads,
> Along with Pleasure close ally'd,
> Ever by each other's side,
> And often by the murm'ring rill,
> Hears the thrush, when all is still,
> Within the groves of Grongar Hill.'[1]

Please let me see *The Mickle Drede* when you can.[2]

As to your 'regrettable diction'. I agree that it must be accepted 'as something inherent'. At the same time I shall always blame it where it seems to me not to be effective. A style may be many things: it must be effective, & I blamed that of *White Nights* because it was not invariably so.

I look forward to seeing your dear Scribe with you in the Spring. So does Helen.

May your logs be fragrant & sparkling, your nuts sweet, your house wind-proof, & your sighs all happy.

Edward Thomas

Bronwen is one of our many beautiful Welsh names. Here are some:—Blodwen, Ceridwen, Mafanwy, Eiluned (pronounced Eileened, a form of Lynette), and Olwen. All are old & all are still used. Olwen! Olwen![3]

*   *   *

I am afraid some letters, or at least notes, are lost here. Between 12 May and 26 May 1903 ET and I met for the first time at 95 Ebury Street. From February 1903 to March 1905 I was free from the lung trouble which dogged me for many years before and after then; and in May 1903 I was visiting London for the first time, staying about a month and seeing ET two or three times.

I can find no letters until March of the following year, when an unhappy Winter for him had evidently intervened: but I must have heard from him frequently in the Summer and the Autumn of 1903,

---

[1] This jumbled selection of quotations seem to be quoted from memory. Cf. ET's *The Poems of John Dyer*, pp. 21, 50, 109.

[2] GB, *The Mickle Drede And Other Verses*, 1896.

[3] ET disclaimed any knowledge of the Welsh language. His father was a Welsh speaker and ET spent many holidays with his father's Welsh-speaking family at Pontardulais. Myfanwy was the name given to his third child.

as I had the proofs of his book on Oxford to read—which he was then writing.

(From that time until I was more ill than usual in 1909 I read all his book-proofs systematically—as a kind of author's reader in contradistinction to the printer's reader. After 1910 I could only do that occasionally, and I believe that John Freeman fulfilled the same regular function after he became Edward's friend in the years immediately before the War.)   GB

*   *   *

7

8 January 1903   *Rose Acre*

My dear Gordon Bottomley,

I hope you won't mind my gilding a newspaper column with your charming beam-verses—Here is the best I could extract from a frost-bound brain, concerning house-mottoes: you need not return it.[1]

Very many thanks for the *United Irishman*.[2] Yeats can do nothing bad, and the play had some thing excellent about it; yet I could not quite overcome my surprise at finding a justice of the peace among the characters. As a play (I am not a playgoer, & have only been to a theatre six times) I should think it was good.

I have at last found a space of leisure. Forgive me for dedicating it to literæ instead of letters.

With our love, Edward Thomas

8

18 February 1903   *13 Rusham Road,*
                                      Nightingale Lane, London, S.W.

My dear Gordon,

Everyone is congratulating me, so I write to you in the faint

---

[1] This *DC* review is attached to the original letter.
[2] W. B. Yeats, *Where There is Nothing: A play in 5 acts*. Issued as a special supplement of the newspaper, *The United Irishmen*, 1902.

hope that you will kindly condole. Briefly, I have been asked to
write a book of 60,000 words on Oxford, to accompany a series
of pictures by John Fulleylove, R.I.; it has to be completed on
June 30; & I have agreed to do it.[1] I came to town a week ago
to seek my fortune, after a spell of bad luck. This work was
given to me on Monday, & I am not only sick at having to
scatter so much ink over the beautiful mother, but panic-stricken
with the feeling that I have not the courage, or the endurance,
or the information that is necessary. So please tell me that you
pity me. I fear you can do little else to help me in the matter. But
please, if you can, let me know of (or lend me) any out of the way
Oxford books, or send me any literary references or any anec-
dotes. I ask in despair, because I can not produce 60,000 words
unaided, & do the extra amount of reviewing necessary to keep
me going for the next 4 months. Of course, I can probably quote
from Matthew Arnold, Newman, De Quincey, Lionel Johnson
&c &c & so delight myself and fill space. Inkitas inkitatum. All
is ink.

And now I have to apologize. First, for not answering your
letter that is now a month old; & second for being about to be
such an intolerable correspondent as I shall be until July. You
were very ill when you wrote, but I believe you are better now,
& we still hope you may come to Bearsted, where I shall return
in the course of a month, & perhaps much sooner. For I cannot
work in London. There are so many conveniences to contend
with—worst of all, the gas fires in every room in this house (my
father's & mother's).

Goodbye. Commend me to your Scribe.

Ever yours Edward Thomas

9

10 March 1903   *Rose Acre*

My dear Gordon,
I can only send you a word to say how sorry I am that your

[1] ET gave the manuscript of *Oxford* to his close friend E. S. P. Haynes, who later
gave it Lincoln College Library. Cf. Haynes's portrait of ET in *Personalia* (1917,
1927) and *The Lawyer, a Conversation Piece*, 1951. See, too, *WWE*, pp. 99–101.

hand is still bad & how grateful I am for your ambidexterity. I think perhaps I shall be able to use the quotations which you have copied from Morris, & the Stevenson's *Edinburgh*[1] might be suggestive. Of course it is a good subject, but you forget that I have to write mechanically, so many words a day,—which does not suit my ways at all. Also, tho I am determined to introduce a great deal of quite unpopular stuff, yet I have to respect the publisher's wish to a small extent. In the short time allowed to me I must make use of facts, & even stale, dull facts. I can't pour forth sound & fury at the rate of 500 words a day for 120 days consecutively. And it will not be wise for me to lay much stress upon the degradation of Oxford in the last 50 years: I must merely throw a little sarcasm here & there. Morris must have had a very eclectic eyesight if he saw a mediaeval city almost entire, when he came up. For Worcester, Pembroke, Jesus, Christ Church, the Radcliffe Camera, All Saints Church, & many other places were 16th, 17th or 18th century buildings almost unmixed. Personally I think that until very recent years all architects have been wonderfully successful in planning churches & libraries & quadrangles in such a way as to make them capable of becoming (in a century or two) excellent younger children of the same old city. I think of architecture in Oxford not as Norman & transitional & classical &c &c, but as either Oxford architecture or not. Poor Fulleylove! I don't know much of his work.[2] He seems to have a good notion of colour. I had his *Holyland* which was a very superior *guide book* indeed. I suppose you miss imagination & motive in his work & I daresay you are right.

By the way, I entirely agree with you about my paper on Epitaphs.[3] I don't see anything in it: never did: but inserted it at the request of a friend who thought it might please, & because the Arbuthnot epitaph is so good.

I think the photograph pretty good of Helen & bad of Merfyn (who by the way is a fine brutal Saxon at present).

I am glad you like Sandys.[4] Ovid certainly is not heavy, but I think GS sometimes is. I have his book of travel here (1632)

[1] R. L. Stevenson, *Edinburgh: Picturesque Notes*, 1879.
[2] John Fulleylove (1845–1908), a water-colour landscape painter, had held successful exhibitions in London of his drawings of Oxford (1888), Cambridge (1890), Greece (1896) and Palestine (1902).
[3] *Horae Solitariae*, p. 25 ff., 'Epitaphs as a form of English literature'.
[4] George Sandys, translator of Ovid's *Metamorphoses*, 1621–6.

which is a good book & a storehouse of classical quotation—

Yesterday I sent off my first chapter of *Oxford*. Now I am busy with a series of character sketches of Oxford people (largely imaginative): & hope you will like some of them.

You see I am in haste which you & I both dislike. So goodbye. I shall look out for your collection of verses. Commend me to your Scribe & with our love believe me

Ever yours Edward Thomas

10

17 April 1903   *Rose Acre*

My dear Gordon,

I have not had time for writing before, & moreover I haven't time now. But I want to say that I am sorry I said nothing about your visit, in my last letter. It was forgetfulness just for a moment. The fact is that we have only one room to spare. But there is a room or perhaps two to be had in a house in the village. Rose Acre would be good for you: it is so high & windy. The village is lower & more sheltered, & I think perhaps you ought not to think of that. Would it be possible for you to come here & for Miss Burton to stay in the village, 8 minutes distant? She would of course come here as early in the morning & leave as late at night, as she wished. I am afraid it is not quite a pleasant arrangement. I suggest it because it is the only one, & we do want you to come.

When I have sent in all the chapters of my Oxford book—at the end of June probably—we are to move to a pretty, old house on the village green, with a pair of lime trees on the two strips of lawn in front. It is covered with ivy & has shuttered windows, and a dormer window in the roof. I hope it will not be thought too sheltered for you to come there some day.[1]

I am working almost as quickly & badly as possible at *Oxford*, & have sent in a chapter 'on entering Oxford', one on Dons, one on 'the stones of Oxford' (which is a medley of history and sentiment), & one on College Servants; & I have one on 'an Oxford day' and one on Undergraduates, in hand. Most of it is

[1] On this house, and ET's many changes of house, see *WWE*, pp. 101–5.

just inkhorn work. But perhaps you will like a page here & there about men & places. I like one or two myself. You will very likely meet Glanvil's 2 or 3 pages on the scholar who turned gipsy, if I dare to quote a matter which will be very irrelevant. The chapters on 'an Oxford day' & Undergraduates are giving me most trouble, because I know most about them & cannot invent as I did in the case of Dons.[1] What I shall say about the Churches I don't know, because I have almost no technical knowledge of them as a foundation. St. Mary's is the church in 'Caryatids'.[2]

I see that I am giving you the lees of an oft-drained brain.[3] So goodbye. Commend me to your Scribe & remember us both.

Ever yours Edward Thomas

I want to have *The Vine-Dresser*. Will you tell me who published it?

11

7 March 1904   *Bearsted Green, nr Maidstone*

My dear Gordon,

It is almost as long since you heard from me as since I wrote to you, & to me that is a very long time. For I ceased to write to you when I ceased to be able to write, & my pen refused to connive at anything but the telegram style. Helen has probably been sending you messages as dismal as my thoughts,—not as dull, I expect.[4] I am hardly at all moved to write even now. But

---

[1] See ET, *Oxford*, Chapters III and IV.

[2] *Horae Solitariae*, Chapter 9.

[3] Reviews of the following books appeared in *DC* during this April: *Thirteen Satires of Juvenal*, trans. S. G. Owen; *The Poetical Works of Thomas Traherne*, now first published from the original Mss., ed. Bertram Dobell; *Hither and Thither*, songs and verses, by the author of 'Times and Days'; *Seria ludo*, by a Dilettante; Israel Zangwill, *Blind Children*; J. Churton Collins, *Critical Essays and Literary Fragments*; Lawrence Alma Tadema, *Songs of Womanhood*.

[4] GB's memory seems to contradict Helen Thomas's recollection (*WWE*, p. 101) that 'with the Oxford book David's [i.e. ET's] luck took a turn, and I do not remember at this time another period of anxiety about money'. Letters from ET to Ian MacAlister (5 September, 1 November, 25 December 1903) confirm GB's statement. The house, however, proved hopelessly insanitary and Bronwen was dangerously ill there. During the gap in letters to GB, May 1903–March 1904, ET contributed the following number of traceable reviews: *DC* (72), *S* (1), *WS* (1). In the spring 1904 he became a regular contributor to *The World*.

two things conspire to produce this page. First, I feel I must show you that I want to write. Second, I began an essay on last Friday night, & in a way you were responsible for it: in this way, that I have had Arthur Ransome staying here & he left on Friday,[1] whereupon the memory of his very pleasant company persuaded me to soil a beautiful white sheet of paper again, the first (excluding *Oxford*) for 15 months, with an essay; & if I hadn't found that he was a friend of yours, I might have failed to discover him. This reasoning is good enough for an essayist. Ransome is a remarkable boy. My only fear for him is that he may become merely five years older than he actually is; that he may become merely old for his age. For he seems to be working, as hard as if he liked it, at pure journalism, tho it is quite clear that he has in him things which can never be expressed in pure journalizing & may even be suppressed by it, at his age. I told him so. But of course there is no reason why he should listen to me, who am an obvious failure. I am. *Oxford* hasn't done me any service. I am not in the least in demand, except in quarters where moderate work is wanted for worse pay. And if I were in demand, I am not in a position to supply. *Infelix sum*: & I will drop the subject, & just ask you to admire the brevity of those two words. I did not believe myself capable of it.

Helen is away on the coast, at Walmer. She has had a wretched time, tho I hope not worse than I have had in consequence. For she fell ill, just as I was learning to work & enjoy at home again. You know that I tried to live in London,[2] to escape the noise of the children? I escaped the noise & fell upon horrible silences, where people talked abundantly indeed & to me, but said nothing to break the silence of my soul. I was the victim of a score of kind acquaintances & even persons I had called friends for years. Work abounded: I could have doubled my income. But I fled & now I am beginning to hear music again, & that is what I wanted to tell you. Yet I must not, for I am going to put it into my essay

[1] Arthur Ransome (1884–1967), author, traveller, and scholar, had known GB before he settled in London as a journalist writer. In 1904 two volumes appeared in The Lanthorn Series: No. 1, *The Souls of the Streets and other Little Papers*, by Arthur Ransome; No. 2, *Rose Acre Papers*, by Edward Thomas.

[2] An expedient ET resorted to throughout his life. (See *WWE*, pp. 108–9.) On this occasion he stayed with Helen's sister, Irene MacArthur. At the end of 1903 James Milne had replaced ET's sponsor, H. W. Nevinson, as literary editor of the *Daily Chronicle* and for a time ET feared that this would be the end of his main source of income.

& then you may hear it some day. In health I am no better, tho I am a few pounds heavier; nor am I less depressed, irritable, but I hope I am getting used to it, which is nearly as useful, tho not so pleasant, as getting rid of it. I believe I shall never be happy unless I become mad. By the way, I was twenty-six last week. I think that authors' ages should always be given to their readers: that is the best criticism.

　　With my love to you & your Mother & your Scribe,

Edward Thomas

12

My dear Gordon,

　　It is not easy for me to think about the future, even about next month. It all seems so improbable, & every day seems to be the last, so tired and unconcentrated am I. But now I promise myself that I will leave here for Cartmel on or about April 13 or 11. It is most pleasant to think of, & I thank you & all yours for asking me. You know I am no traveller.[1] I am always wanting to settle down like a tree for ever. But I have, except my body & clothes, already spent so much life at Cartmel that I feel I am not untrue to myself in taking them as well. You will let me have an hour or two a day for work, won't you? It may be quite unavoidable.

　　You will find me, I fear, somewhat hard of speech & hearing in the matters you & I really care about. For all my life I have been in the hands of those who care for other & even opposite things; & they have tried to teach me—or by my own imitative nature I have tried to learn—to say much & smartly about things I care nothing for. Perhaps after all they are the only things one can ever sum up & be satisfied with in conversation. And this reminds me of what you say about your own isolated position, away from fellow artists. I know well the desire & the apparent need; for work that depends always & entirely upon a man's own invention & impulse always lets the artist down into deep waters of misery now & then, & at those times I have sought the company of many and various men, & yet I have always been alone

---

[1] Earlier this year ET had refused a commission to write a travel book about Holland.

& unaided; all I have got from them has been experiences which I never use. I have talked my soul empty to a man who (as I had not the wit to discover) answered me with his tongue; not one man, but a score: I suppose, as I hinted just now, that my talk was obscure—in 'clouds of glory' if you like. Well, are you likely to have better luck? Your work seems to me to be a far lonelier flower than mine, & other artists might change you or swamp you, but couldn't help you to develop.—I think—for the mere health of the brain, a variety of social intercourse should be good: & I wish you were able to try it. But with me, social intercourse is only an intense form of solitude, and as solitude is what I have to avoid, the means are yet to be found.[1] Does this uncomfortable talk comfort you at all? But your poor wrist—that is worse than all my ills—It is a horrible, plain fact that might appal a Berkleian.

I am glad you like 'the rapture of the fight'. I hardly ever do. I look forward to writing & look back upon it joyfully as if it were an achievement & not an attempt—very often. But while I write, it is a dull blindfold journey through a strange lovely land: I seem to take what I write from the dictation of someone else. Correction is pleasanter. For then I have glimpses of what I was passing through as I wrote. This very morning the sun was shining, wide & pale gold & warm as it has done for two weeks, & the church bells suddenly beginning to ring were at one with it a part of Spring, & they set me writing; for I could not go out, as I have a touch of Helen's illness & am over-weak; but at once, I became dull with the dulness of ecstasy (I suppose). I don't know what the essay—which pretends to be an episode— is going to be like, but some day I may publish a volume & give an essay to each of my friends, as Lionel Johnson did with his verses, & this shall be yours. It is called 'The Skeleton'[2] & is (roughly) two pictures: first a beautiful, many-sided youth in Spring, & next his skeleton in Autumn, & I, or the teller of the

---

[1] Edward Garnett, who became Duckworth's 'reader' in the autumn of 1901, recalls how W. H. Hudson 'formed the habit of lunching with me, nearly every Tuesday' at the Mont Blanc in Gerrard Street; 'literary acquaintances that I made about this time would also come to the Mont Blanc, and in this way a small circle of habitués was formed, among them Thomas Seccombe, R. A. Scott James, Stephen Reynolds, Edward Thomas, W. H. Davies, Hilaire Belloc, Muirhead Bone, Ford Hueffer, Perceval Gibbon, occasionally John Galsworthy, and rarely Joseph Conrad.' See *The Athenaeum*, 16 April 1920.

[2] Eventually published in *The Venture*, No. 2, ed. John Baillie (1905).

story, have murdered him. It is so simple in scheme that it will be difficult to make it effective. Also, I am hampered by my long silence, for I have accumulated so much material that I am tempted to use too large a part of it.

Your letter makes me think you do not know how much of *Oxford* is imaginary. Only one of the dons is taken from life, & he is the one like William Morris: the original is F. York Powell, a distant cousin of mine, as I have just discovered.[1] The college servants are all imaginary: so are the undergraduates, except the one who 'achieved everything but success'. Of the College Garden only a fragment is visible & that is Wadham Garden. Philip Amberley (are you sorry?) never lived & never died, & never taught me this easy script—which is descended from a style founded on a 14th or 15th century monkish hand & sometimes used by a brother of mine who has been trained as an artist.[2]

Helen is just back & looks quite well. She and I send our love to you all.

Ever yours Edward Thomas

13

24 April 1904   *Bearsted Green*

My dear Gordon,

As you will suppose, I got to London safely on Friday—for which I have to thank W. B. Yeats's plays rather than the L.N.W. Railway.[3] I spent Saturday morning in dull business and reached home at tea time. It was a perfect day, full of the sound of cuckoos & nightingales and the scent of cherry blossom, & my

---

[1] *Oxford*, pp. 82–4. 'He moves about a little uneasily, like the late William Morris, and as if he would rather use deeds than words.' GB had probably commented on the absence of a drawing by Fulleylove to illustrate Chapter VII, 'In a College Garden', pp. 209–17.

[2] The portrait of the imaginary Philip Amberley is the sixth and longest description of 'Present Dons', pp. 85–93. It was lifted out of ET's note-books. His artist brother was Ernest. E. S. P. Haynes states (*Personalia*, p. 6) that his copy of *Oxford* from ET was annotated with the names of Hilaire Belloc and Raymond Asquith opposite two of the portraits of undergraduates.

[3] Helen and ET had paid a visit to Well Knowe. As always ET worked at his reviewing even on holiday. W. B. Yeats, *Plays for an Irish Theatre*, vols. 2, 3, reviewed *WS*, 18 June.

welcome was just as tender as my farewell at Cartmel. But I should not have been so glad to be at home again so calmly glad, if I had not been glad to be away with you all at Well Knowe. I was such a gloomy and languid beast very often when I was with you that I fear you didn't know how often I was as contented as I am ever likely to be, and all because I liked you and your father & mother & Miss Gordon so well.[1] (By the way, I am now Helen's rival as an admirer of your mother, & we spent some pleasant competitive moments in remembering her.) Will you please say as much and more (in your unique & expressive, if regrettable diction) ? I really can't say it myself & want you to translate out of my silence for me. For yourself, you do not need my words on paper. Our happy intimacy needs no compliment, & I dare to think that perhaps you have some recollections—I have many—that make thanks unnecessary. Well Knowe is going into my memory, along with Oxford and the Pilgrim's Road and the Surrey & Wales & Wiltshire I knew as a child.

Today I have already been busy at reviews,[2] for there were more books awaiting me at home. Also Helen & I are both busy thinking about a new house. We may, after all, go to the Red Brick country. It is convenient & I have to remember that if I found a place worth settling in for ever I might have to leave it soon, with my uncertain income. So I just seek a healthy house, near town, at a moderate rent, and leave perfection for a happier future. This house is looking its best now & the green plants are so fresh & various that we don't miss the flowers.

Bronwen is wonderfully well, looking exactly as in her best days, and with an increasing command of lucid & effective English. Helen & Merfyn are perfectly well, & I believe I am decidedly better.

I hope to see you in London, & your next visit must be to us. With Helen's love & mine to you all.

I am Ever yours Edward Thomas

---

[1] GB's maternal aunt: his mother's maiden name was Maria Gordon.
[2] The following reviews appeared soon after this date: W. Warde Fowler, ed., *An Oxford Correspondence*, *WC*, 27 April; W. Barry, *Newman*, *DC*, 5 May; A.E., *The Divine Vision, and other Poems*, *WS*, 7 May; Herbert W. Tompkins, *March Country Rambles*, *DC*, 16 May; Walter J. de la Mare, *Henry Brocken*, *DC*, 17 May; Horace G. Hutchinson, *The New Forest*, and Mrs. Willingham Rawnsley, *The New Forest*, *DC*, 18 May; the Rev. Henry L. Thompson, *The Church of St. Mary the Virgin, Oxford*, *DC*, 24 May; and Hilaire Belloc, *Avril*, *DC*, 26 May.

I will send Symons's *Cities* & Jefferies's *Field & Hedgerow* tomorrow.[1] Was there another book?

14

12 May 1904   *Bearsted Green*

My dear Gordon,

I have again been looking at the Book,[2] & the more I look at it the more I understand it and like it. At first I confess I was astonished in an unsympathetic & uninterested way by what I read. Evening after evening I took it up and threw it aside sometimes in sorrow & sometimes in anger. At last I must acknowledge that I have seen some very fine things in 'The White Watch' & 'Vision of Giorgione' & 'Harvest Home' among others. But after all, my dear Gordon, the book is not for me unless you can perform an operation upon my silly skull. Your moods in these poems (if I understand them aright) I am often in deep sympathy with & time after time you express things magically that I have barely experienced. But. But. But. The writing makes a very weak appeal to me, tho I see that it is capable of strong & high appeal to others—So if I should get the book from the *Chronicle* you will understand if the review is unintelligent or if there is no review? I am sorry: both because I am so narrow minded a reader and (above all) because I can't like everything you do tho I like everything you are.

I fear you partly anticipated this dismal tale. But tell me you pardon it.

I am busy, tired & neuralgic & haven't found a house. With Helen's love & mine,

Ever yours Edward Thomas

I heard from Baillie[3] this morning & have written to Haynes[4] about him.

[1] A. Symons, *Cities*, 1903; R. Jefferies, *Field and Hedgerow: Being the last essays of R.J., collected by his widow*, 1889.

[2] GB's *The Gate of Smaragdus*. Three versions of 'The White Watch' and four songs from *A Vision of Giorgione* are printed in *Poems of Thirty Years*.

[3] John Baillie, who was editing *The Venture*, No. 2.

[4] E. S. P. Haynes, who was a writer as well as a lawyer. ET reviewed E. S. P. Haynes, *Standards of Taste in Art, DC*, 29 June.

15

26 June 1904   *Elses Farm,*[1] *The Weald, Sevenoaks*

My dear Gordon,

What is the use of writing to you—though being written to is good—when I have wished for hardly anything in some of the calm evenings here except you and a spinet and 'Somer is icomen in'? So you see that we like the place. I have had terrible moods here & long fits of despair & exhaustion, but the short intervals have been very sweet, tho, as I say, I wanted something even then. But your last letter is dated a month ago & I must write something especially as I know you will give me something back—

I have killed my man. One day last week I sat down & vowed I would not rise till he was dead, and so it fell out, but it is a bad death. Whenever I have to deal with facts & incidents I begin to sprawl or else to be very plain & blunt. Well, as I approached the death, I got nervous & simply said that I killed him (Philaster his name is) & then, in spite of my plans, I only gave about 5 lines to a description of the skeleton. And after all I don't know that I will let John Baillie have it & I feel as if I would never try to write again.[2] There is no form that suits me, & I doubt if I can make a new form. At any rate, I must avoid long things. Perhaps the 'man & a landscape' plan has a future for me. It is really my physical weakness that spoils my work. I can't write more than a small page at a time: then I am interrupted for a week: and so I wander & sprawl.

Since I came here, I have been very busy with reviews.[3] *The World* has asked me for signed articles 3 weeks running, on very poor books, & that means much writing & little said. I wonder will they let me have *The Gate of Smaragdus*, & why is it so delayed?

[1] For Helen's account of Elses Farm, see *WWE*, pp. 105–9.

[2] It was published in *The Venture*.

[3] *The World* increased its coverage of new books from April 1904 until December 1905 by using signed articles and reviews as well as its causerie, 'Pages in waiting', which was signed 'P & Q'. During this time ET contributed 12 signed articles (or reviews) and innumerable paragraphs included in 'P & Q' which can be identified from the letters to GB. His signed reviews were generally given pride of place. In this letter he refers to *The Love of Old Books*, 14 June, p. 1039, *Eighteenth Century Sidewalks*, 21 June, and *On Country Books*, 12 July.

Now I have to go to meet Haynes & I think I will send this as it is rather than wait & make you wait.

Helen & the children, who are well & happy, send loves to you all. So do I—

Ever yours Edward Thomas

16

1 July 1904   *Elses Farm*

My dear Gordon,

Why didn't you let me know that you were to be in London again? I was up for a few hours on Wednesday, & if I hadn't been so hesitant, I should certainly have called at 95, for I thought of it twice in my wanderings.

I am very sorry to hear of the misfortunes of your book, & hope they are over. Still the nasty little Unicorn is dead. Crosland seems to have been kind. Elkin Matthews should be all right.[1] He is not only poor but honest—a wonderful combination of virtues especially in a publisher. But what does he know about me?

I will think about sending the story of Philaster to Baillie. But to copy out such a thing will require much vanity or much self-denial.

Yes, what of Ransome? I asked him to come here, but have not heard from him for 5 weeks, tho I heard he was in the North. Whose reader is he? Also, why does he want to publish a book, & a book of essays, & above all of essays written out of malice aforethought?

I am again rather busy with a long article on country books to be written for *The World* &c.[2] But I am much puzzled by Yeats's *Tables of the Law*.[3] Does he see the point (if any) of the

[1] '*The Gate of Smaragdus*: with eight illustrations by Clinton Balmer (Small folio, pp. 66), bears the imprint of The Unicorn Press, 1904, but was transferred before publication to Mr. Elkin Mathews and published by him in the same year. An additional leaf bearing his imprint was inserted opposite the title-page, without any excision being made to accommodate it. (400 copies).' [See 'Note' to *Poems of Thirty Years*.]

[2] See Letter 15, note 3.

[3] *The Tables of the Law* and *The Adoration of the Magi*, reviewed *WS*, 13 August, and *DC*, 15 August.

3a Berryfield Cottage

b The House at Wick Green built by Geoffrey Lupton

4 Edward Thomas in 1907, from a photograph by F. H. Evans

two stories? Or are they records of experiences to which he hopes that the reader may discover a point? I like them especially the *Adoration of the Magi*, but they seem to me full of gaps, unless of course they are simply records of experiences. Tell me what you think—

But I have 9 volumes of verse at my elbow—two dramas &c— and must work.[1]

I shall not easily forgive you for not giving me a chance of seeing you here or in town—

With Helen's love

Yours ever Edward Thomas

Did you see the *Saturday's* attack on my hysterics, forced humour & imitation of Chesterton? Another case of constipation, I suppose—

17

6 August 1904   *Elses Farm*

My dear Gordon,

I have just come to the end of a review of minor poets, and I have another one in hand.[2] So you will know how to forgive this letter. To thank you fittingly for yours I ought to have your command of a jewelled and blossomy vocabulary. I was not only very glad to get it, but I am glad I have got it still; which does not often happen with letters, does it?

First & before I forget it Mr. Arthur M. Ransome lives at 1, Gunter Grove, Chelsea, S.W. He has quite a good room with a bed delicately suggested by a tapestry cover, and other things suggested by a Japanese screen. His books, some portraits, drawings by Colman-Smith & some of Balmers, are there, & on the mantelpiece some of the drawings of 'An I.P.' and a great bulk of his landlady's glass & china decorations, & in the midst thereof a large earthenware pot, with tap, containing Ginger Beer, which his visitors always spill into his landlady's fender &

---

[1] An unsigned review of seven volumes of minor verse appeared in *DC*, 4 July, and a signed review of 3 volumes of verse and 2 verse dramas on 25 July.

[2] Probably the ironic unsigned review of five volumes of minor verse, 'Poets born and made', in *DC* of August. ('We are not worthy to deal with the work of a man who has heard the nightingale in Autumn.')

on to her Japanese umbrella which conceals the fireplace. There are also three chairs, a table & a floor. Here smiles Ransome, whether in the company of his dreams or in the solitude created by visitors who do not always smile. Also he says 'Bother' and even 'Damn'. He gets younger every day & in September he produces a book—which you may have seen. I have seen it & have laughed & sighed & wondered. I suppose that if a man can write such things he should be encouraged to publish them. That he should want to publish them, amazes me. In book form, I can only endure them when I think that he has made a tolerably good mould of sentences &c into which he may some day find something to pour. I know something about sugar in prose, but this is prose in sugar. . . . I am going to try to understand it before it is received by the *Chronicle*.

By the way, along with Ransome's comes a book with my name on it. You know how little I want to publish even when I like what I write. Well, this Publisher's Adviser lured me into letting him have 10,000 words of bad, old published stuff, mostly written before *Horae Solitariae*, just because he wanted to start with 3 or 4 books & couldn't if I refused. So I am trying to comfort myself by calling it something like 'Experiments'. If there is anything in it that you like, I will dedicate it to you.[1] Perhaps I can send a proof.

I look at *The Gate of Smaragdus* often, & am anxious to see it published so that I may be forced to think about it more clearly than I have done yet. Why send copies to any papers except the *Athenæum, Spectator, Academy, Chronicle, Daily News, The World* & *The Monthly Review*?

The *Saturday* is amusing. I laughed at the notice of *Oxford* & now the review of Belloc comforts me, for my laugh wasn't quite cheerful. But it would be impossible to justify more than one or two of the pilloried sentences, don't you think? H.B. used to write for the *Saturday*.

'The Story of Philaster' is not copied yet. But I have promised to send it in before the end of the month. It is very bad & I have destroyed much already. I decided, by the way, that my murder was bad, & have cut it out. Since I finished it, I have written two

---

[1] *Rose Acre Papers* (No. 2. The Lanthorn Series), 1904, was dedicated 'For Gordon Bottomley, Poet'. On the back page there are notices of '*The Souls of the Streets*. By Arthur Ransome. Just Published.'

short papers, one a kind of story (without incident except a silent death) called 'The Listener' & the other 'A Complaint' (at the destruction of an old suburban house I knew for twenty years). I like your suggestions for myself very much. Tonight I am going to sketch 300 words for a *petite poéme en prose*: but it is not for me to be 'concise, carven, jewelled', my dear Gordon! Mistery is mine. Also I shall not forget The Imaginary portrait, with or without a landscape. But I don't think I can do imaginary Conversation: what is more I can't attempt it. You see, I am no talker. When a person talks with me there are two monologues to be heard, not one dialogue. By the way I am now known as *The Eagle Cock* (who blinks & blinks on Ballygawley Hill): which is cruel of you.

I will not believe that Shelley is diffuse & effusive except in 'Laon & Cythna', 'Rosamond & Helen', 'The Sensitive Plant' & a few more. Also I will not prove that he wasn't. For I don't read him. He is part of myself.

i.e. I agree with you entirely.

You are quite right (about *The Tables of the Law* & *The Adoration of the Magi*.) But they have a grave & purposeful look about them which does not quite suit their real irresponsibility. And, as it stands, *The Tables of the Law* is not of a piece; it might easily have been longer or shorter.

8 August 1904

I can't go on as I meant to do; I was interrupted by an unexpected visitor yesterday, & have much work lingering. I attempted to do the poem in prose, but my inability to see clearly what I am writing about, —i.e.to see anything as a whole & not merely as something with detail here & there,—makes it a failure at present. And even in detail it takes me long to get past the obvious or Conventional epithet &c to the right one & one that is more right. How true Sturge Moore's detail is: I am just reading *Pan's Prophecy* his last booklet.[1]

Goodbye & give Helen's love & mine to all at Well Knowe.

I am ever yours Edward Thomas

---

[1] ET had consistently admired Sturge Moore's poetry. See *The Gazelles and Other Poems*, reviewed *WC*, 21 April. T. S. Moore, *Pan's Prophecy* was given a full column review in *DC*, 24 August, entitled 'An admirable poet'.

18

26 August 1904   *Elses Farm*

My dear Gordon,

I wanted to write to you as soon as I got your letter (for no
other reason than that I liked it). But I was just off to Walmer
with Merfyn. We stayed with a friend there and Merfyn was
introduced to the Sea—which he liked. My host was an amiable
old man, once a neighbour of ours at Bearsted, who spends every
evening of his life in dressing for dinner and playing Patience.
He seemed to like it, but I got quietly and solemnly bored and
took to swallowing overmuch beer at dinner and thus ensuring
somnolence until I could go to bed, where I read de Musset's
Confession d'un Enfant du Siécle. Have you read that book? The
magniloquent way in which he mistakes reverie for thought reminded me of myself, as also his glorious and elaborate sorrow
at nothing at all. I read it for the first time & was surprised to
find that, tho he said it finely, he said much the same thing about
his own generation as I have said about ours: so that I conclude
that all decrepit young men think the same about their generation.

Since I got home I have worked hard and unwillingly at two
enormously dull books which I had to review at length for the
Chronicle—the *Life & Letters of Edward Byles Cowell*, and *Dukes
& Poets at Ferrara*.[1] But I find almost all books dull now, because I have to write about them. I have let myself in for an
article on Sturge Moore's four recent volumes,[2] tho I really have
nothing to say about them except that they are very fine and that
I like them. If other critics are half as unwilling as I am, no
wonder that they are so bad. As usual, I am trying to think how
long I can go on turning out one or two thousand words of
'criticism' every week. By the way, Milne wouldn't give me
Ransome's book[3] partly because two other people (including
Snowdon) had asked for it, & partly because it was so small &

---

[1] George Cowell, *Life and Letters* etc., reviewed *DC*, 29 August; Edmund G.
Gardner, *Dukes and Poets* etc., reviewed *DC*, 3 September, both unsigned.

[2] *The Centaur's Booty* and *The Rout of the Amazons* (1903); *The Gazelles and Other
Poems*; *Pan's Prophecy*, reviewed *WS*, 1 October.

[3] *The Souls of the Streets and other Little Papers*. James Milne, literary editor of
DC, and ET never saw eye to eye on literary subjects; Milne preferred the bland
generalities of reviews by Arthur Waugh. Keighley Snowdon, like GB a
northerner, was a regular contributor to *DC* literary columns.

mincing in appearance. I am thereby saved a masterpiece. I hope
he won't treat my own companion volume in the same way. By
the way, I am dedicating it to

Gordon Bottomley

Poet

How bizarre it looks! The first proofs were mostly errors & I
hope I may have a second batch. I suggested calling it *Horæ
Solitariæ* (Second Series) as it belongs to that period of history.[1]
But will Duckworth object?

Last night I brought the 'Skeleton' to an end & sent it to
Baillie. It is a failure, and my bringing it to an end was as purely
an exercise of will as the original murder was. In the last
sentence but two he is alive and well; in the last two he is dead
& makes a most attractive skeleton. I have murdered my original
scheme. Your laughter is too kind by far. But I will never compose in that way again. Already I have done one of the short
things you suggested, tho unhappily it was snatched away before
it was finished, by the *Chronicle* Editor who wanted a 'Country
article' & got a fantasy about Pan (of course) instead. But I
can't get the confidence necessary to copy out my recent things,
when once I have corrected & finished them. I have half-a-dozen
things in this state now, some 18 months old. Shall I borrow the
Ransome typewriter? It is warranted to produce an essay in $1\frac{1}{2}$
hours, & a review in rather less. I think, by the way, that he will
have to stick to Literature because he has already allowed two
ridiculous errors to be printed in prospectuses: e.g. 'the gem
will be as dainty as possible' instead of 'the form &c'. That
stamps him as a literary man at once, surely; perhaps a genius.
He was here recently and I liked him much. He departed in my
trousers, having muddied his own.

I must make the middle the end, as usual.

Helen & I send our love to all of you at Well Knowe.

Ever yours Edward Thomas.

30 August

I had to go town last Saturday. There I saw Ransome &
arranged to call the book *Rose Acre Papers*,[1] such a pleasant title

---

[1] In 1910 ET published a selection of essays from *Horae Solitariae* (always written
Horæ Solitariæ in these letters) and this version of *Rose Acre Papers* under the
latter title.

(to me) that I wish the things were better & more deserving of you and it.—I am sick of London & people & am wanting to be more of a hermit than before, if I can—But now, this moment, as I hoped I was settling down, the servant falls ill with something that will perhaps be alarming, & I am off to housework and irritation again. Pity me.

Good news: the *Chronicle* has rejected my 'Pan' etc. as I hoped and thought it would.[1]

19

28 September 1904   *Elses Farm*

My dear Gordon,
    I can't write. For today I leave home and tomorrow I start life in London lodgings. I found that my work—even my bad reviewing[2]—was suffering more & more from a silly but unavoidable nervous interest in the children's movements in & out of the house, & equally silly but unavoidable interference in little household things, & a continual wearing irritation. This affected my temper and I thought it wise to try the effect of a change. So I am leaving on a wonderful calm autumn day which I ought to enjoy profoundly, tho the very nervousness that fits me for it unfits me for it except in quiet & solitude. Alas.
    My room is in Ransome's place at

1 Gunter Grove
    Chelsea
        London S.W

Secretly I hope I shall be forced to return soon: as I may well do, since it will cost me an extra 15/– a week to live in one room in town, so that I shall have to make £40 a year more than usual.

---

[1] Although this particular article was rejected, two others were published: 'A Village Chronicle', *WS*, 30 July; 'The Country in August', *DC*, 6 August.
[2] Reviews published in September include A. C. Swinburne, *A Channel Passage and Other Poems*, reviewed *W*, 6 September; *Susperiosae cogitationes*, by the author of 'Poems and other verses', reviewed *DC*, 10 September; Stephen Gwynn, *The Masters of English Literature*, reviewed *WC*, 19 September; *Westminster Abbey*, painted by John Fulleylove, described by Mr. A. Murray Smith, reviewed *DC*, 27 September.

But congratulate me on my second triumph this year. In February I was asked to do a book on Holland & I refused: last week I was asked to do one on Marcus Aurelius or on Swift & I refused. Few authors have a nobler record of performances left undone.

Many independent people see me in 'The Man who knew Himself'.[1] I can see about 4 remarkably apposite sentences; but as it was written when he had only seen me 3 times or so I can hardly suppose he modelled it on me unless Duncan Williams supplied the information. But I have an unlucky way of showing my own character to everyone.

I have just asked again for your book from *The World.*

What do you think of this photograph to be looked at from about 3 yards away? It is by the well known F. H. Evans who did Beardsley. He asked me for some sittings & this is one of the results—technically faulty. If you don't like it, return it and he may do a better one soon—

With Helen's love & mine to you all

Ever yours Edward Thomas.

20

20 October 1904   *1 Gunter Grove*

My dear Gordon,

I have not been able to find a pleasant hour for writing to you from here. For I have done much work, my room is so hideous & homeless that I have been able to attempt little else, & after work I have rushed to some distraction, seldom to books, seldomer to writing. And now I am worse off than ever.

For I have just been asked to write a book on Wales for Blacks.[2] The fools of course have waited until the last moment

---

[1] Ransome's *The Souls of the Streets,* pp. 37–44, 'A man who knew himself', called 'Merlin'. 'The keenness of his intellect has been sharpened on himself. . . . He pierces in half an hour to the heart of a book, and sees what the author had arrived at, how far he had failed and why. . . . He sees so clearly the pettiness of others that he cannot believe in the greatness of himself.'

[2] *Beautiful Wales,* painted by Robert Fowler, R.I., described by Edward Thomas. In Black's Popular Series of Colour Books; other volumes included *Oxford,* by John Fulleylove and ET; *Greece,* by Fulleylove and the Very Rev. J. A. McClymont; *Holy Land,* by Fulleylove and the Rev. John Kelman.

& I expect to have less than three months for the whole. So I am off to Wales next week to see some of the country I know & to make plans & to get into condition. Meantime I have work to finish & plans for travel to make & people to see; & there can be no letter. I am very sorry indeed. But do help to keep me alive by sending me a letter sometimes.

It is pleasant to live close to Ransome, by the way. I don't know what I should have done without him, with no other human being within 3 miles.

I asked several times for *The Gate of Smaragdus* at *The World* office, & don't suppose it ever got there. I will try again. If Matthews[1] sent it to *The Week's Survey*, I would try to get it from the editor. What do you think?

By the way, if you have anything to lend that might help me in *Wales*, do send it (to Elses Farm, not here, tho I shall be here for another week).

I am glad you like the photograph, & much surprised & amused at the supposed resemblance to Beardsley.

With my love to you all.

Ever yours Edward Thomas

21

1 November 1904   *C/o Mrs. Phillips,*[2] *Oaklands, Amanford*
R.S.O., Caermarthenshire

My dear Gordon,

Why don't you write? At least, now that I have left Chelsea, you need not confuse me with my late exuberant, rash, & Protean housemate. He was full of a letter about Baillie which he had written to you but was most secretive about a letter in reply: so that I was inclined to suppose that he might have swept me into the matter.

But I write now to ask if you would be willing to look at the prose version of two (very simple) Welsh songs, & to make a verse or two out of them to be set to two sweet tunes which I think I told you of. If you will, I shall send prose & music

---

[1] Elkin Mathews, the publisher.
[2] Cousins on his father's side. For a vivid description of a childhood visit to these paternal relatives see 'Home' in *Light and Twilight*.

together. I want to include them in *Wales*. Your name would be mentioned if you were pleased with the verses.

The book doesn't grow at all. I have not written a line or made any complete plan. But I am making notes. This is a wellknown county to me, & Helen & I walk in it all day. Helen stays till Friday—we came down last Friday: & then in a day or two I start off alone into mid Wales on foot & hope to reach Cader Idris or Llangollen in a week.

With Helen's love & mine to you & all at Well Knowe

Ever yours Edward Thomas

22

13 November 1904   *Elses Farm*

My dear Gordon,

I had to put an end to my mountain walk on the 4th day, because I got blistered & strained. But it was a splendid time— the people so hospitable & the country so magnificent—& someday I may write the better for it. Nevertheless, it has only made my present incompetence seem the greater and I cannot write a word. I even think I may have to give it up after all. Still I am reading hard & making plans just as if I were quite confident. Do let me have the Welsh book you speak of.

Oh, I don't know what to do, & I haven't at present the courage to do just what I like, regardless of the publisher; nor if I did, would it be for much use, since it would be so little.

You should have seen the mountains of Cardigan—and the hundred rivers—& the peat & birches & white farms & deserted houses & orchards—and five miles without a man or a house in the mist. In fact the mountains I crossed were so wild & wet that few of the farmers had ever been far over them: there were ravens & badgers & otters there.

I am promised the prose translations of the Welsh songs soon & will send them on at once, with the music. I will mark the internal rhymes for you & such regular alliteration as there is. It should make a fine patch on my hasty page.

Money difficulties make it impossible for me to live in London just now & I don't want to if I can avoid it. And yet you can't guess how the little things of life here trouble me & incapacitate me. Merfyn fidgetting is worse than a brass band practising at Chelsea: truly; tho I am not sure why. So I may not meet Balmer just yet. I must be in town to use the Museum, however, in a week or so, & then—if he is arrived—I hope I shall see him: if you give me a letter I will call on him—no, just his address is all that is necessary.

Goodbye. I hope you will write in spite of all discouragement from me; I believe that I am what I am because I am perplexed by Wales & by the reviewing I have to keep up as usual & by problems beside which these are amusements.[1]

Helen & I send our love to you all.

Ever yours Edward Thomas

23

12 December 1904   *Elses Farm*

My dear Gordon,

I couldn't write so soon if I hadn't just received the Welsh translations, in spite of your letter & your gum.

The simplicity of the things in translation is rather frightening to me. I wonder what you will think.

The 'Maid of Llandebie' goes like this:[2] & by the way Llandebie is 4 syllables, the first & third being accented: but the 4th is so unlike anything English that you can't rhyme with it. I put the accents on the proper names as they come.

(1) 'I love a maid of Llándebíe, & she loves me also. Of all the young maids of Caermarthen(shire), there is not one so fair

---

[1] His reviews at this time included the following: *Tom Jones* and *Joseph Andrews*, reviewed *DC*, 14 October; John Davidson, *The Testament of a Prime Minister*, *DC*, 22 October; *The Poetical Works of Longfellow*, *WS*, 29 October; *Natural History of Cambridgeshire*, edited by J. E. Marr and A. E. Shipley, *DC*, 5 November; T. S. Osmond, *Scattered Verses*, *DC*, 5 November; Hilaire Belloc, *The Old Road*, *W*, 22 November, and *DC*, 13 December; T. Sturge Moore, *Toleda and Other Odes*, *DC*, 27 November; C. E. Farrow, *The Cinematograph Train and Other Stories*, *DC*, 27 December; *The book of the aseygnements and techynge that the Knight of the Towre made to his daughters*, *DC*, 29 December; *Poems of D. G. Rossetti*, edited by W. M. Rossetti, *DC*, 2 January 1905.

[2] *Beautiful Wales*, pp. 47–9, 'and one of the songs was "The maid of Landybie" by the bard, Watcyn Wyn. Here follows the air and a translation by an English poet [i.e. GB].'

as she. On her cheeks are roses, white & red, the tints all blended. She is the only maid I desire, & she will have none but me.

(2) 'I love one maid of Llandebie, & she also loves but one. The tender maid remains faithful, pure of heart, & lovely to see. Her beauty & comeliness have won my love & my life; for the sweet & blushing & kind fair one has no one comparable to her in all the world.

(3) 'While there is lime in Cráig y Ddínas; & while there is water in Pánt y Llŷn; & while the waves of shining Loúghor (Lucher) walk between these hills; & while there is a belfry in the village, & the sound of its bell pleases the countryside, the maid of Llandebie shall have her name held in sweet remembrance.'

There is no internal rhyme, at least not a regular one which need be followed. You will see how the lines rhyme from the stanza given with the air.

I am sorry we have only the air in sol-fa of 'The Maids of Caermarthenshire'.[1] The last syllable in the first line of each pair of lines rhymes with the 4th in the second. Here are some of the verses:

(1) 'The song & the harp desire to sing the praise of the maids of fair Wales. And lads have no theme which is so dear to them. And there are no maids in the land like the Maids of Caermarthenshire.

(2) 'Their pretty cheeks bear the bloom of the rose. Their complexions have also the white sheen of the lily. And the fairest roses & lilies adorn Caermarthenshire itself.

(3) 'All beautiful & loveable are they; as fleet as the wind when on its wings: of modest look & nimble foot, how swift of motion are they ever! Ay, the maids of Caermarthen dance it through the world.

(4) 'There is a pure heart in each breast, & a happy nature with it. They are up with the dawn & sing with the bird; for the maids of Caermarthen are full of the songs of the true Muse.

(5) 'Sweet is the song that rises with the day from the happy heart; sweet the air which blows at night from the heath; sweet is it to hear the clear voices of the maids of Caermarthen.

(6) 'It is the desire of the man who would love a maid to love one of them, for one of them, I say it in earnest, is worth two or

[1] Ibid., pp. 134–5.

three of the usual ones. If I take a wife, I shall surely take one of the maids of Caermarthenshire.'

I can't write any more tonight,—my hand is tired by copying *Wales*.

---

13 December

I came back yesterday from three days in London where I worked & also saw Balmer. I like him, but he was so shy & silent that I can't say I was happy. But I shall see him again. He tells me that Robert Fowler (a friend of Ashcroft Noble's) is illustrating *Wales*—[1]

It is pleasant to know that you like some of *Rose Acre Papers* & that we agree about its faults. But I am surprised that you liked my cat story.[2] And by the way, O lover of Cats & therefore of mine, I do not think the gum[3] is quite the soul of you:—or perhaps my tobacco incapacitates me.

Then about Grieg & the *Didone*.[4]

I did like Grieg 4 years ago: but as a matter of fact I ought to have said Chopin in that place. 5 years ago I heard a *Didone abandonnata* at Oxford—liked it—& forgot its composer. But I always liked music, only as a rule I was compelled to hear it in a crowd & hating the crowd I had no fit ear for the music. Surely you know, & knew that I liked to hear you play & often want to hear you.

I liked the pictures in *The Venture*, but especially Shannon's. I thought the Ricketts too small & didn't look at it.[5] 'Tresses of the Surf' pleased me much & more than anything else of Balmer's except the 'Apple Gathering'. By the way, I was very glad to hit upon De Quincey as an author for him to illustrate when he asked me to suggest something; for he had already thought of De Quincey & of the same passages as I, and it has never been done.

Your suggestion for *Wales* is not quite definite enough but it

[1] Robert Fowler, R.I. (?1854–1925), was educated at Liverpool College. His 'Conway Castle' was exhibited at the Royal Academy in 1903.

[2] The second paper (pp. 13–23) about Cleopatra, the cat of 'my friend Oliver now called a poet by half the critical world'.

[3] A box of storax, which burns like incense. [*GB*]

[4] Clementi's sonata called *Didone Abandonnata*. [*GB*]

[5] The painters, Charles H. Shannon (1863–1937) and Charles Ricketts (1866–1931), who were also interested in printing, illustration, and lithography. Clinton Balmer had already illustrated GB's privately printed books.

may bring forth. I have now done far more than a quarter of the whole, but not anything that I want to do so far. I have no time except for outlines & hurried phrases & cheap epithets.

This morning I wrote a bad review & did housework. This afternoon I roamed about the house looking for disorder to put straight & now I am fit for nothing yet must do 1,000 words of *Wales* and copy another 1,000. How then can I write to you?

Goodbye with Helen's love & mine to you all

Ever yours Edward Thomas

I haven't had time to see *The Venture* again.

24

30 December 1904   *Elses Farm*

My dear Gordon,

Very many thanks for your letter, your portrait, & your reminder[1] that there are hundreds of persons named Edward Thomas.

I have only just got your letter. For we all went to London on Friday before Christmas, which was foolish, because I had influenza, & then Helen got it, & now I am back here entirely alone, trying to cook & work at the same time, so that my usual haste & stupidity are doubled. Your letter painfully reminds me that they are doubled. For I want badly to write, but obviously cannot. Nor have I any calm to look forward to, since Helen may return tomorrow & we have no servant, & the wind is shaking the house.

I don't see how I am to hear of the *Didone Abandonnata* at Oxford, for I know nobody there. But perhaps Haynes will tell me when I see him next, tho he likes Scarlatti best, I believe.

I shall see Balmer again, & I pray that I shall hear you playing in his room. For it is a good room, & every day I remind myself that I have not heard you play or even somebody else.

About 'The Maid of Llandebie', the Loughor (in Welsh Llwchwr, which is almost Hloochoor) is a lovely river: & the Cráig y Ddínas is a great hill covered with hazels, from which wealthy people get lime.

[1] An article on social work signed with his name, and amusingly unlike him. [*GB*]

I shall call the portrait, Gordon Bottomley the younger. It is a good likeness but when has a reviewer & hack to get time to copy the portrait needlessly in words?

Ransome reviews me quite cleverly in *The Week's Survey*,[1] but is so anxious to show that he is cleverer than I that he says my work is composed of *sentences*, whereas it is at least composed of paragraphs, that are inconsequent, tho pleasant in themselves. He was over anxious about making his point.

I hear that *The Venture* is having rough seas.

I wish you a happy recovery from Christmas, and a constant belief that I shall some day write a letter.

By the way, could you lend me Samuel Palmer's Welsh pictures?[2] I am now doing 12 landscapes, one for each month,[3] & am hard up, & think they might help. Or lend me a poem to set me going.

With love to your Mother & Aunt Sarah and your father, from your broddling[4] but ever yours

Edward Thomas

25

11 January 1905   *Elses Farm*

My dear Gordon,

You pretend admirably. But I wish you wouldn't pretend that you thought I didn't like your poetry very much & more & more. Nowadays I only read (except Welsh & review books[5])

[1] An unsigned review in *WS*, 24 December.
[2] Samuel Palmer (1805–81), a famous and original landscape water-colourist. Many of his exhibitions contained paintings based on tours in North Wales in 1832 and 1843. Late in life he turned to book-illustration and to etching. ET probably refers to a portfolio of reproductions of his Welsh pictures.
[3] *Beautiful Wales*, Chapter V, 'Wales Month by Month', pp. 99–199.
[4] 'Broddling' was a word improvised by my mother to describe a bad dentist working away at extracting a tooth in little pieces. Edward said it was a great invention, and said it over and over with delight when he first heard it. ⌈GB⌉
[5] ET means books about Wales; he sang Welsh songs but never claimed to know the language. His father was a Welsh speaker but his Monmouthshire mother had no Welsh. However, it would be surprising if his tutor at Lincoln College, Sir Owen M. Edwards, had not encouraged him to take an interest in the Welsh language. Helen Thomas has told me about her visits to Wales with ET where, on occasions, they had to use signs to obtain lodgings in the farm houses of monoglot Welsh families. His friend, Thomas Seccombe, is probably referring to ET's passive knowledge of Welsh in his letter to the *T.L.S.*, 16 April 1917 (later reprinted

the *Aeneid* just before going to bed, & yet for three evenings I
have struggled with your capitals & the only irritation I had
came of the feeling that your things would expose me too much
if I quoted what I like. And now you almost compel me to quote
your 'Apple Gathering' as well as 'Apple-Bluth',[1] and that too on
a day when for your sake alone I put all my modern poets on
shelves over the fire in my study. (I have just been reluctantly
moving my books upstairs to the room I have worked in, to
avoid the noises, since I left Wales: it is not a good room and it
faces north.)—Well, please send me something to quote.

Many thanks for Palmer, which I have not yet opened. And I
will try to keep tobacco smoke out of it.

I am very glad you like the song, & contrite that I should have
done it harm through mumbling it. I believe you think me rather
a classical beast. I wish I were; for not being that I am nothing
— About the versions of the two songs. I have just been with
great disgust & cramp copying out the wretched chapter which
they are to adorn. This chapter now goes to Black who will, I
hope, send me back a type-written copy, to which I can add the
songs at any time before the end of February, or say the middle.
But the sooner the better & don't hesitate to put two verses into
one, in the lively song.

I should like to see any really good (not necessarily lauda-
tory) reviews of the *Gate of Smaragdus*:[2] but not the literary
World. And has any reviewer said anything about you or me in
The Venture? I don't get press cuttings & have heard nothing
about *Rose Acre Papers*, of course, which is a comfort, since
praise would be annoying & ridicule unnecessary.

About London, I paid 10/- a week for my room at Gunter
Grove, & extra for washing, light & coal. I fed myself anyhow.
But now the landlady offers full board & the room for £1 a

---

as a Foreword to *The Last Sheaf*. Essays by ET, 1928): 'Thomas had what are
vaguely called "Celtic" characteristics; he was, as his name betokens, Welsh,
and he sorrowed at times over the loss of his birthright in the Cambrian tongue;
. . . *Wild Wales*, he savoured intensely, and I expect he knew nearly as much
Welsh as Borrow.'

[1] *Poems of Thirty Years*, p. 19 and p. 24. See *Beautiful Wales*, p. 130.
[2] *Poems of Thirty Years*, pp. 177–88 contains extracts from 'Press opinions of Mr.
Bottomley's work'. They include reviews in the *Daily News*, 21 October 1906 by
John Masefield; *Literary World*, 6 January 1905; *The Speaker*, 7 January; *Pall
Mall Gazette*, 8 February; and *Manchester Guardian*, 10 February.

week, which I should accept if I could afford to go & work in town. You will have no difficulty in getting a room for 10/- or less at that distance from town & probably board for another 12/- or 15/-. When will you come? And will you stay here a little while? I know you won't stay a long while.

And now my wrist & my second finger remind me of *Wales* & will not let me go on writing much more.

Wales gets worse & worse & as I copy chapter after chapter I am furious with myself. Think of yourself publishing the first drafts of the poems in *The Gate of Smaragdus*—the very first: think of me writing often 1,000 words a day & then with practically no correction copying them out, & this too when many of the things are of a kind I should usually—chew for a month or more for each 1,000 words. I have just done a wintry white & lonely mountain.[1] It took 2 hours & is just a series of notes: but I must copy it out in haste & either leave much out or not amend it at all. If I had succeeded the result would have been as much like a poem of yours as verse can be like prose. Merely to fill space I had to quote a long piece from Shelley that was not in the right mood. Honestly, I do think we aim at very similar things & you nearly succeed & I never come even so near as to fail. How I could envy you your leisure if I did not know that I should waste it.

Goodbye. Helen's love & mine to you all.

Ever yours Edward Thomas

Please return these proofs when you have looked at them, tho I am only in haste for the letter which will come back with them.

Isn't the new Sturge Moore—*Theseus & Medea*—magnificent?[2]

26

My dear Gordon,

Your letter & the translations & the music of 'The Maids of Caermarthen' (with Fowler) have just come, and I am made very

[1] *Beautiful Wales*, pp. 99–108.
[2] *Theseus, Medea, and Lyrics*, reviewed *DC*, 5 January.

glad. But perhaps I shan't be able to say so because to tell the truth I am now so pressed by work & so unable to acquire concentration naturally that I have taken some of the devil (and take it sometimes thrice a week) to help me, & if I dally long it is not a help, but a great hindrance, so I must be quick.[1]

I have already planned to use 'The Maid of Llandebie', I mean your translation. Of course it is not you, & it is not the Welsh lyric, but it can be sung & it has already reminded me of the original. Therefore, without your name, but with your apologies, I have inserted it in my 3rd. chapter.

So far I haven't made a place for the other, but I certainly will.

The spondees are heavier tho not much slower than in the original. Your remark about spondees tempts me. But I must only recall that a classical master once said to me 'There is only one spondee in English & that is beef-steak as it is usually pronounced'. Your version has the disadvantage that it does not look quite so well without the music as the Welsh does, & perhaps the internal rhyme is not inevitable in it. But I quite see why you prefer it, as I do, to 'The Maid of Llandebie' which comes near to facility instead of simplicity.—No, I have not time. I am already nervous & heady. But I don't follow line 4 of stanza 2, 'And quick as such scent of blossoms'. Is it to stand there? Also, I dislike 'zestful'.

Before I forget it, the woman & the room at Gunter Grove were clean. I haven't time to say 'how clean'.

I shall rejoice over *Wales* just because it includes these songs & I fear for that reason only. I hope Blacks won't refuse to print the airs. If only you would send me a poem, something perhaps in the mood of *The Crier*,[2] which I am tempted to quote in my 'November' or 'February'.[3]

True, I haven't violence. The nearest approach to it is the sham humour which I insert in order to make it clear that my feeble seriousness is as ridiculous to me as to others. I shall not fight against it.

No, you are not getting old, because you are not settling down. I sometimes fear that I am settling down—with nothing underneath.

[1] The reference here is to opium which ET had experimented with as an undergraduate. He resorted to it only rarely and, one suspects, as an aid to concentration. There is no hint that he was an addict.

[2] *The Crier by Night.*

[3] Sections of *Beautiful Wales*, Chapter V.

The rough waters of *The Venture*—I meant the poor reviews.

I was glad I went to Balmer.[1] I have lent him some De Quincey volumes, I fear in vain, perhaps they are not so good as my vision of them in his studio. Is he getting on? I feel quite sorry & angry that I cannot help him even by suggestions.

You are right about Fowler. Conway might be quite fine in the original. Between us we shall not make another fortune for the Scotchmen. Did you know he was a friend of Ashcroft Noble's?

Perhaps then, your 'Ohohey' comes from the Greek *euoi* which is *evohe* in Latin.

I have already made one attempt at Palmer's suggestion, & tho I have failed I am going on. I can't be at once so clear in detail & so large as he is, without more time: so I have to give up the detail & my largeness usually comes to vagueness.

How odd of you to like my criticisms, & what criticisms? You can't have seen my things on Sturge Moore in the *Chronicle*—4 or 5 at different times: & I get worse.

Theseus & *Medea* are so unlike Tennyson & so much better that I can't find fault with them, except that the two are curiously little people in my imagination, after reading his poems.

I must be quick if I am to work tonight. It is now 8, & I must write my 'May' for the book.[2] It is hard because Cartmel & the larches keep coming in.[2]

Helen sends her love with mine to you all. She envies me my letter & so should I envy her if it were hers.

Ever yours Edward Thomas

27

17 February 1905   *The Weald*

My dear Gordon,

Yes I am going to be happy (a ridiculous word for my heavy glum restlessness which continues) traditionally. I am already quite surprised by myself. But I have temptations continually,

[1] Clinton Balmer, who illustrated *The Gate of Smaragdus*.
[2] See *Beautiful Wales*, pp. 135–42, especially pp. 131, 136–7.

twice I should have taken the thing if it had been at hand. Still, my work & my opinion of it does not improve noticeably

You heard nightingales at Bearsted. At least I did when you were there. Perhaps you were thinking about my excellent dog. Yes; you shall hear them here. They will be singing well on May day and for a week or even a fortnight before. But I shall see you here or in town before then.

I fear you won't like the script of *Wales*. It is untidy & far worse than this in places.[1] It is now coming back slowly from the printers and is dirty. By the way, Rathbone's air was quite wrong and I don't understand it.[2] I only found out yesterday that it does not represent the sol-fa at all.

The early part of *Wales* is worst. Some of it appals me even in the state in which I return it to the printers. It is sometimes saucy, sometimes dull, & often unintelligible & displaying my unique power of making the obvious appear subtle & then ridiculous.

I have just got an advance copy of Oscar Wilde's *De Profundis* to review by the day of publication.[3]

By the way—you see how confused I am—I have had to leave out some verses of 'The Maids of Caermarthenshire', which perhaps you will not mind, as those you did were only part of the original. I will cut out 'Apple Bluth' if you like: but I shouldn't like to. I don't like it nearly so well as other things, but I wanted to please myself by using something of yours, & that was easiest to use. Would you rather I forced your name in? It would have to be forced.

I look out for your bucolic.

Ransome will not return to Gunter Grove, I think. His mother gives up London very soon, but I hope he will not follow to Edinburgh.

Goodbye. I am about to write the last pages of *Wales* and I

---

[1] The mss. of *Beautiful Wales* was given to Cardiff University College Library by GB. In a letter to GB, dated 8 April 1905, omitted from the present collection, ET writes, 'I write immediately. That is why I am so brief. But here is *Wales*. Keep the M.S.: I wish it were a better one. I hadn't the energy to clean the printer's marks from it; but you will if you ever read it. You will prefer to read it first in the proof which I enclose—a proof which I have improved in a hundred small ways, tho I shall still make use of your suggestions if you make any.'
[2] A friend of GB and a collector of folk-songs to whom ET makes acknowledgement in his *Pocket Book of Songs for the Open Air*.
[3] Reviewed *DC*, 23 February.

have only 10,000 words left to copy. But I shall be busy if I get all my work in before March 1, the appointed day. Did I tell you I had decided to omit all history? So there goes all my Museum work and my fifty close pages of notes. And I have to do a signed review of dear Nevinson's latest book[1] which is a not very good collection of newspaper reviews etc.—a very hard thing, especially as I am nearly 20 years younger than he & much in his debt and much liking & admiring him.

    With Helen's love & mine to you all

Ever yours Edward Thomas

28

2 February 1905   *The Weald*

My dear Gordon,

    You are an excellent moralist. That is to say, I agree with you. Moreover, I am apparently on the way to a more sensible mode of living. I burned my opium (as I often have done) and did not buy any more. But I am grateful to the Devil, because under his influence I easily acted the amiable man: Then I threw it off, and such is the value of tradition, I am still amiable, & consequently a more cheerful member of this family. In fact, I have had a wonderful sweet mouth, that is how I explain it & every day I am practising self restraint in temper which used to be impossible. Isn't it odd? & I get quite hopeful about the future—not as a literary cove of course—but as a little man. My great enemy is physical exhaustion which makes my brain so wild that I am almost capable of anything & fear I shall some day prove it. A busy day in London yesterday so wearied me that I only just did not spoil everything. I saw Ransome, & he has been bad & looks bad.

    At last in my 'April' I have quoted all your song of 'Apple Bluth'—the book is nearly at an end & I have only to copy it and to write 'October', 'November' & 'December'. Shall I send you the manuscript if it falls to me? For the book will be in a sense I

---

[1] H. W. Nevinson, *Books and Personalities*, reviewed *DC*, 4 March. ET owed his employment on the *DC* to Massingham and Nevinson.

have no time to explain—yours.[1] I told you—I think—that I was doing landscapes for each month of the year. They are marvellously irrelevant as a rule: so are the 7 or 8 characters.[2] And I am giving up the notion of writing history: I shall put all my history into my 'December' probably.

We have a pretty good servant now. Helen said to her a few days ago 'Look at the pretty sky!'

'Yes' she said 'that is what you call a sunset, isn't it?

We send our love to your mother & Aunt Sarah & your father & you.

Ever yours Edward Thomas

29

27 February 1905   *The Weald*

My dear Gordon,

Of course I only meant to say that I thought it just possible (tho I know that I was wrong too) that you would like to have the credit of verses of yours in *Wales* even if they were quoted in such intimate relations with the context that it would be difficult for me to mention your name. I have thought since of putting footnotes to give sources of all quotations from contemporaries —the others being Sturge Moore and Ernest Rhys. I think it would be only fair. But you do transfix me as you say you wish!

Yes, I wish I had reviewed your poems[3]—The enforced task would have enabled me to read them more carefully than I do now, so that I, if not you, might have been the better for it. But you annoy me when you praise my reviews, which are best when most irrelevant, & even then poor derived stuff tho whence derived I am not at present sure. I often wonder whether

---

[1] Like another friend, Ian MacAlister, GB believed that some of ET's best work was in these 'Colour books'. 'The gentle austere beauty of his prose in such books as *Oxford* and *Beautiful Wales* makes its own claim for posterity's attention; and there is injustice in the failure to reprint them.' GB, 'A note on Edward Thomas', pp. 166–78, *The Welsh Review* IV, 3, September 1945.

[2] *Beautiful Wales*, Chap. IV, pp. 55–98. [Mr. Jones, the minister; the landlord of the 'Cross Inn'; Mr. Rowlands, the minister; the poacher; Llewellyn, the bard; Azariah John Pugh, a schoolmaster; Morgan Rhys, and others.]

[3] *The Gate of Smaragdus*. A reference back to the review by Keighley Snowdon, *DC*, 3 October.

my later writing is clearly derived—e.g. 'The Skeleton' and the *Oxford* characters. Sometimes I think not.

I saw Ransome last night & he says you have been eloquent against descriptions. What will you say of my 25,000 words of landscape, nearly all of it without humanity except what it may owe to a lanky shadow of myself—I stretch over big landscapes just as my shadow does at dawn, right over long fields & hedges into the woods & away! What will you say? And I hardly care what anyone else says, too.

Rathbone was right. But he misunderstood Helen's writing; her r's often looked like t's and so he took them. We have got the thing right now. But I defy you to discover why I omit some of 'The Maids of Caermarthen' by *what* I omit. I have kept 3 verses, including the petticoat verse, and the first & the last. Now, why? And supposing you are right, do you approve?

I have just copied the last 2,000 words of the book. I am, you see, capable of anything. But I am neither happy, nor relieved. Task work is good for me. I am a thing of habit, & the regular[1] work of these last three months has been far easier than the irregular[1] which has been not half of it in bulk. So now I shall not have any more leisure than before, I fear. But I can always steal a day so long as I leave home or start early for a walk (which is seldom). So I shall see you several times in London, I hope, before you come here. I think you will find the right place for hearing nightingales either in the fields or in bed: last year in the calm nights we heard them from the house continually. I do want to see you soon. Where shall it be? It must not be at a picture gallery or a restaurant where we know people—I mean not with Ransome or his acquaintances or mine. But I am too possessive.

Helen's love & mine to you all. It is 1 a.m. & I want to read a little before bed because tomorrow will be all reviewing. Where shall I hear 'Somer is icomen in'? Oh, at Balmer's, of course. I haven't seen him for weeks now.

Yours ever Edward Thomas

---

[1] ET has glossed this sentence with asterisks: 'regular'='Wales'; 'irregular'= 'reviewing'. During the period January to March, I have traced 14 reviews in *DC*, and 5 in *W*, with probably 4 others in *The Academy*, which, under new management, increased the space devoted to books (including signed articles) on 11 March.

30

16 March 1905   *The Weald*

My dear Gordon,
    Ohohey! your letter.
    You come to London next Wednesday: so should I in any case, & as you will be there I shall stay until Friday or Saturday. But I see it is impossible for us to meet as I wish. So, I suggest that I meet you on Wednesday and join you or not as seems best then; and that I spend Thursday or Friday with you, doing exactly what you want to do. Will you let me know which day? Then I will call for you at Ebury Street at 10: perhaps in the evening Balmer would admit us both? If you decide to see pictures on the day I am with you I can go out & have a drink if I am bored by the pictures—But let us go to something old if you like:— the National Gallery and the Museum. But I am in your hands except that I know a place for lunch—Let me know in good time how this strikes you.
    Thank you for your poem. Let me have time. I may not be able to open it for a week, because I have to review[1]

Thomas Moore by Stephen Gwyn
The Grey Brethren by Michael Fairless
William Bodham Donne & his friends
Peeps into Nature's Ways
A Country Diary
Travels round our Village
A folio Chaucer
A new Keats

[1] This letter marks the beginning of a period when ET was able to make a substantial income (£5 a week at least) by reviewing for 4 or 5 papers at the same time. The same book is often reviewed in different periodicals from different angles and at varying lengths. In this way, and because he systematically sold review copies to the booksellers, he derived some profit from the devoted thoroughness with which he read all books for review. I have traced the following reviews of the books mentioned above: *Thomas Moore*, and E. de Selincourt, *The Poems of Keats*, reviewed *W*, 28 March, and *DC*, 3 May; Catherine B. Johnson, *William Bodham Donne*, reviewed *W*, 4 April; *The Grey Brethren, and other Fragments in Prose and Verse*, reviewed *DC*, 27 March, and *W*, 15 April; *The Works of Geoffrey Chaucer and others, Facsimile of 1532*, edited by W. W. Skeat, reviewed *DC*, 24 March; the three nature books, reviewed *DC*, 12 June.

Also to correct proofs, sow beans, peas, brussels sprouts, leeks, radishes . . . and walk much with a visitor this weekend.

Why should I want to write about FitzGerald any more than about Browne, Hardy, Pater, Cowley, Yeats, Hawthorne, Borrow, Patmore, Shakespeare, Milton, Verlaine, Euripides, Virgil? I don't want to. I don't want to write at all, but if I do write, it must be about myself & I had rather do it *apropos* of landscape & imaginary people than popular authors.

You are right about Wilde, & I hope you understand the first sentence & know which sentence is Milne's.[1] The fact is I was in haste & the book never was anything but a review book. I can hardly bear to look at it again but I rather think it is very poor except the Christ interlude. Also I never did more than admire Oscar Wilde.

I didn't see Beardsley's letters.

Now I am disturbed & I try to propitiate you by sending mutilated proofs of *Wales*. If you have not time to look at them now, will you return them at once? Make any suggestions you like & forgive 'The Hay Waggon'.

Ransome isn't coming. His fickleness annoys me.

I must go.

With our love Ever yours

Edward Thomas

*　　*　　*

Between this letter and the next I came to London and settled down in rooms to try to live and work there; but I did not remain quite a fortnight, for my lung broke down again after a week of N.E. wind. My two years' immunity was, in fact, over.　　GB

*　　*　　*

31

3 May 1905   *The Weald*

My dear Gordon,

I should have written before if I had thought it necessary to

[1] Reviewed *DC*, 23 February. Milne was the literary editor who frequently altered ET's copy.

say thank you for your letter. Yet now I have little more to say. For I have had several people to stay here lately & have also not been well, so that all my good time has had to go to my reviewing. The Cottage turns out well & I go there to business for 6 hours regularly every day when a damaged ankle allows.[1]

Are you wanting *Midsummer Eve*?[2] I read it once, ten days ago, & that is not enough to make sure of my likes & dislikes. I took a sinister joy in the names of your persons and the gross rusticity of some of the detail & conversation, as contrasted with the pure Gordon of the greater part. Of course like anybody else, I quarrel (on first reading) with the dramatic form, and enjoy the lack of any sense of time & place. At present I don't like—or rather I don't see—the whole, but I like most of the lines. But the fact is I am only moved to say I like many lines & believe I can like the whole in time.

A thousand thanks for what you said of *Wales*. But

(1) I didn't forget the women: I was afraid of them. I will try someday, if only for your eyes.

(2) It was too late to add other verses of 'The Maids of Caermarthen'.

(3) I hope to have a chance of correcting the misprinted line in your poem.

(4) I regret you don't like the landscapes. For landscapes are what I seem to be made for, considering that I have tried for 10 years to do them, & am always trying. Say whatever you think of them whenever you think of them. I believe I am sincere enough & earnest enough to make use of criticism. What I want to know is the effect produced. Then I can compare it with my intention & see what to change. I have, by the way, seen Garnett's *Imaged World*.[3] It is stupid, without power & without effort.

---

[1] He had rented a small cottage in Egg Pie Lane for half-a-crown a week and he walked there at 9 a.m. every morning. Cf. *WWE*, p. 109 and a letter to Jesse Berridge dated 16 April 1905: 'By the way, I now work in a little cottage $\frac{1}{2}$ a mile over the fields from here. An Oxford friend of mine—whom you will perhaps like—has rented it and comes for weekends or so.'

[2] *Midsummer Eve*, a one-act play in verse, mingles the supernatural with the country life at Cartmel; printed in a very small edition in 1905 by James Guthrie at his Pear Tree Press. Not included in GB, *Poems and Plays*, 1953. GB described the play as a 'poem of earth and change' in verses sent 'To Yone Noguchi, with a copy of *Midsummer Eve*.'

[3] Edward Garnett, *An Imaged World* (Poems in prose), 1894.

O God, the *Chronicle* asks me to do frequent 'prose poems' on the country.[1] What am I to do? I patched up a May Day out of *Wales*, but badly & in haste. But when *Wales* is out, I don't know what I shall do. I can't do the usual newspaper country article, & I don't believe I shall be able to hurry myself into doing my best at regular intervals. I want to have subjects given to me *which I must use*. Have you any? The subject—or the title—must be obvious; my treatment will be as usual. I dare not refuse. A confession of inability would have been mistaken for insincerity and rudeness. The money I could learn to do without. If only Ransome & myself could be combined for the time being. His flow & confidence! His movements puzzle me. I shall end by refusing to be interested. Yet I owe him much humility on account of a superior review of his lamentable *Stone Lady*.[2]

Now I have to try to say something about the *Decameron* & the *Heptameron* for the *Speaker* which despises my usual manner & frightens me into attempts at being sensible.[3]

Helen & Merfyn are away. But their love goes with mine to you & your people.

Ever yours Edward Thomas

32

13 June 1905   *The Weald*

My dear Gordon,

Have I ever left a letter and a long one unanswered for a month, before now? But the truth is I have been busy; my days and nights full of writing and reading. I have done a good deal for *The Academy*[4] which suddenly shows me unmitigated kind-

---

[1] Two such articles appeared in *DC*: 'The making of Spring', 1 April, and 'A Mayday', 1 May.

[2] *The Stone Lady*, ten little papers and two mad stories, 1905. Review untraced.

[3] *The Decameron*, translated by J. M. Rigg, and *The Heptameron*, translated by Arthur Machen, reviewed *S*, 22 July.

[4] During June and July the following number of reviews can be traced: 13 in *DC*, 10 in *A*, 2 in *S*, and possibly 7 in *W*. Books reviewed in *A* were *Works of Charles and Mary Lamb*, edited by E. V. Lucas, vols. 6 and 7, 10 June; R. Bridges, *Demeter, A Mask*, 10 June, also in *DC*, 4 July; S. Baring-Gould, *A Book of South Wales*, 17 July, and *DC*, 26 June; G. K. Chesterton, *Heretics*, 24 June; *The Rhymer's Lexicon*, compiled by Andrew Loring, 1 July and *DC*, 19 June; *A Modern Mystic's*

ness; some for the *Speaker* & *Outlook*, too, as well as for
Chronicle & *World* as usual. In fact I have had little to think of,
except the various reasons for and against making over £5 a
week, as I easily could. I have decided not to try to make more
now, chiefly because it would be murdering my silly little
deformed unpromising bantling of originality, and take away the
one thing in my life that resembles a hope—a desire, I mean. So
I nobly remain moderately rich. And yet since *Wales* has been off
my hands, I have done & attempted nothing but reviews & that
too in spite of invitations from the *Chronicle* and *Country Life* to
provide 'essays' for the world. For I haven't done a stroke towards
my 'prose poems on the country' for the ½d. press. I can't try.

 Also I haven't read your play again, nor anything outside my
work save the *Aeneid* and a ballad or two. ——

 What you say about the 'unrelated masses' of landscape in
Wales is horribly true. It had not occurred to me how much harm
the economical publishers have done me by printing the landscapes as close together as pips squeezed out of a fig.[1] If they
had each begun at the top of a page they would have had a chance;
or if I had told the reader to take only one or two before going
to bed or after a meal. Secretly, I rejoice to have seen Edward
Garnett's Prose Poems,[2] because they do not show that I have
suffered by being born 10 years after him.

 I begin to envy you your Ransome at the back of the house.
By the way, I may not be able to answer his postcard of last
week:— will you tell him he should stay with me when he comes
to town? If only his writing truly would reflect his high spirits!
But only his friends understand the connection between high
spirits and his diluted ginger beer. Your comparison with Kate
Greenaway is adroit. ——

Way, 8 July; George Gissing, *Will Warburton*, 8 July, and *W*, 27 July; *De Flagello
Myrteo. Thoughts and Fancies in Love*, 15 July, and *DC*, 4 July; W. B. Yeats,
Stories of Red Hanrahan, 22 July; *The Scenery of London*, painted by Herbert
Marshall, described by G. E. Mitton, 29 July. (ET's extended contributions to
The Academy from June to December contain some of his most perceptive literary
criticism.)

[1] *Beautiful Wales*, Chapter V, 'Wales Month by Month'; ET's 100 pages of text,
interspersed by 48 of Fowler's paintings, are run on without regard to their form.
Each month contains at least two distinct sections—some have three or four—and
each section is a separate essay on a new theme. The effect, as ET notes, is
rather disjointed.
[2] See Letter 31.

It would take a stupid long time to say why I thought your pastoral should not have been in dramatic form—The pure rusticity—e.g. the girl and the newly dead cow—is excellent: so are the names; but I can't or couldn't harmonize them with e.g. landscapes which are straight [out] of your 'head' and not through their heads at all (as it seemed to me).

Oh, the oaks & hazels & nightingales, Oh this Spring—and no Gordon—often Helen & I have said, now if Gordon were here! or, as often, if only Gordon were playing 'Sumer is icomen in'! For I don't know whether I most wanted to enjoy you here or to have you enjoying the being here. And now in the mist after a week of rain the last nightingales are singing. Dare I ask you to come all the way from Cartmel to stay here?—

Don't insist on my praises of *Polyphemus*. They are 3 or 4 years old; also I don't know how much of them was due to the mire of verse out of which I picked it.—

(I have read Baring Gould's *South Wales* tonight—it being now 11 p.m.—and review it tomorrow morning. Hence . . .)

I hope you didn't take my Gorky[1] seriously and literally as perhaps Ransome did. Its misty irony was intentional. But I wish I could mind my own business.

Helen's love and mine to you all & my remembrances to the lamp chimney.[2] Also our love to Arthur.

Yours ever Edward Thomas

Here comes *Demeter*;[3] shun the alcaics & all thought of them.

33

30 June 1905   *The Weald*

My dear Gordon,

I don't believe I shall ever read your play through again however long I keep it. For I really can't read anything nowadays that I have not got to read. Even your 'September' excited as I

---

[1] *Creatures that once were men* and *Three of them*, reviewed *DC*, 12 May.
[2] Which had lasted two years—or some similar time that stirred his incredulity. [GB]
[3] R. Bridges, *Demeter*.

was by the idea of your using that mode, I read as if I was to review it; saw its faults & determined to say nothing about it.[1] The result of all my reviewing seems to be that I lose all power except of saying what a thing is not—a power I always had but could once upon a time keep under. You don't know what it means to make £5 or £6 a week by reviewing. This week for example, I read review books all day on Monday & Tuesday, interrupted only by my little lots of housework, lessons to Merfyn & meals. Then until tonight I have been reading & writing all day with the same interruptions & also about ¼ hour to Virgil; the only other books opened being the Keats and Shelley from which I give Merfyn his Shelley lesson. And now I am so tired that I was amazed that I could merely enjoy some sea tales by John Masefield—also for review—an hour ago.[2] My opinion therefore is worth nothing (except money). I greatly fear I cannot keep up to even my old standard. Original writing I dream about, but never get so far as to get out paper & pen for it. . . . and yet you expect me to write about *September* & *Midsummer Eve*. Why, I forgot that it was Midsummer Day this week—tho I was sentimental enough to remember that I must celebrate it a few days before. One nightingale sang for a minute as I walked to my cottage on Tuesday. It was the last. The cuckoo is almost silent. The year has passed; the Spring has done without me; I have not had one good hour of standing still & forgetting time. But I make over £200 a year, or can expect to.

You are good in your attitude towards Ransome, & clever to keep it up. I have long had to drop it & to like him largely because he reminds me of my oldest friend, now in Africa these three or four years past. But I like him, & could still like to hear his plans. He ought to have come here to worry me. I could have stood him better because I fear I have a bit of the stupid patron in me—e.g. I have just set an old college friend going in journalism, made him think of it, told him how I had done it, & sent him round Fleet Street & rejoiced when he cackled over his first book to review.

I wish I could read *Demeter* not as a reviewer & one or two other books I have lately had—e.g. & above all a 'period play'

---

[1] Untraced.
[2] *A Mainsail Haul*, reviewed *DC*, 2 August, and *A*, 5 August.

called *Borgia* anonymous & published at 3s. 6d. by Bullen. It has
no arrangement, but it has a hundred fine dialogues & you would
like some of it if you could pardon a slack Elizabethanism in the
cadency of the man's blank verse.

But how should I know whether a book is good when I have
this week reviewed these?—[1]

(1) *De Flagello Myrteo; Thoughts & Fancies on love*—aphorisms,
good or pretty all. (Elkin Mathews)
(2) *Borgia*
(3) 3 other plays & an epic
(4) *The Spiritual Life* by Lady Dilke
(5) *Confessions of Lord Byron*
(6) *My Garden in the City of Gardens* and one other book; &

I have ahead of me[2]

(1) *A Mainsail Haul* by John Masefield
(2) *The Scented Garden*
(3) *The Dog from Clarkson's*
(4) *Will Warburton* by George Gissing
(5) Swinburne's *Tragedies*
(6) Verse
(7) *Influence of Feeling for Nature on Medieval Poetry*
(8) *Confessions of Byron*—again
(9) Article for *Academy* on feeling for Nature in 18th century
poetry.

Sombrely, I am glad you like *Polyphemus*. Sombrely, I have
not read *Penthesilea* But as much of me there is
Is yours ever Edward Thomas

[1] (2) O. Wilde, *Borgia*, reviewed *DC*, 19 July; (3) including Bridges' *Demeter, DC*,
4 July; (4) *The Book of the Spiritual Life*, by the late Lady Dilke, *A*, 29 July; (5)
by W. A. Lewis Bettany, *W*, 4 July, and *DC*, 18 July; (6) F. W. Burbridge, *My
Garden in the City of Gardens* and *The Book of the Scented Garden*, *W*, 1 August, and
DC, 7 September.
[2] (3) Desmond F. T. Coke, *A Vagary*, reviewed *A*, 22 July; (5) a 150 word notice
in *W*, 25 July, p. 166; (6) Untraced; (7) Alfred Brese, *The Development of the
Feeling for Nature in the Middle Ages and Modern Times*, *DC*, 14 August; (9)
This article cannot be traced. A signed article, 'Eighteenth century sidewalks',
appeared in *W*, 21 June, and a review of six country books, with some wider
reference to the place of nature in English writers, in *W*, 12 July. This theme is
further developed in ET's short introduction to *The Book of the Open Air* (1907).

34

24 July 1905   *The Weald*

My dear Gordon,

Helen has just gone away for two or three days with Merfyn and left me with Bronwen & myself. I have lately been more miserable than ever in the intervals of entertaining numerous acquaintances & friends. In one month we have had here Irene, my father & mother, Mary, Jesse Berridge, Duncan Williams, Tom Clayton, Dalmon, & my grandmother.[1] And now I have no money in the bank, and I have laudanum inside me, and it is a fine sad evening, and I can no longer read a German on *The Development of the Feeling of Nature* & a Frenchman on Charles Lamb.[2]

If only somebody who wanted to, would look after me—somebody strong, not too tender. For I am sure I get worse & worse (N.B. I haven't taken opium for several months until today) & no week,—hardly a day,—passes without my thinking that I must soon cease to try to work & live. But I am so irritable & restless that even if I go so far as to resolve not to work, in a few hours out of sheer ennui I get down a review book & a little later perhaps write a review. If I have now & then ten oblivious minutes at sunset or midnight, I am very lucky; for at all other times, whether I am reading or writing or talking or trying to sleep, I am plagued by such little thoughts as how much I shall earn this week or what train I shall catch tomorrow or whether I shall have my letters by the next post, & such big thoughts as whether any thing is worth while, whether I shall ever again have hope or joy or enthusiasm or love, whether I could for any length of time be quite sensible in taking food, sleep, drink &c & whether if I could be, I should be any better. You see—I must have some motive & to be honest, my responsibility to Helen & Merfyn & the dear & joyful Bronwen is not a motive. I must believe in myself or forget myself and I cannot. I get more & more self-conscious every day—of the little good in myself &

[1] Mrs. Irene MacArthur—Helen's sister; A. D. Williams—a journalist; Tom Clayton—a school friend; Charles Dalmon, a recent friend and poet, whom ET described as 'a modern Herrick' (*The Last Sheaf*, pp. 71–7).

[2] Jules Derocquigny, *Charles Lamb*, reviewed *A*, 26 August. ET read French and German as well as Latin and Greek.

work,—of the much bad,—of the futility of reviewing,—of my insolence in Reviewing any book,—of my way of doing things,—my way of speaking,—my very attitudes, dress, expression—Shall I ever have the relief of true and thorough insanity? Oh, for some one to help, instead of being surrounded by people who see that I have many things & am some things which they would like and therefore conclude that I ought to be happy or that I am 'affected' or wildly exaggerating, just because I can jest and walk a good many miles & do a good deal of work. But do not think I am foolish enough to believe that anyone will or could be expected to save me. . . .[1]

I can't go on. There is much I want to say but I am too critical & self conscious & could never satisfy myself or you in saying it. So goodbye.

Yours Edward Thomas

35

6 August 1905   The Weald

My dear Gordon,

Your letter was very good to have. I shall not survive my gratitude for it.

I was having 3 days in town when it came. I returned on Thursday, then had to work, &, instead of writing to you, on Saturday noon I started with Freeman (my neighbour) to walk to Canterbury along the Pilgrim's Road.[2] We spent Saturday night sleeping & trying to sleep in the fields, sheltered by corn sheaves. It was good. But this morning we had to turn back after going 25 miles because my feet were no use. So I am back, fretful & tired, aware that I ought to be careful—that carefulness is troublesome & dangerous—& that I shall never be careful enough. I don't think you are quite sound when you urge me not to be self-conscious; nobody could be more so, or more conscious of it: & that way will always lie misery, dissatisfaction, imperfection, perhaps 'tragedy' or tragic farce rather. Still, I like every word you say & know it ought to help me but doubt it will etc.

I meant to see Balmer in town & on Thursday I called on him,

---

[1] 97 words omitted.
[2] Martin Freeman, a Lincoln College friend.

but he was flown to Chelsea & I had not time to follow him in the rain unprotected.

As far as I know, I have thought out my relations with Ransome carefully & come to a conclusion pleasing to him & me.

—also tho I am the Confessor,[1] I can never confess everything to one man, even to you—I find I have unconsciously arranged my confessions according to the person & so each one of three or four is frequently surprised and put on a wrong scent. I fear you are so mistaken by my fault, & yet—now at last—I can not even try to put you right. But know, that only a revolution or a catastrophe or an improbable development can ever make calm or happiness possible for me. Still you need not be afraid of an abrupt fifth act, because I am too distracted & undetermined ever to do more than be perplexed in the extreme & in vain.

Meantime, I have got behind with my work & that troubles me,[2] & I must go.

Goodbye. Ever yours Edward Thomas

36

4 September 1905   *The Weald*

My dear Gordon,

I wonder can you like any of this thing (excluding the name). It is recent—2 weeks old. I have a notion that it ought to be a more complete picture than it is, & that it fails because it hovers between the neglective & the picturesque without combining them. Since writing it I have done two others—one suburban (a beggar suggesting to a boy all travel & adventure & liberty as he passes down the street), & one a dawn. It annoys me that I stick so to short things now—between 500 & 900 words—By the way, put a pencil mark alongside what annoys you & explain or not, as you like.

How odd that you find the Electrician 'healthy but limited'— 'like Sanitas'.[3] I saw him twice last week in town. Certainly he is limited. Perhaps I alarm him by advice—did you know I gave

[1] I had called him Edward the Confessor. [*GB*]
[2] In August and September 16 reviews appeared in *DC* and 6 in *A*.
[3] A quotation from a contemporary advertisement for a lavatory pan disinfectant.

advice? Anyhow, he gives me confidences so obviously imperfect that I wish I could never see him again.

I saw Balmer, too, & took Freeman with me. But Balmer was interrupted as well as shy & in 10 minutes there was nothing to do but to go in a serio-comic atmosphere of my making. I promised to go again next day & couldn't manage it.

Someday I shall collect my small things & call them *Illusions*, with the sub-title (my own) of *Ejaculations in Prose*. You shall see my others when they are copied & have been duly rejected by the world the press & the devil. Why will no one print me?—

Edward Garnett has introduced me to Joseph Conrad's work.[1] His *Youth* is magnificent—a young shipwrecked sailor in a small boat worn out, lying in the bottom of his boat & getting his first view of the East (palms & men) at dawn.

Perhaps I shall write tonight—an *Illusion*, not a review—so I hurry off. Send me back this M.S. when you can—

With my love to all of you—and Helen's.

Ever yours Edward Thomas

37

15 September 1905   *The Weald*

My dear Gordon,

I am glad I sent you my ejaculation. The condemned sentence was bad & just as you said. So I have pulled it together & am now almost satisfied with it. But I wonder are you right about the form. You are my kindest critic & you tell me to drop the form because it doesn't give me opportunity enough. Edward Garnett—who was here today & yesterday—finds the form all right but says my sentiment is not always consistent—that details are sometimes out of keeping—& that I often make the reader want a picture & do not satisfy him. If he were not so damnably infallible I should be inclined to believe him & to persuade

[1] Garnett was a frequent visitor to the Thomas household and has left some vivid memories of their association. See especially *Selected Poems of Edward Thomas*, with an introduction by Edward Garnett, The Gregynog Press, 1927, and Garnett's entry in *DNB*.

myself that really you both agree. But I can't give it up yet. I am always wanting to do such things; & they are not indolent either —the ideas are spread over the long blank period since I began to do *Oxford* & only now can I use them; so I think I must. No other form ever occurs to me, tho I see that I may come to stories of some kind—not plotty cathartics, but episodes ending suddenly & soon; & that a novel is possible, & fine on account of its difficulties. Once or twice, I have thought of a suburban novel to be called *A Suburban Education* but vaguely, & I don't like great blocks of autobiography. But stories & novels seem far off & what am I to do? I can't force myself as you can. For instance, I can't tell myself to do portraits & I dislike action and psychology.—The fact is that you want me to use what experience I have had more explicitly than I do, don't you? But I must learn to do so by growth, not by executing poetic justice upon the remnants of a childhood that never existed. How important it sounds!

Can you have Helen as well as me? She must have a holiday & she wants me to join her & I cannot go to you & elsewhere with her now that the publishing season is beginning. But I should like 10 days or a fortnight with you far better than anything else —The little bedroom will do perfectly. (I am very rude.) Helen will be 'never a third'.

I saw Arthur for an hour or two this week.[1] He still talks about literature, but I was glad to see him & yet afraid that his chief occasion for liking me is a belief that I am interested in him. We sang

> We're off to Rio,
> We're off to Rio,
> Then fare you well,
> You bonny young girl,
> We're off to Rio Grande.

[1] Arthur Ransome. I have omitted a few unkind and personal references to Ransome from the last three letters which suggested that a brief estrangement had existed between them. ET was so lonely in his chosen occupation, so proud and yet so eager for like-minded company that, at times, he gave himself without stint to a new friend. ('My liking for [Ransome] was never without artificiality. I cherished him because he was the nearest approach to a blithe youth I happened to know and it is natural that I should be angry with him for a rather speedy disillusionment.' Letter to GB 24 August 1908.) Helen Thomas has recalled for me the colour, laughter and extravagant fantasy that the Ransomes brought to the Thomas household. ET was going through a bad patch this summer as his three letters to

It has a glorious tune which I prefer to Westminster Abbey just now.

Goodbye. Helen believes you & sends her love with mine to you and all.

Ever yours Edward Thomas

38

19 September 1905   *The Weald*

My dear Gordon,

I don't know why it should be possible for you to think I might take offence at the perfectly clear objection to my coming with Helen. Of course, I don't. Whether I can come alone, I dare not say; but I will try, & it is quite possible. Let me know when you can, what date will suit you best. Meantime, Helen will probably go away on Monday & deposit the children in various places.

Also pardon me for saying you forced yourself. I thought I was echoing you when I said it. So I was but inaccurately. I ought to have known better, especially as I am never so conscious of growth as to be able to say 'that is of yesterday', far less to feel that I am actually pretending to be 23. I don't believe I am. And aren't you a little harsh about the 'form'? Except that my things are nowadays always between 400 & 1,500 words long, & always in prose, they have no 'form' in common; unless you are thinking of the ubiquitous first personal pronoun. It is probably reviewing that makes me so jerky. Short things are all I have energy both to conceive & to extrude. Here, e.g. is a suburban one.[1] It is at least simple—a virtue so unusual in me that perhaps I exaggerate its merit here. Garnett quoted a good thing (which I did not

---

Jesse Berridge show (dated 25 July, 8 August, and 16 October 1905). The last one begins, 'My dear Jesse, you really ought to write to me. You know what I am doing perfectly well.—grumbling, and wearing my clothes and doing reviews for the million.'

[1] Some of these 'ejaculations' found their way into *The Heart of England*, 1906. The following reviews appeared in October: E. V. Lucas, *Life of Charles Lamb*, *A*, 30 September; *Poetical Works of R. Bridges*, vol. 6, *A*, 14 October, and *DC*, 17 January 1906; William H. Davies, *The Soul's Destroyer and Other Poems*, *DC*, 21 October; *English and Scottish Popular Ballads*, edited from the collection of F. J. Child, *S*, 28 October.

remember) from Joubert, saying that it is possible to exaggerate
the moral qualities of things, but impossible to exaggerate their
physical qualities; & he quoted it against me. But if I were to
stick to the physical qualities of what I see, I should have to wear
glasses. I don't see their physical qualities very often; so I am
at least an honest fool in refusing to stick to the physical:—or
ought I resolutely to leave out my 'atmosphere' of fancy etc.?

How distracted I am! For three weeks I have had sudden
visitors (not always welcome) in the middle of a week, so spoil-
ing my work, & now I have to go to town to an *Academy*
dinner—a bright thought of the Editor's 'for discussing what is
about to appear' in the paper. I can't discuss, because I want to
suppress the greater part & to be better paid. Freeman & I are,
however, getting in a lot of impressionism amongst the heavy
stuff & make a point of refuting other contributors time after
time under cover of a review. I wish you could join. By the way,
would you write a review now & then if a book were sent to you?
I can't promise but I think I might get something from the
Academy if you let me know what sort of thing you would prefer
or, if possible, the names of books coming.

In haste; for it is evening & I always expect to do something
in the evenings when they are still. With Helen's love & mine.

Ever yours Edward Thomas

39

24 September 1905   *The Weald*

My dear Gordon,

Helen goes away tomorrow for at least a fortnight. So if I can
get away to you, I shall not be free until about October 10. I
hope to come, tho I expect I must bring books with me, if I
may.

What an excellent plan I have got of catching letters from
you—by sending my M.S.S. And many thanks for what you say.
I think you are right when you say that 'masses of such visions
should be piled & reared together': yet I am too feeble & stupid
to think hard about the remedy. My excuse—that I am too much
disturbed by reviewing & household troubles—might fairly be

condemned as a pretext; & yet if you knew my almost daily agonies of fury, despair, violent resolve & dull resignation, perhaps you would not blame me much for sticking to purely minor prose. I try to force myself not to spend more than a few hours at a time because I invariably subside then into the cushions of easy intercourse with people as idle, as silly but not as miserable or (may I say) ambitious as myself. Then I think that this would be impudent & lofty. So I do nothing. Just now I am so sick of books & literary people that I do not think of writing even my ejaculations.

I was at an *Academy* dinner on Thursday at a gilded restaurant that made me feel like an unfortunate woman. Sturge Moore sat opposite;[1] I was not introduced: but I sat next to the Editor of *The King* who told me that George Newnes' new buildings were the finest business buildings in London 'tho he knew nothing about architecture'. N.B. Unless you get on to the roof of Covent Garden market you cannot see these buildings at all, they being to a most narrow street as a precipice.—I didn't get on: the rest being reviewers (who went about asking whether *Academy* dinners were to become as famous as *Punch* dinners) and creatures who were females if one may judge from their stupidity & the purple colour which $\frac{1}{2}$ a glass of champagne gave to their cheeks.

Next time I am at the *Academy* I will give your name & address to Harold Child who is assistant & practically omnipotent editor. He is a Winchester & Brasenose man; a friend of Lionel Johnson's; once an actor: a kind, clever, uninspired, somewhat academic man, apparently. I see that it might be a good thing in the end if you got a little work from him, & I will do what I can. By the way, all reviews are anonymous.

I grow very very dull. I am always talking about personality & looking for it in others & envying it in its most varying kinds, & am so conscious of my own lack of it & so disgusted that daily (I think) I give myself less & less chance of ever putting forth a little of it.

———

Ransome told me he had decided to give up his romantic way of life as he considered it, & ceasing to stew his plums, to live

[1] ET had reviewed T. Sturge Moore, *The Little School. A Posy of Rhymes*, *A*, 2 September.

near Balmer. I hear he has been instructing Balmer in my true character.

I wish I had that table piano but it is impossible.

I am now about to write the 3rd article of 2,000 words on Charles Lamb which I have had to do in 3 months.[1] Lamb was glorious but he can't be written about & it annoys me to have to do so, especially as he doesn't deeply touch me—So how can I write any more to you? tho thereby how I could write what I have written is made clear. Forgive the reviewer.

Yours ever Edward Thomas

40

21 October 1905   *The Weald*

My dear Gordon,

We were very glad to have your good news & we believe that your father goes on getting better.[2] There is nothing else to say until I know that you are comfortable again. But by the way, have you heard of *The Acorn* a quarterly for the benefit of Yeats . . . and Chesterton?[3] As for me, I have just been rejected by *Country Life* and expect to be rejected (as far as articles go) by *The Academy*. One way & another, I do get on: by the time I am forty I shall be quite unprintable.

With our love to you all.

Ever yours Edward Thomas

41

14 November 1905   *Elses*

My dear Gordon,

I am very glad to hear from you again in spite of your little

---

[1] See Letter 38, note 1; Letter 34, note 2; Letter 32, note 4. There is no shade of annoyance in the admirably balanced review of Lucas's *Life*.

[2] In a note to an omitted letter, dated 7 October, GB writes 'My father had dangerous pneumonia.'

[3] In each of the 3 letters to Berridge (Letter 37 note 2) ET excuses himself from a

bit of bad news which was I hope untrue by the time it reached me. But I really am busy now. For three weeks I have been preparing & writing an article on Jefferies for *Temple Bar* & now I have only 4 days work left before I take a short holiday in Wales & in those 4 days I must write on Tchaikovsky's *Life & Letters*, *The Anatomy of Melancholy*, Turgeniev, & more on Jefferies.[1]

But about your book.[2] I daresay it will come to me from *The Academy* & I will try for it from the *Chronicle*. Don't send a copy to *The World*. They never review verse or practically never & I only annoy them when I ask them for it—as I many times have done & in vain. Send it to *The Speaker* & I may get a few words on it there. Of other papers I can only suggest *The Outlook*, *The Independent Review*, & *The Manchester Guardian*. Can't you—I should be grateful if you would—send me an advance copy so that I can prevent Keighley Snowden? In any case I ought to know of the earliest probable date of publication. It sounds fine.

You don't say that Child has sent any more books—so I suppose he hasn't: but ask, when you can hear of a forthcoming likely book. Your prose poem really had no chance. Their verse is their only exception to the rule that their matter is 'critical' in the narrowest sense.

I must take a short holiday and a friend invites me to Swansea, so I go on the 21st for about a week (after 3 days in London) & hope to get some walking in Caermarthenshire. From there I hope I shall write to you. But I am unusually plagued as well as busy & feel as if I ought to fall in a heap on entering Wales: probably I shall only drink beer though.

Please send my love and sympathy (if you can) to your Mother and Father, & give it to Aunt Sarah with Helen's.

Goodbye. I am ever yours

Edward Thomas

---

meeting with Chesterton which Berridge was trying to arrange. *Acorn*: An Illustrated Quarterly Magazine devoted to Literature and Art, numbers 1 & 2, 1905–6.

[1] Possibly, 'Thomas De Quincey', *Temple Bar*, April 1906, pp. 289–300; *The Life and Letters of P. I. Tchaikovsky*, edited by Rosa Newmarch, reviewed *DC*, 23 November; *The Novels and Stories of Turgenieff*, translated by Isabel F. Hapgood, reviewed *DC*, 13 December; *The Anatomy of Melancholy*, reviewed *DC*, 3 March 1906; and E. Gosse, *Sir Thomas Browne*, reviewed *DC*, 26 December.

[2] G. Bottomley, *Midsummer Eve*, drawings by James Guthrie.

42

23 November 1905   C/o *John Williams,*
                                        Waun Wen School, Swansea

My dear Gordon,

I got a promise at *The Academy* and *Chronicle* of your book &
probably I shall get it from one of them.[1] That was on Monday.
On Tuesday I came here & I have been fiercely bored ever since.
Swansea is a big rather notably ugly town & what with my not
very intimate acquaintance with my host I am being reduced to
inanition. Everything is against me. A mile off lives an old Aunt
whom I remember seeing when I was 4: two miles off is an old
Lincoln friend whom I had not seen since 1900. I have seen them
both & they have plunged me into languid & unpleasant remi-
niscence, & altho the Welsh mutton is good my food is thus not
altogether bracing. Also the merriest man I ever knew—Watcyn
Wyn[2]—the bard who wrote 'The Maid of Llandebie' & 'The
Maids of Caermarthenshire'—is to be buried today: and on
Sunday I am to be taken in my bowler hat & collar to a Welsh
chapel in the town. And I have still a lame foot & cannot con-
fidently start a long walk. Of all those blessings my temperament
makes the best as you know it would. So how can I write?

I saw Balmer on Monday & enjoyed an hour or two with him
& his brother. His brother is charming—his clean & reddish
hands, his shining collar, cheeks & eyes, the perfect white parting
of his hair, as he sat at the piano, were fascinating in a way. On
Tuesday morning I saw Ransome for a little while. He read me
a story about a tramp, a clay pipe & a wife in which a small pretty
notion was insisted upon to distraction. He also talked about the
Lady whom he has promised to marry. He complained that he
could not 'get anything of himself into' his stories: a natural
complaint.

My host is a schoolmaster. The school is adjacent & now I
hear a master's whistle assembling a crowd of ragged children
& see him with miniature ferocity giving silly little cuts with the

---

[1] Reviewed *DC*, 26 February 1906.
[2] The bardic name of Watkin Hezekiah Williams (1844–1905), a Welsh schoolmaster, poet, preacher, and popular lecturer. He was the founder and principal of
Gwynfryn School, Ammanford—a seminary for preachers.

cane to boys who are healthy enough to ignore his commands.
So I end.

Remember me.

I am ever yours Edward Thomas

43

22 December 1905   *The Weald*

My dear Gordon,

What is it you reproach me for? For my prose my manners
or my last letter or what? As for my prose & that inopportune
letter from Swansea I do apologize. I expect you really referred
to my *Chronicle* articles.[1] You could not reproach me for not
writing at once when your news came. I only once congratulated
a friend[2] & that was because he seemed likely to turn out an
enemy & I could not afford an enemy just then. In your case, the
printed announcement came as I was setting out for a walk in
Wales and I thought 'Oh well. Gordon is all right' and of course
it did not occur to me that I had a duty to perform, & I don't
believe it occurred to you.

I am rather badly off altogether just now. I am full of reviews
& yet I have made £20 less than usual this quarter.[3] Also I have
been thinking. Also, Hodder & Stoughton have asked me to edit
a list of popular natural history in 12 monthly parts & I am going
to accept because I believe it will be discipline—(this is hypoc-
risy).[4] Also, Fisher Unwin says he thinks I am a great man &
I must write him a book. And now two visitors are descending
on us in 2 hours time for a 5 days stay & when I want to do some
more thinking & gardening. It may seem odd to you that 5s. in
cash as a Christmas present for Merfyn has just proved most
useful to us.

[1] From October to December, 22 reviews appeared in *DC*, 4 in *A*, and 5 in *S*. ET
assumes, I think, that GB refers to the severe review of *The English Lakes*.
painted by A. Heaton Cooper, described by W. T. Palmer, and of L. W. Bailey,
The Outlook to Nature, *DC*, 4 November.

[2] I had lately been married. [*GB*]

[3] In January appeared 10 reviews in *DC* and 1 in *A*.

[4] Subsequently bound in 2 vols. as *The Book of the Open Air*, edited by ET, 1907.
A single de luxe volume was also published as *British Country Life in Spring and
Summer* and, later, a companion volume for *Autumn and Winter*.

Well then, how can I do more than send you this book and ask you to forget that if it is Tennyson & water so was Tennyson? You may like 'Heraclitus'.[1]

Ever yours Edward Thomas.

I am enjoying *Midsummer Eve*. Last night the first 4 pages seemed to me perfect & new.
Will you write 957 words on 'Pond Life in January' for my natural history? Pay is $\frac{957}{1000}$ of £1:2:6.

44

11 January 1906   *The Weald*

My dear Gordon,
   Along with my Natural History job I have accepted the position of collaborator with Frank Podmore in a series of articles on 'Apparitions, Thought Transference' etc., for *The Grand Magazine*.[2] He exudes information and I string it into ropes & coils of pearls. For this humble office I am paid 31/6 a 1,000 words. There was no choice: I cannot pay my rent or anything but daily expenses just now, & my prospects—since Harmsworth bought *The World* & *The Academy* took to the paths of virtue which lead but to the grave—are bad.[3] Yet you desert me and cannot produce a prose poem on 'Pond Life in January'.—So far I have taken no notice of Fisher Unwin. I thought of saying I would do a book on the South Country—with more landscapes & persons—but after all, why should I?
   I read *Midsummer Eve* the other day with complete delight & shall struggle to say so in a way that will please you. I shall not review you with the Multitude: so you may have to wait. *The Academy* sent your book elsewhere in spite of my request & their

[1] The poem 'Heraclitus' in William Johnson Cory, *Ionica*, 1858; third edition 1905.
[2] Frank Podmore (1856–1910), a prolific writer on psychical research and related topics. His *Robert Owen* was published in 1906.
[3] From January 1906 both *The World* and *The Academy* ceased to publish signed review articles and reduced the space devoted to literature. It is still possible, I think, to detect ET's contributions, much reduced in length and consequently less well paid. (The last newspaper cutting ET preserved from *The Academy* was for 14 April 1906.)

promise. The levity with which they treat *Chronicle* reviewers is worthy of a better newspaper.

If I can't read Virgil to you at Well Knowe I shall have proofs of articles on stoats, reptiles etc. In any case I should like to come—and I do know a few more songs which you may be able to enjoy.

But I have only been able to do three days work since Christmas until Tuesday last: so I must haste to a little ambuscade on that fat abbot—Churton Collins[1]—& some preparation for my Ghost articles. So goodbye to the lady & you & our love to all & a happy new year to the lamp glass[2]

Edward Thomas

45

24 January 1906   *The Weald*

My dear Gordon,

I suppose you did not see my page of quotations from Davies in the *Chronicle* or you would not have asked if I had his book.[3] He has become a friend of mine since I first saw him in early November or late October in the Borough. We have corresponded; I saw him in Wales; & yesterday he was to have taken possession of part of my cottage—for he is very poor & being one-legged & I think a poet he finds work at a trade impossible. But unluckily I was given notice to leave my cottage at the end of this week & I had suddenly to put him off. I fear he may once more drift about the Borough 'tasting the various ales': he says he is going to a Rowton House this very week. It was sad that my worst bout of poverty should come when he most needed help, & when all I could send him was little more than enough for his fare to London. I wonder what you will think of his best things. I think he has immortal moments.—By the way, I some-

---

1 *The Plays and Poems of Robert Greene*, edited by J. Churton Collins, reviewed *DC*, 25 April.

2 'The same one still' [GB]. See page 86, note 2.

3 William H. Davies, *The Soul's Destroyer and Other Poems*, reviewed 21 October 1905. ('He can write commonplace and inaccurate English; but it is also natural to him to write, much as Wordsworth wrote, with the clearness, compactness, and felicity which makes a man think with shame how unworthily, through natural stupidity or uncertainty, he manages his native tongue.' In all, ET mixes shrewd praise with many quotations in his two-column review.)

times give him books: if you have any spare copies of even the most elementary poetry I should be glad to transmit them. When I saw him he had only a 6d. Wordsworth & Shelley—which it must have been fearful to read by the light of a coke fire—& one or two strange miscellanies & gifts (of their own works!) from reviewers (not from me, I assure you). I have given him a Wordsworth, a Sturge Moore & I forget what else: I am taking him a Byron and a Cowper.[1]—Well, I enclose his book & the *Borgia*.[2]

Be patient when you see my review.[3] It exceeded the length allotted to your book & it may be cut by the Blind Man. Also it was done in furious haste—as I do all things now. Oh, I have lost my very last chances of happiness, gusto & leisure now. I am swallowed up. I live for an income of £250 & work all day & often from 9 a.m. until 1 a.m. It takes me so long because I fret & fret. Even my daily walks to & from the cottage are solid lengths of uncomfortable misery. My self criticism or rather my studied self contempt is now nearly a disease. But do not be anxious. I am a docile dog. I shall go on until accident or old age stops me. N.B. The one thing that engrosses me—now that fishing is impossible—is the making of walking sticks. If I could be [as] serious over prose poems I could perhaps please Edward Garnett. Did you see my 'Pride of the Morning' ?[4]

The copy of your book sent to the *Chronicle* was defaced by 'with the publisher's contempts' in a bad handwriting.

How you would like Ernest Rhys, by the way. I see him now & then—an absolutely devoted lover of all gentle & fine things both by temperament & accident. But such consistent people with

---

[1] ET sold most of his review copies .and gave duplicates to his friends. *The Poetical Works of Byron*, edited by E. H. Coleridge, reviewed *DC*, 13 February; *The Poems of Cowper*, edited by J. C. Bailey, reviewed *DC*, 21 March.

[2] The *Borgia*. See Letter 33.

[3] Of GB, *Midsummer Eve*. 'The blind man' was one of ET's names for James Milne. The review, signed 'E.T.' is one and a quarter columns long. ('Here, as in his other poems, whether in lyric or dramatic form, he has gone to the deepest wells of his own personality, and though the draughts glimmer a little in the light of sun or moon or stars, they retain the incalculable and haunting gloom from which they came.')

[4] This is either a reference to *DC*, 11 January, when ET's reviews (of E. V. Lucas, *The Open Road* and *The Friendly Town* and Arthur Symons, *Spiritual Adventures*) occupied the first three review columns of the literary page, or to *DC*, 25 January, when the first column was a signed review of *Poems in Prose from Charles Baudelaire*, translated by Arthur Symons.

real characters nearly always annoy me who am destined to reflect so many characters & to be none. What a barber was lost in me!

I use boot trees now—also plates with Monograms. If I live 20 years longer I shall be well-dressed. The pity of it is that I don't sincerely want to be. I am buying a dinner gong with my last sovereign.

It is possible—I think likely—that we shall be turned out of this house in 6 months time: which I cannot look forward to with ease. But Merfyn will need a school in a year or so especially as my time & temper for informing him are shortening fast: so a change is inevitable within 2 years.

This seems a large enough chapter of my autobiographical remarks for one household. But not therefore do I cease. I have to write on De Quincey, on Telepathy, on Byron, on Blake, on '100 Years Hence by an Optimist', on Leland's *Itinerary in Wales* etc. etc.[1]

Yours ever but in confusion now

Edward Thomas

P.S. Ransome took *Midsummer Eve* off *The Academy's* hands. He is getting clever. He bought my *Horae* for 9d. & sold it in an hour to A Friend for 2s. He is just resting after his sixth (serious) affair of the heart.

46

1 March 1906   *The Weald*

My dear Gordon,

I would have sent you at least a word before, but for a tussle with Dent which has been added to my other amusements. He promised by word of mouth (I can't say to my face, because he has never looked me in the face) that I should have 100 guineas for my book,[2] or 35s. a 1,000 words. Then I gave way & said he should have more than 60,000 words. Finally he wrote & without

---

[1] 'De Quincey' (see Letter 41, note 1); *Blake's Poetry*. A new text by John Sampson, and *The Lyrical Poems of Blake*. Text by J. Sampson, reviewed *DC*, 31 March. The remaining reviews cannot be traced.
[2] ET, *The Heart of England*.

explanation & assuming that I should agree, & said that I was
to have £100 instead of guineas. I had 5 minutes to decide & no
one else in the house; so I said no & feared the reproaches of my
elderly minded friends for refusing £100 in my present condition. But he has given way & I am to have my £105. So what a
Summer I have to look forward to! I confess that I was secretly
rejoicing at the possibility of a careless holiday with you; but
now I must take some long walks round Cartmel and try to get a
tradesman to drive me about. By the way neither you nor I said
anything about the length of my holiday. May it be 10 days or a
fortnight? I want you to do a small thing for me—to order the
Daily Chronicle at the shop where I had it before.[1] Will
you? . . .[2]

Ransome has been seeing Sturge Moore, which is lucky for
him. He says S.M. was talking against those who write about
'Lamb & FitzGerald & others who don't count': so I shall hardly
dare to meet him, since such writing is my profession & I don't
like explanations.

William Davies thanks you for the Browning. He looks most
solemnly happy whenever I pass through his room to mine, &
he says he is happy. But I leave him mostly to himself; we are
not born for one another. He says he has been writing verses.

Goodbye with my love to you both.

Ever yours Edward Thomas

47

17 March 1906 *The Weald*

My dear Emily & Gordon,
   This is not a vain attempt to thank you fittingly for making
my 10 days a holiday & the most pleasant I can remember since

---

[1] Although ET consistently pooh-poohed his work as a reviewer he seems to have
kept a fairly full file of all his substantial reviews. Helen Thomas had 6 bound
volumes of reviews, many of them indexed by ET and annotated where his own
text had been sub-edited. Between St. David's Day and 17 March, 3 full length
reviews appeared in the *DC*: *The Anatomy of Melancholy*, 3 March; *The Poems of
Cowper*, 21 March; and Lafcadio Hearn, *The Romance of the Milky Way, and
Other Studies and Stories*, 22 March.
[2] 31 words omitted here.

I was a child (to use an expression that makes Emily laugh). But I write just to say that I have got home to my work again & am glad in a fine warm day & the happiness of Helen & the children. It seems clear, by the way, that we have soon got to move.

I have written 10 letters & have now got reviews & articles & books to write & Belloc's portrait to paint:[1] for these my chief present qualification is a headache, so you at least I will not endeavour elaborately to afflict but just send what books I could remember by the Alienobarbe.[1] Let me know that you are well. Goodbye.

Yours ever Edward Thomas

P.S. Let me have the proofs of Doughty back & I will send the book itself if it is possible.[2]

Will Gordon write 1,000 words on some of the flowers of Cartmel valley?[3] £1. 5. 0.

Will Gordon or Emily describe the dress etc. of any pace-egging boys[4] that were striking—just a rough note for me?

48

26 April 1906   *The Weald*

My dear Gordon,

William Platt has sent me the book containing his 'Goneril's defence'[5] to send to you, & here it is—you will find it too long, lengthy, & evangelical perhaps. I have just shut up my MS. book

---

[1] A tribute two and a quarter columns long appeared in *The Tribune*, 10 September 1906 ('His writing has something of Hazlitt's gusto; the writer is, in a sense, the equal of his heroes. So, too, in his criticism. Of criticism in the tremendously Arnoldian sense, he has nothing; his criticism is simply an interpretation of enjoyment.'). 'Alienobarbe' is possibly a nickname for Belloc or Conrad.

[2] Charles M. Doughty, *The Dawn in Britain*, vols. 1 and 2, reviewed *DC*, 30 March; Vols. 3 and 4, *DC*, 18 August; Vols. 5 and 6, *DC*, 7 February 1907.

[3] See *The Book of the Open Air*, vol. I, pp. 209–12, 'A northern valley. By GB'. In an omitted letter from Devon, 31 March, ET writes 'In a day or two I will suggest one or two additions to your flower article.—e.g. to suggest dates definitely; also to hint more definitely at configuration of the land, nature of the rock, characteristic trees'. He was a scientific editor.

[4] In the north of England children, dressed in mumming costumes, raced their coloured Easter eggs ['pace-eggs'].

[5] William Platt, *The Maid Lilias*, 1904.

of *The Heart of England* to write a little moan to you. Why can't somebody help me in this awful labour? I work continuously at the cottage from 9.30 to 4.30 every day & squeeze from 1,000 to 1,500 words out of myself, & the result is to be my worst book. There are plenty of landscapes & 'spurred lyric'—in fact ¾ of the book will be of this kind, & far inferior to *Wales* because I have less impulse & less material. The rest is pseudo-genial or purely rustic—Borrow & Jefferies sans testicles & guts—except one short love story told just before a fox-hunt which I think pretty good. There are 2 scenes in church, both secular in tone: my Virgilian Schwabism does not come off.[1] And so by wonderful & contemptible determination I have written about 20,000 words this month & have 10,000 words of old stuff that I can use. There remain 30,000 words. Even now I would give up if I dared & lose the £100 cheerfully. I pray it will be my last book if it ever become a book. Henceforth I cease to write 'about the country' & become a reviewer with a wife & family, *tout court* & no deception. Still I hope to do the 30,000. What shall it be about? I can't do the village at all. My old customs would go on to a page with large margins. Also I can't use all the songs which Freeman & Williams & I know[2]—already I have got in 'Poor Old Horse', the haymaker's song, & *'Las! il n'a nul mal qui n'a le mal d'amour'*—of which, by the way, the 4th line is not as I suggested, but (after *'au pied de la tour'*)

'Qui pleurë, et soupirë, et mène un grand dolour'. If you can get the air copied out for me I should be grateful. But can you help me? Give me a string of subjects (excluding the beautiful con-sumptive girl & the hermit)? Or must I fall back on gentle clergymen who are fond of gardens & old books & of course possess sun-dials? Save me if you can. Is there anything in *Wales* I could re-write, do you think? I am sure you will not mind helping an imposter especially as I shall try to explain my impos-ture in a light preface.[3] And yet this April has I know been splendid while I have sat blaspheming it in vague English.

    Give my love to Emily

Ever yours Edward Thomas

[1] Randolph Schwabe (1885–1948), etcher, draughtsman, book illustrator.
[2] Martin Freeman and Duncan Williams.
[3] See the conversation between ET and the watercress man in Chapter I, 'Leaving Town'.

49

3 May 1906   *The Weald*

My dear Gordon,

Your letter etc. came when I could not answer it; then I had
to be in town two days, & today has been as busy as ever, but
suddenly this evening, in the midst of reading about hallucina-
tions I thought I would write to you. Helen and Merfyn are
away for a few days, & I get very lonely when I am so much
busied about unnecessary things.

I showed your letter at once to Davies & I enclose his answer,
hoping you can read the poem.

I don't object to 'loins': only I am sure that most people,
perhaps remembering 'the fruit of his loins' will be slightly uncomfortable at the word, & I know that *Literature* once cut into
a translation of mine from Flaubert which spoke of a swimmer's
'loins'.[1] Probably I shall substitute 'flank'. And many thanks for
re-arranging & supplementing the article which now does well.

> 'for which they scorn & hate them worse
> Then dogs & cats do sow gelders'

says *Hudibras*: but I don't know whether sows ever were gelded
as bitches sometimes are.

Doughty—I am reading him again & find hardly any difficulty
in the performance. No doubt he is wrong, tho I believe he could
not have done otherwise. I feel that his total effect is finer than
that of any long English poem except *The Faerie Queene*; but I
haven't time to find out why. Hueffer wrote well about him in
The Tribune, & someone unknown in *The Times*.

I ran into Ransome in town. He had intended not to let me
know he had come, but was affable & explanatory. Apparently,
he has been convincing publishers with words.

Will this book suit Rathbone? It is one of the best solemn
literary books I have had.

We have many nightingales here, but after this year we shall
not hear them again for we have just had notice to leave at

---

[1] 'Loins'—an obscure reference to something GB had sent to ET. See ET's article,
'Flaubert in the fields and on the shore', *A*, 29 March 1902.

Michaelmas. We don't know what to do. Helen won't take a
neighbouring farmhouse because she must have the responsibility
for Merfyn shared by a schoolmaster: yet we can't really afford
a good school, & so far have not heard of a house near Bedales.
It upsets my work. Still I go on & now I think I have less than
⅓ left to do for *The Heart of England*: it seems likely to be the
worst third. I seem like imitating *Wales* rather badly.

Oh, I have asked Dalmon for the poem,[1] but he has not
answered.

I am nearly asleep.

Here comes a poor Rhys[2] & if I can find it, the Sturge Moore
you want.

I am sick at heart because I am writing badly & much, because
I am getting little money, because I am leaving here, & because
I am always laughing at myself & yet truly I am still the same
funny sentimental egoist that I was before I learned how to
imitate laughter. I am remorseful after my hours with Freeman
& Clayton when I did nothing but imitatively laugh at things I
can cry over when nobody is looking. And yet I went gravely a-
Maying on Tuesday morning. I wonder what I really am? Well,
I am Emily's devoted &

Yours ever Edward Thomas

and I thank Emily for remembering me even in words.

50

17 May 1906   *The Weald*

My dear Gordon,

This can't turn out to be a letter for I am behindhand with
several pieces of work & weary after a day in town when I saw
many people, drank much wine & sat 1½ hours for my portrait to
a colourman.[3] But my thanking you will fill a page perhaps. And
first for the letter, it was very good to have.

---

[1] Charles Dalmon.
[2] Ernest Rhys, *Lays of the Round Table*, reviewed (with other volumes of verse)
  DC, 25 January.
[3] Probably Frederick H. Evans, a society photographer.

The subjects you suggest are all good, but even if they had come earlier I don't think I could have used them because they are difficult & I have to do easy subjects or at least such as I already have material for. So I doubt if I can use them, though I will try the imaginary Saint perhaps. Now for the French song: but I seem to have varied from my usual way of singing it, for the time is wrong. Nevertheless I have got it right with your version as a basis.

Don't thank Platt. He sent the book to be forwarded to you, but without having heard your name, so do not trouble. I quite agree with you about him.

Dalmon promises his poem but has not sent it yet.

I expect William Sharp praised 'Dinadan' because he knew Rhys: & I have not heard of any other poem of the same name.

No, we shall not take the neighbouring farmhouse. Helen goes to Petersfield tomorrow to look about. It is near Selbourne & will have many nightingales near.

I wish I could offer you another subject, but I can't think of one. Have you a suggestion? If so send it please.

It is cold & moist, & I am overwhelmed by a sense of incompetence (& its importance) & don't know what to do. My last chapters have been dreadful. I still have 8,000 words to do & no subject except an orchard by the sea, which will make my 27th landscape in this dreadful book. I wish I were not divided between healthiness, 20 mile walks, humour etc. and small decadence. Was ever anyone more perplexed?

By the way, I wonder can you tell me if the place names in the 'Hunting Song' which Rathbone played—it is in the little book—are spelt rightly? Grass-gards, Ulpha, etc. Dunnerdale etc.[1]

The Bard is still happy & I think I shall give him a room in my next house unless I get a cottage there too. He has shown me 40 pages of his recent verse & it is painfully mediocre & pastoral, with usually just a faint gleam of original feeling that has come through his shabby words—for his style is throughout at the level of his poorest in the printed book. It is distressing & I have to tell him what I think.

---

[1] *The Holm Bank Hunting Song*, given to ET by George Rathbone, is quoted in full in *The Heart of England*, pp. 211–2. ET pays a handsome tribute to the musical knowledge of George Rathbone and Martin Freeman in the 'Note' to *The Pocket Book of Poems and Songs*.

> With our love to you both & my apologies for being what I am
>   Yours ever Edward Thomas

Supposing Helen & I were free & rich at the end of June, could
we come to see Emily & you?

51

12 June 1906   *The Weald*

My dear Gordon,

This is bad news, & I look for good very soon. Yesterday as
Helen & I were walking in the fields after Supper & hearing the
last of the nightingales—almost the last—we were wondering
whether you were in London then & why you did not come
straight here & take us by surprise. That made me sorrier this
morning when I got Emily's letter—which I thank her for.
Expectation of seeing you both quite robs me of the little letter
writing I had in me before. And I had been arranging for you
& Emily to go to Evans on Wednesday or Thursday & then to
Hooton[1]—Well these things don't matter if you are going to
get well quickly. But you made me your debtor by a letter on
the 23rd of May—also your creditor (by telling me I could not
come to you this Summer). I didn't answer because of the book
which still demands a month's copying & I fear some more
chapters. And now while I am uncertain how you are, how can
I laugh with you about *The Academy* & Harold Child's school for
backward boys who have not read Newnes' other publication,
Tit Bits—or that the man who is painting me is only a kind
Welsh fool? No I will wait & hope that Emily will again let me
know how you are. Helen & I send our love to you both. I am
ever yours

> Edward Thomas

[1] Harry Hooton, who had married a friend of Helen Thomas, was one of ET's
earliest and closest friends. Most of the extant letters written by ET at Oxford
were to Hooton. The Hootons and the Thomases exchanged frequent visits.
Hooton was one of ET's favourite walking companions (see the dedicatory note
to *The Icknield Way*) and a member of the group of friends who met on alternate
Wednesdays at St. George's (a vegetarian restaurant) in St. Martin's Lane.
At this time the Hootons lived at Minsmere.

111

52

3 July 1906   *British Museum*

My dear Gordon,

It was good & surprising to hear that you were down & much
better again. I was fearing you might be helpless & Emily too
busy to let us know. And I did not write because I had not nearly
recovered from *The Heart of England* (which I sent in yesterday)
and was more stupidly melancholy, weak, & incapable of work,
rest, or pleasure than ever before. Now I think I am going to
return to the old lofty level by the help of iron, quinine &
strychnine, though I know I shall soon be bald, impotent &
finally precipitated at the bottom of the tumbler for all to admire.
Yet I have a chance of editing a collection of folk songs &c. for
the 'open air' which a publisher asked me to prepare on the
strength of a *Chronicle* article, & shall accept if the price is toler-
able.[1]

Dalmon has not written to me for months & I have not met
him. If I remember I will write to ask him for the poem. I am
glad the anthology increases & pleases you. Whom are you
including that I do not know. Miss Buckton's 'Starling'?[2] There
is a goodish new man named Gerald Gould.[3] David Nutt published his 'lyrics' a month or so back & there is one nice impetuous
illusive piece called 'Romance' & one or two good things in
which I have perhaps mistaken neatness & freshness for beauty—
I often do, being jaded & down at heels myself. . . .[4]

Here I am interrupted by books to be read.[5] Goodbye.

7 July

Since I began I have had no time, as you can guess. For that
day Ernest Rhys suddenly asked me for an introduction to
Borrow's *Bible in Spain*[6] & I have been re-reading it and reading

---

[1] The 'article' was the review (28 June) of *Traveller's Joy*, compiled by W. G.
Waters.
[2] See Alice Mary Buckton, *Through Human Eyes/Poems*, 1901.
[3] Gerald Gould, *Lyrics*, reviewed *DC*, 22 August.
[4] 35 words omitted here.
[5] Between 4 July and 1 August, 7 reviews appeared in *DC* and 1 in *S*.
[6] In *Everyman's Library*, 1906.

large pieces of Knapp's *Life*.[1] Also I have been negotiating with
Grant Richards, a long troublesome business. As the result of a
review of mine he asked me to edit an anthology of songs for
the open air.[2] So I am in 6 months to produce a collection of
ballads & songs, but especially folk songs, to a large number of
which I shall give melodies. It will be mainly English but will
include some Latin & some French. I like the idea: at least I
should like to possess such a book. Of course I must avoid the
Golden Treasury obviousness, but that will mean hard work if I
am to produce something very good. Probably I shall include no
one living unless his work has some excellent music to it which
is unlikely. All the pieces will not be about the country of course,
tho many will be. A large number will be such things as I like to
think about when sitting down or walking in the country. When
anything strikes you as good & not obvious, I do wish you would
jot down the title or first line & let me know. Also, will you ask
Rathbone if he can let me have the music & words of a song in
the last Westmoreland festival book, beginning

> 'As I was walking one Midsummer morning
> A-viewing the meadows & to take the air.'

I should be grateful if you would.

At last I have, I think, got a house at Petersfield. We shall go
to it about November & so have 2 months existence in other
people's houses after Michaelmas.

Alas! I have overestimated what I did for Dent & I have to
set to work to do another 3,000 words. Yet I have a feeling in my
head as if a bullet had got into each temple. . . .[3]

Give my love to Emily.

I am ever yours Edward Thomas

P.S. I am in town for 10 days or so, until the 12th because our
house is invaded by a friend of Helen's, 2 children & a maid.
I wrote to Dalmon.

[1] W. I. Knapp, *The Life, Writings, and Correspondence of George Borrow*, 2 vols.,
1899.
[2] *The Pocket Book of Poems and Songs for the Open Air* was first published by Grant
Richards in the *Books for Wayfarers* series.
[3] 51 words omitted here.

53

28 July 1906   *The Weald*

My dear Gordon,

Your second letter has just come & your revised letter to Dalmon sent off. He will no doubt choose a title or let you do what you will.

Many thanks for your suggestions for my *Anthology*.[1] I shall use them.

Meantime tell me if this song ought to go in my strange collection—

The pedlar tall doth cry:
True hearts, false hearts! come buy!
I am Love, it is May, come buy them!

There is another verse, but it is inferior. Would you care to write 3 or 6 lines for the music of which I will not divulge the distant source until you have said if you like it. I will let you know soon whether I can find anything in the *Gate* or elsewhere for my anthology. By the way Gerald Gould assents affably. I hope you like him & I am delighted with your joy in 'Flower & Leaf'.[2] I am including 'Come Pretty Phyllis' in my anthology.

I return your 'Maids of Caermarthen' in case you care to look over them again.[3] I shan't ask Black's for leave.

[1] I have omitted letters written on 18 July, 11 and 19 August. They are all concerned with ET's 'Book of songs'. I retain this one letter as a sample of the close collaboration between GB and ET. Bottomley's 'Anthology' was never published.
[2] By Charles Dalmon. [*GB*]
[3] Enclosed with this letter is GB's translation of Watcyn Wyn's Welsh poem.

Here comes Walter Ramal or De La Mare with 'Lovelocks' in it. I regret that I saw nothing in any except the nonsense pieces in 1902, while I now see that it is poetry.[1] The romance has no verse in it, I think.

I got Housman's leave to print a short piece from *The Shropshire Lad*—but through Richards himself.

It is very sad & surprising to hear that you find this glorious (but unenjoyed) Summer damp & not good to you. But at any rate I hope England will content you. If only the Hampshire chalk downs would do what you want. And as to myself, can you really think of 10 years hence when 'Merfyn will be grown up' & I shall be 'young with large expanses of life left'? Then you are more wonderful than ever.

Well now I must return to my *Anthology*. I get no reviewing nowadays[2] & I must do something in order to feel that I am really a wage-earner. I have already got about ¾ of my poems from the Standard Authors.

By the way, Davies will stay on at the cottage during the winter—if I can pay his rent. Also he has broken his wooden leg & needs a new one & they are very costly. Do you know anyone from whom to beg £1 or so to be repaid in another world? If so, get it & send it to me. I am collecting.

I have actually included Beddoe's translation 'Under the Lime Trees'—'Tandaradei'—& along with other things it will make my book a wonderful Aphrodisiac: I have also put in part of his 'Invitation to Oxford'.

With our love to you all

                                    Ever yours Edward Thomas

54

24 August 1906   *The Weald*

My dear Gordon,

Many thanks for your letter & the poems & I shall certainly

[1] Presumably Walter de la Mare, *Poems*, reviewed *DC*, 9 November. ET had reviewed Walter Ramal, *Songs of Childhood*, along with six other volumes of verse, in *DC*, 14 August 1902.

[2] In August, September, and October, 10 reviews appeared in *DC*, 2 in *S*, and 1 in *The Tribune*. ET's name is included among 'Some Contributors' to *The Bookman*,

use all except 'Nancy Dawson', which is doubtful because I shall have to pay for it very likely. I already have leave to use O'Shaughnessy, but Chattos want £1. 1. 0 for a poem by Stevenson.

I am glad you like Belloc. No. I chose 'July' & may take others if I have room, but not 'Auvergnat' ∵ Lucas has it in *The Open Road* & I do not like it very much. I am using the drinking song too.

I got leave from Noyes & now can find nothing in him good enough! But I must use something.

The Academy note simply means that the paper is tottering through lack of advertisement—Child admitted so much.[1]

I hope you sent your protest against printed references to mixed bathing to the Editor of *The Daily Chronicle* & signed yourself 'Married Man'.

Then I will use Yvette's '*Quand la feuille etait verte*'.

Of course I have 'Summer Dawn' in my anthology & probably I shall use one or both of the 'Hollow Land' poems & one from a later volume of Morris which you recommended.

Also I have 2 things by Ramal who wrote & said he read me.[2]

I wrote an obscure Corinthian prospectus! Used the phrase 'romantic realism' to cover the artist & me & our pet lambs.

CHALKY HAMPSHIRE will certainly do.[3]

How did you hear of Ensor whom I faintly knew at Oxford?[4] He is a Fabian & a barrister & a Toynbee Hall man & a *Manchester Guardian* leader writer—a fine character, I believe. His verse did not greatly move me, & I did not think it really was verse, though his thought is often interesting.

I shall include a page or two from Doughty Vol. III if I can. There are some glorious things in III & IV, as fine as anything in the *Iliad* as it appears to me not a Greek.

---

vol. XXX (April–September 1906) and in every volume thereafter, but there are no signed reviews by him in the above period, although many reviews in the column called 'The Bookman's Table' reflect ET's taste, interests, and style.

[1] A reference to H. H. Child who left *The Academy* in 1907.

[2] 'Ramal' is Walter de la Mare who constantly paid tribute to ET's qualities as a reviewer-critic. See de la Mare's foreword to ET's *Collected Poems*.

[3] Reference untraced.

[4] Sir R. C. K. Ensor (1877–1958) was at Balliol College, Oxford, and a leader-writer on the *Manchester Guardian* 1902–4. He published *Modern Socialism*, 1903, and *Modern Poems*, 1904.

Milne surpassed Milne yesterday.[1] If you see a *D.C.* review
of *Early English Dramatists* look for 'Villar' instead of 'Villon'
& admire.

Here are my first proofs.[2] Any merely verbal suggestions—in
addition to corrections of slips & printers errors—I shall be very
grateful for. But don't attempt to cure any banalities, for as you
see, Dent is shirking the galley proof and I can make no serious
change in these pages. The opening will amuse you. You will see
Bellocisms in my 'Watercress Man', I fear, also in a sentence or
two in 'Faunus'.[3] The sooner you return the proofs the better, I
think, as Dent talked of publishing next month.

I have collected £7 for Davies already, & I think I have got
a publisher for his autobiography, which has some fine things
in it.

But I have an old friend still here & we usually rise at 4, fish
until 9 & then walk, & in the intervals I edit & write letters &
read a lot of 3rd rate old country poetry with sweet feeling in it,
lent me by W. H. Hudson—Hurdis & the unhappy peasant
John Clare. Also *Pastorals & Other Poems* by Elinor Sweetman
(pubd. by Dent, 1899 & remaindered) which has a good
'Pastoral from the Meadows' & some really pleasing stuff as far
as I can gather at a glance. I can't begin regular work till next
Tuesday. On Thursday I go to Hampshire for 4 days with a
naturalist—G. A. B. Dewer.[4] Then I expect Nevinson & then
work & then the move.

Can you tell me the publisher of Manx songs in which
Dalmon's 'O what if the fowler' comes?

Goodbye.

Yours & Emily's with love from us all.

Edward Thomas

---

[1] Literary editor of the *DC*, and a constant butt of Edward's. [*GB*] *Early English
Dramatists*, edited by J. S. Farmer, vols. I–IV, reviewed *DC*, 23 August. ET
compares 'The disobedient child' unfavourably with Villar's [*sic*] most famous
poem: the sub-editor reinforces his error by entitling this paragraph 'Villar's
Way'. In his scrapbook ET pencilled in 'Villon' without comment.
[2] Of *The Heart of England*. 'The Watercress Man' is on p. 2.
[3] *The Heart of England*, Chapter II.
[4] Dewer contributed articles to *The Book of the Open Air*.

55

27 August 1906 midnight   *The Weald*

My dear Gordon,

Many thanks for your letter & my proofs.[1] I am relieved & more than that by your liking things in the first chapters. In fact your letter lifted me up until this evening when I got this 3rd lot of proofs, which include the horrible 'Village', 'Frieze at the 4 Elms' and 'August'. I don't know how you can forgive them. They were written in 1902 and in part as early as 1899 & I had them by me—Dent insisted on 6,000—& so I had to throw them in. They make a nasty mess, though they include a few (recent) sentences which are not bad. They and the length of my work today have quite put me out.

In each case I have done what you suggest. The 'ands' are gone, though one was not quite wrong (the other was a printer's invention). Also I have re-written the first sentence of all, which now stands: 'Sunday afternoon had perfected the silence of the suburban street' which I know is heavy & parsonic. I thoroughly admire your openings of 'Lady Gwendolen's Flight' etc. Why not continue the stories? I want to know about the French-polished dress-box.

It is very nice of Marriott to read me—you don't say 'like'.[2] I believe he is good, but I never read *The Column*. Did you? Walter Ramal reads my reviews & remembers them.[3] Isn't he versatile? I am printing his 'Child in the story awakes' & 'Bunches of Grapes' (ending ' "A bumpity ride in a waggon of hay for me" says Jane') not because they are the best, but on the whole the fittest. 'Reverie' (beginning 'When slim Sophia') is lovely: so is your choice.

I feel sure you are right about Ensor. But don't worry about Doughty. He seems to me now very big but although I did not say so I do hesitate about him & feel that he may turn out a Southey after all. Remember that Edward Garnett gave me a good start towards my admiration for Doughty. And positively

---

[1] *The Heart of England*. Part II 'The Lowland' contained 'August' (Chapter XIV) and 'The Village' (Chapter XXI): the second section of the latter is a romanticized rustic description of 'The Tale of "The Four Elms" '.

[2] Charles Marriott, *The Column, A novel*, 1901.

[3] See Letter 54, note 2.

Doughty is an antiquarian. Admitting that, perhaps I am not so far from you. Also, it is very rapacious of you to demand that all beauty shall come into your sight! But you should read his love-scene of Esla & Cloten—she covering him with her mantle & rising from his embrace at dawn not knowing 'she hath known a man'—[1]

I am too tired to go on & tomorrow I have many books to review & then I go away & then hurry until Michaelmas.

Tell me what you would like me to put into my *Anthology* of yours—not necessarily from *The Gate of Smaragdus*. I don't mind a passage from one of the plays or an unpublished poem. It should not exceed 24 lines by much if at all.

Bad versewriters now send me their books gratis because I said something about modern poetry lately.[2]

Helen & I send our love to Emily and you.

Yours ever Edward Thomas

I hope the next proofs will be a better lot. They are very ill printed, I think.

56

4 September 1906   *The Weald*

My dear Gordon,

I can't tell you how glad I am of your letters & your proofs.— My delay is due to my being away from Thursday until Tuesday.—Your praise has delighted me & I feel that I can hardly ever be quite down-hearted again. It was—you will understand —particularly good to have you sharing my own preferences. The articles you like best I also thought best & you do indeed fortify me in some timid measure of confidence. I think the 'Earth Children'[3]—the old man & his wife—the best thing of all,

---

[1] The story of Esla and Cloten in Doughty, *The Dawn of Britain*, Book IX.

[2] ET generalizes on modern poetry in two reviews: Joan Davidson, *Holiday and other poems*, DC, 1 August, and *Lyra Britannica*, arranged by Ernest Pertwee, DC, 10 August.

[3] *The Heart of England*, Chapter XXV; apart from the introductory chapter ('Leaving Town'), 'Earth Children' is the most extended piece of prose in the book. It seems to recall the old Wiltshire couple with whom Edward and Helen spent their honeymoon. (See *AIW*, pp. 43–50.)

& am only surprised that you seemed to think I should disagree.

The way you have corrected my proofs is wonderful. I adopt every suggestion that you make, & only where you are uncertain have I left things as they are—once, I know, to the detriment of the sense, but that can't be helped. Do you notice how careless of the minutiæ of form I get—long rambling sentences, which I know to be imperfect? I hope it means that I am getting into a truer method & not merely becoming a pure journalist.

I know you are right about the piling-up of landscapes—but then could I in the time I had have made a good book as well as make good chapters? I am not sure about the formality of my murderer's talk. It was so easy to throw it into colloquial forms that I hesitated. But I can't feel sure that the dialogue is really natural.

About 'Adelaide' in my 'Golden Age'—there is no reference to anything except an episode at the time of writing it & I have therefore killed her & thrown her away.[1]

Thanks for Hardy. I hesitate between your choice & 'A Darkling Thrush' in *Poems Past & Present*. 'Tranter Sweatley' is too long.

I will look at Allingham's poem. Of Barnes I already have the 'Great Old Oak' and a description of an old farmhouse, both pretty good; yet I will look at 'A-comen down from Gramfer's'. Davenant's poem is too well known, and I have never felt it to be very good.

About yourself, I think 'The Dairymaids to Pan'[2] or something from *Midsummer Eve*, but perhaps the Sheep-Shearing Girls,[3] in which I can't altogether like the rough rusticity of the intention. 'Sanctuaries' I like, expecially verse II, yet so far (in haste) I quarrel with 'one fluttering mote & blond' & seem to allow more fulfilment to the idea than you have really got into such a small space.

I can't agree with you about your expecting to salute all beauty in English things any more than you could salute beauty in what is loveliest in West Africans or Australian aborigines. It

[1] Ibid., Chapter XX contains no reference to 'Adelaide'.
[2] From *The Gate of Smaragdus*. It was included in the 'Evening' section of *The Pocket Book*, p. 273.
[3] 'Shearers' Song' in GB, *Poems of Thirty Years*, p. 100.

is too godlike—not for a claim—but for an achievement. You
shall have Doughty soon. He refuses in admirable English to let
me use a page of him in my anthology.

———

You will see that I have tried to get away from oast houses in
these last proofs. Shall I cut some of 'em out? You will dislike
all the mountains, but not all the sea,—& will you care for 'The
Fox Hunt'? It has been doctored a little by a gent. who says he
knows how short stories should be wrote.

I must see *The Column.*

Yes, you told me about Dalmon.

By the way, can you use anything of the magnificent Lady,
Laurence Hope, in your anthology?—See her *Indian Love,
Garden of Kama, Stars of the Desert* (Heinemann). Or Morley
Roberts' *Songs of Energy.*

Goodbye. I have already written 4 letters to naturalists, one
to Fisher Unwin (who wants a book once more), & many more,
since I got home, & it is still 'speechless heat'. Forgive me for
being short.

Helen's & my love to Emily & you.

Ever yours Edward Thomas

P.S. Dent is in a hurry for the proofs. Can I have them within
a week?

57

10 September 1906   *The Weald*

My dear Gordon,

I have just sent off the proofs. Your suggestions are most
useful. Where I could—in my haste—I made use of them. I
admit your rightness in every case. But you alarm me by reminding me of the terrible carelessness of my long sentences, often
irremediable. I suppose the *Daily Chronicle* is part of my infir-
mity. As to *The Morte D'Arthur,* I never realized how wretched
the Temple Classics edition was.[1] I could not alter it seriously as
I have sold my good *Morte D'Arthur.* How did I come to use
that passage? I expect in the same way as you came to love it

[1] Sir T. Malory, *Le Morte d'Arthur,* 4 vols., 1897 (Temple Classics).

most. For we do resemble one another, in spite of my opinion of your pastoralism.

And your praises. If only my work did not get so entirely outside myself as soon as it is finished I should become languid with joy and vanity. I feared the Waggon might be melodramatic & too much talked about—Oh! how I do talk about things, producing not works of art, but remarks about works of art that someone else will do.

But you ought not to praise my Mountains. I fear they are mere collector's work, & where they are not that, too vague.

Is the Schwobism really right?[1] It has no outlines. It is not seen. There is no reason why it should not have been half or twice as long, I feel. It is too moral & not visible enough.

As to 'The Fox Hunt'—no, my editor only suggested & sketched the interpolations in the *old man's* narrative & he invented (& I unwillingly adopted) Enid.

I am using your 'Carol'.[2] I had seen it before but almost forgotten it. It is very beautiful & I wonder how it came to be written. It is too perfect for a folk song: in fact Morris—would have liked to write it.

I am sorry you can't use Laurence Hope—Heinemann does not charge for her poems, I find. I cannot tell you whether Morley Roberts is a Canadian, but I see you are not an Imperialist, though you include Rhys. Also I do not possess Roberts: he was only lent to me by his friend W. H. Hudson.

You ask about 'In lofty numbers let us rave'—it is Drayton's, cruelly dismembered by me from one of his lengthy pastorals, but I cannot trace 'The woods of Arcady are dead'.[3]

Yes, I admit. Carbonek is Penard castle in Gower. Don't review me and betray it to those who think it matters.

I must leave out 'Adelaide'. But she shall not die.

You will pass quite near to Petersfield in going to Bournemouth, I expect. I wish we were to be there to intercept you.

[1] 'Schwabism'. See page 107, note 1. 'Enid' is the betrothed of the nephew, the old man who tells a long story before the meet; the narrative is interrupted a few times by references to Enid's reception of the tale. ('The Fox Hunt', Chapter XXXI.)

[2] 'A Carol For Christmas Day Before Dawn', *Poems of Thirty Years*, p. 5, was not included in *Songs for the Open Air*.

[3] Drayton's poem is quoted in *The Heart of England*, Chapter XXXIII; 'The Song of the Happy Shepherd', by Yeats, in Chapter XLIV; 'The Castle of Carbonek', Chapter XLVI contains a long quotation from Malory. ET here refers to the description of Penard Castle which begins the chapter.

5 Gordon Bottomley, a drawing by John Nash, in 1922

6 Edward Thomas in 1913

But we do not know yet when we can get into our house,—perhaps in October, perhaps not until December. I hope you find that Bournemouth is the right place (for a short stay, because I should not like you to live in Hampshire & not within a day's walk of me.)

It is odd about 'The woods of Arcady are dead'; but I cannot think of a possible source just now.

Oh Comforter, goodbye. It is in my mind today that you are alive & quite real & that—well, very few others are with whom I exchange talk & letters. Give my love & Helen's to Emily & take ours yourself.

Ever yours Edward Thomas

58

27 September 1906   *13 Rusham Road, Balham, London, S.W.*

My dear Gordon,

Only a word to let you know that we were turned out completely yesterday, all but one nail which I could not wrench from the wall. We stay here until tomorrow, when Helen & I go to Wiltshire for 3 days & then to South Wales for a fortnight or else. Your Aunt of Cartmel I forgot until too late, I am sorry. Please keep Doughty III until we get to Petersfield. Freeman lives near here & has a copy, & I shall be back here in a fortnight or so working, until we finally move. I daresay you are right about him, but I still think that his war (I forget if there is much of it in III) is far & away the finest that ever got into poetry, though I will confess that I compare it (favourably) rather with the great histories than the great poems.

Oh, I had a nice naïve letter from Pádraic Colum & I gathered from it that you were using something of his. Can you tell me the edition of *New Songs* which I ought to see at the Museum?[1] I seem to remember a fine 'Drover' & he promises an unpublished poem. He and Maurice Hoy are quite important in Dublin, I hear.

I have been asked to write an article on Sonnets for *The*

[1] *New Songs. A lyric selection*, 1904.

Saturday Review:[1]—also a history of English poetry for Fisher Unwin which—if he will allow me not to pretend to scholarship, philology, grammar &c—I may do in a few years' time.

Elkin Mathews is to publish William Davies' 2nd book of poems early in November so the poor bard was not utterly sad when we left him, especially as his leg & his Rent are fully paid up. Did I tell you Bernard Shaw is reading his Autobiography & will introduce it if he likes it?[2]

I wonder could you do an article on outdoor poetry in English for my Natural History? showing the changing (or permanent) attitude towards wild life & scenery. You could quote a lot but you would have to get a lot into not more than 3,000 words. Think of it. Freeman may do Country Songs, but that will leave you free to touch the Ballad. It is a subject I should like, but I am too busy & I should be too pohetical.[3]

Oh, will some really good man praise my 'Ship, chariot & plough', my 'Earth Children', 'Metamorphosis' &c?[4] I feel that perhaps they are really good & I am almost sure they are new. But who knows?

When does the Anthology come?

By the way, 'The woods of Arcady are dead'—those glorious verses quoted in my 'Marsh' which you asked about—are in Yeats' *Poems*!

Yours & Emily's ever Edward Thomas

59

2 October 1906   c/o *John Williams, Waun Wen School,*
Swansea

My dear Gordon,

Thank you for your letter. It is raining hard & our respectable

---

[1] *A Book of English Sonnets*, reviewed *SR*, 10 November.

[2] William H. Davies, *New Poems*, reviewed *MP*, 3 January 1907, *B*, January 1907, and *DC*, 24 January.

[3] 'Nature in English Poetry', by GB, *Book of the Open Air*, vol. II, pp. 206–16; 'English Country Songs', by A.M.F., ibid., vol. II, pp. 167–74. At this time ET was a busy reviewer as well as an editor and anthologist; he reviewed regularly for *MP*, *DC*, and *B*, and frequently reviewed the same book in all three papers.

[4] 'The Metamorphosis', Chap. XXIV is a genuine prose poem. It is a single page

severe hostess intimates that we must not get wet through &
cumber her with dripping clothes, so we stay in with the
antimocassars. That does not suit letters but I write just to
send time along until the weather clears. Understand & forgive.

About your Essays. Yes 1,000 or 1,500 on the painters
might make a fine quintessential thing—English painters.[1] I can
give you until the end of December for the two, but if they come
earlier all the better, because I shall certainly have many other
contributors delaying & calling for the goad.

Yes, Freeman is the Doughty specialist on *The Academy*.

In 6 weeks we may very likely be at Petersfield. If not, then at
Balham.[2] In either case shall I see you? Could you have a week at
Petersfield if we are there? When we are there, I will send the
address.

Thanks for news about Colum. Maurice Hoy is important
because of (1) his tie or bow, (2) his reputed good looks (3)
his flow of quotations from second-rate writers & talkers on art
&c. I am thus rude ∵ he never acknowledged a M.S. prose poem
('The Hay Waggon') which I copied into the *Rose Acre Papers*
which Mrs. Podmore sent to him.

The other day a man wrote to me asking for the Welsh original &c. of my 'Eluned'.[3]

Do you know any good Irish songs (with possible words) for
my Anthology? We have now got 50 very fine songs, including
mediæval words & melody on the coming of the Ass out of the
East.

The rain continues, but so does my disability.

Helen's love & mine to you & Emily & your father & mother
& Aunt Sarah.

Ever yours Edward Thomas

---

description of 'a proud ash shedding its leaves after a night of frost' and anticipates,
more clearly than any other passage of his nature prose, some of ET's poems.
The passage beginning, 'The ship, the chariot, the plough, these three are, I
suppose, the most sovereign beautiful things which man has made in his time, and
such that were his race to pass away from the earth, would bring him most wor-
ship from his successors', is the second paragraph in Chapter II ('Faunus').

[1] *Book of the Open Air*, vol. II, Chap. XXXIX, 'Nature in art' by GB.
[2] His parents' home.
[3] A poem, supposedly translated from the Welsh, by ET; see *Beautiful Wales*, p. 82.

60

11 November 1906   *Berryfield Cottage, Ashford, Petersfield*[1]

My dear Gordon,

This house & the country about it make the most beautiful place we ever lived in. We are now become people of whom passers by stop to think: How fortunate are they within those walls. I know it. I have thought the same as I came to the house & forgot it was my own.

But I am oppressed again by overmuch reviewing for *Chronicle World Bookman* & *Morning Post*[2] & cannot find an hour to sink into myself or to write to you and Emily. You alone know how I felt at your words of praise & happiness after getting my book. All other copies ought to have been destroyed, for *World* & *Standard* have been saying what a cheery knowing companion I am for a day in the country & *The Academy* that I am affected & that in 'the heart of England' people do not speak so. I ought never to do colour books again. People can't believe there is anything in them at all.

Before I forget, 'New College Gardens' is to be found in *Songs of Love & Empire*. I didn't copy it out because I was very busy & I did not feel sure that you wanted it. Don't trouble about 'Goatfoot' now, I have copied it. A quarter of my anthology has gone to printers. The songs are glorious—You should hear Campion's 'White lope, blithe Helen & the rest', more religious than anything I know, & then 'Greensleeves' & 'Rio Grande' & Louis XIII's 'Amaryllis' & '*Orientis Partibus adventavit asinus*' (*La fête des fous*). It will be the best short collection in the world. I wish I thought as well of the poems.

How well you paint Bournemouth for me & the two windows & the cough.

To the Cymric enthusiast I only said that there was no Welsh original for 'Eluned' & that therefore he wd be disappointed

---

[1] For Helen's account of the new cottage, see *WWE*, pp. 112–7.
[2] ET had preserved cuttings of a large number of reviews between 1 November 1906 and 9 January 1907; 15 from *DC*, 4 from *MP*, 1 from *SR* besides the undated ones in *B*. The criticism is of his highest standard and the authors discussed include Shakespeare, Blake, Hudson, A. Symons, Jusserand, E. V. Lucas, Maeterlinck, Yeats, W. de la Mare, and W. H. Davies.

because anyone can make a pseudo translation that suggests a noble original.

Goodbye Emily & Gordon. Helen sends her love with mine. I am yours ever

Edward Thomas

61

9 December 1906 *Berryfield Cottage*

My dear Gordon,

Thank you very much for the songs.[1] I shall use 'Somer is icumen in'. It seems to be quite excusable. And I will add Masefield's version, but must retain that in the minor. Cecil Sharp (who knows) says no *old* sailor would sing the major tune that Masefield gives, & it was he who gave me the version I am using. It is not obvious but I have learned to like it well. 'All round my hat' is obviously from B-Gould, because verse 3 is almost entirely the work of his collaborator (Fleetwood Sheppard): so he must have his guinea.

As soon as I had had your letter I wrote to Rathbone on the subjects you mentioned. I do hope it won't mean a lot of work for him & the disfigurement of the M.S. because it all ought to reach Grant Richards on the 20th & I want my money very badly. I believe the printers will put the 'idiom' right. About '*La fille du Roi*'—if you really do like my version will you send it to Rathbone & I will use it? Please.

By the way, I have lately enjoyed some scores of little poems by Father Tabb.[2] They are exquisite epigrams nearly all—Mrs Meynell's selection—& I have asked for his leave to print one (on 'Silence') but have not got it yet. I send you William Davies' new book & should be most grateful if you would tell me what *favourable* things can be said about it.[3] It is (as I knew all along)

---

[1] *Songs for the Open Air* is liberally sprinkled with melodies, many of which had never before been printed. (ET's informed interest in folk-music illustrates the depth of his decision to live a country life and has almost passed unnoticed by critics of his poetry.) 'Masefield's version' refers to 'Spanish ladies', not 'Somer is icumen in'. [*GB*]

[2] Alice Meynell, *A Selection from the Verses of J. B. Tabb*, reviewed *DC*, 21 January 1907.

[3] See Letter 58, note 2.

far below the first book, & yet I find some beautiful things in it. I am troubled to think that the book will be neglected or slighted in reviews and almost certainly not very widely sold—because I dared not discourage Davies by telling him boldly what I thought. He is pretty well & contented, but the reception of this book will very likely upset him. He has no idea of proportion; nor can he ever understand the Press.

Yes, do the Poetry first & then think about the Painting afterwards if you like. As a matter of fact I shall probably be able to give you plenty of time; & yet the sooner I have all my copy in hand the better. I see your difficulty. I knew but did not realize at the time I wrote how painting had not gone on parallel lines with poetry. I am so busy now that I can hardly make any kind of suggestion about the Poetry.—Freeman by the way probably will say something about the musical aspect.—You had better insist a little yet again on the commonplace about the importance of Nature in all great English poetry, &, if you can, indicate the development of our kind of feeling for Nature after the old merry acquaintanceship & companionship. Oh, no, I am too much muddled even to write a *Chronicle* article on it.—I hope you did not see my article on Blake's *Job* etc. last week.[1] Milne, having to work in some pictures, cut out the last $\frac{1}{3}$ of my article & with it not only what was best but also all reference to Job. I wrote to Binyon to apologize.

I have 3 jolly unpublished sailors' songs for the Anthology: also 2 little known songs from *The Compleat Angler* one by H. Lawes the other 18th century: a noble one which I fitted to Peacock's '3 men of Gotham': also Browning's 'Kentish Sir Byng' fitted (by me) to Lilliburlero,—rather monotonous in the opening: & the famous mediæval '*Meum est propositum*' fitted to the blithest of Welsh tunes: & the 3 or 4 songs from Westmoreland. These are the (almost) entirely new things. I do want them to be correctly printed. But in my endeavour to keep clear of what Lucas & other open air anthologists have used I daresay my poetry is not all good & not all popular enough & I shall not make £1,500 out of it as Lucas did out of his genial *Open Road* anthology.

---

[1] Alexander Gilchrist, *The Life of William Blake*, edited by W. G. Robertson, and *William Blake*, vol. I, with general Introduction by Laurence Binyon, reviewed *DC,* 7 December.

How funny of Rathbone to buy my Guinea Book.[1] It must seem a lot of money.

Merfyn is now going to school & is a much happier boy, but I am not always patient of his petulancy & invertebrateness & his rather large & curious head, though (I should be not entirely parodoxical if I said—because) he is very much like me.

Goodbye. Our love to you both.

Ever yours Edward Thomas

62

Berryfield Cottage

26 December 1906

My dear Gordon,

The photograph is very good & a good picture too & Helen & I were glad to have it this morning & send our thanks to Emily for it with our love. But I may still regret that you didn't meet F. H. Evans & get him to inspect you.[2] Perhaps you will this next year. At any rate I wish you the health for a journey. It is nearly a year now since I saw you at Cartmel & I reflect that I have had one sight of you per annum since we began to write. Then with luck I may see you 30 or 40 times again—which makes the future seem quite a desirable reversion. But the present is of the old sort; even a little worse, since I have had but one visit from a friend since I came here, have had so much work that only twice have I been able to walk all day, & for some reason have attained a degree of selfconsciousness beyond the dreams of avarice (which makes me spend hours, when I ought to be reading or enjoying the interlacing flight of 3 kestrels, in thinking out my motives for this or that act or word in the past until I long for sleep). Certainly I have a devil as much as any man I ever read of. But if there are devils there are no exorcisers, tho a kind friend wrote to me lately to point out the security & sweetness of his refuge in the fat bosom of the Church. I feel sure that my salvation depends on a person & that person cannot be Helen because she has come to resemble me too much or at least to play unconsciously the part of being like me

---

[1] *The Heart of England* was published in a separate 'de luxe edition' at one guinea.
[2] The photographer who produced a studio photograph of ET for *The Bookman*.

129

with a skill that could make me weep. It is unlikely to be a woman because a woman is but a human being with the additional barricades of (1) sex and (2) antipathy to me—as a rule. And as to men—here I am surrounded by schoolmasters,[1] while in town I can but pretend to pick up the threads of ancient intercourse, a task as endless as the counting of poppy seeds or plovers in the air.————————————————————————

I think you are right about Davies. But there are fine things in the new book, 'The Likeness', 'The Ox', 'Music', 'Parted' & others, & I like 'Catherine'. He will always observe & always feel, I think & whether he grows much or not, it seems likely that he will often attain simplicity unawares. I must think out a just & yet genial comment for his private eye. In print I shall praise him mainly because a reviewer has to shout like an actor if he is to be heard by the audience.

How is your Anthology? I have half expected Guthrie to call (at your instigation).[2] Do you think we could do anything with one another?

Oh, thank you for *The Gem* & the Prayer.[3] I wonder is that Miscellany worthy of its great aim. The soft paper anticipates part of a great millenial scheme of my own.

I have written to Dent asking that a copy of my book be sent to the *Courier*[4] but it has very likely gone there & into other hands already. If not Dent will send it & I trust your man[4] will get it. Salute him for me. He belongs to a very small & very secret society. So far my only intelligent review is from *The Athenæum* &[5] that is not favourable. It objects to my 'sensuousness', 'love of colour', 'lyricism'. So far no one has discovered 'The Ship, the chariot & the plough' except you & me.

It is all right about your Poetry article.[6] As a matter of fact I am being hurried on by the publishers, but I have only the first $\frac{1}{4}$ to get ready at once & there will be no literary articles therein.

[1] Merfyn was at the nearby Bedales School.
[2] James Guthrie, the artist-poet-printer who had illustrated *The Gate of Smaragdus*. ET used to walk over to visit the Guthries at Harting, Sussex.
[3] Probably *The Gem Library*, 23 March 1907–13 April 1929.
[4] *Liverpool Courier* whose literary critic ('your man') was Dixon Scott. (*Liverpool*, painted by J. Hamilton Hay, described by Dixon Scott, reviewed in *B*, October 1907.)
[5] Unidentified.
[6] See Letter 58, note 3.

With our love & good wishes to you & Emily & your father
& mother & Aunt Sarah.

Yours & Emily's ever Edward Thomas

63

21 January 1907   *Berryfield Cottage*

My dear Gordon,

I am glad you are better and hope you will be well by the
Spring. If we could come to you in June! We will try hard.

I had to wait a day or two before reading your article. But
it is all right except for that funny reference to an essayist tho I
shall leave it in because so many will think that it applies to them
& so will make you admirers. You couldn't have taken a better
line in so short a paper, I think.

Thanks for Guthrie. Having been to Oxford, I can attack it as
well as he & I don't think I shall mind his Wemmickality. We
shall see. You might mention that Ashford is in the parish of
Steep. He may not know, tho he must know the valley of beech
& yew, juniper & apple trees & mistletoe.

When you write next say if your Liverpool man reviewed my
Heart of England. You will mourn to hear that AMR is doing
my life & letters for a *Bookman* article (with portrait).[1] He
offered himself & as he was just visiting me & the Editor had
accepted him I had just to giggle. He's doing a book on *Bohemia
in London*.[2]

But now I have to review a play on Sir Walter Raleigh & the
last of Mr. Doughty's Epic.[3] So goodbye with Helen's love &
mine to you both.

Ever yours Edward Thomas

[1] Arthur Ransome, 'The Bookman Gallery—Mr. Edward Thomas'—in *B*, vol.
XXXI, March 1970, pp. 244–5, with a photograph by Frederick H. Evans.

[2] Arthur Ransome, *Bohemia in London*, reviewed *MP*, 3 October. Belloc became
literary editor of the *MP* in October 1906. ET was a regular reviewer until 9
January 1911.

[3] H. A. A. Cruso, *Sir Walter Raleigh: A Drama in Five Acts*, reviewed *DC*, 25
February; Doughty, *The Dawn in Britain*, vols. 5 and 6, *DC*, 7 February, and *B*,
March, pp. 267–8.

64

16 February 1907   *Berryfield Cottage*

My dear Gordon,

This will probably only be a word or two. It is the end of the day's work—10—& as Helen happens to be out still I seize the moment. I saw Guthrie yesterday. I had done 3 long day's reading & writing & the morning being lofty and blue I walked to South Harting, about seven miles & met him & his wife & 3 children & found myself infinitely more at ease than I usually am with strangers. We seemed to hit it off in a lazy way quite comfortably & he walked back with me in the evening as far as Petersfield which lies midway. I saw lots of his work & I like his landscape more & more.[1] His *Poe* is going to be good. And aren't his little verses for children good? Also his prose is never unnecessary. If I hadn't liked him I might have depicted him for you in a few ill chosen words, but as I feel we may become friends that is impossible. Your portrait & your handwriting were a large part of the decoration in a not over decorated house. Shall we ever have him & you here together? You will admire his tall straight wife with a noble neck & engaging frankness. Both have a rather sweet Scotch accent.

Thank you again for the books. I have just finished the 'Critic as Artist'[2] again & am astonished to think how much I owe to him, & in fact I am not sure if there is ever anything but him in my criticism—anything worth having. I will be careful with the books.

Never mind about the Landscape in Painting.[3] Your letter suggests a good book which you will never write nor read.

Now here is Helen back from dancing at Bedales & I think it is better to post this now than to keep it a week in the hope that it will grow, especially as I go to town on Monday. Then our love to Emily & you. I am Ever yours

Edward Thomas

---

[1] *Some Poems of E. A. Poe*, with drawings by J. J. Guthrie, 1901; *Songs and Verses selected from Edmund Waller*, 1902; *The Elf*: a magazine of drawings and writings by J.J.G., 1902 and 1905.
[2] By Oscar Wilde.
[3] A reference to GB's 'Nature in art'. See page 125, note 1.

65

7 March 1907   *Berryfield Cottage*

My dear Gordon,

It is very sad, but I think you will get well and at any rate you don't have to correct proofs of natural history articles, measuring them with a 2-foot rule, and to discuss a prize competition to advertise a book you are editing. That is what makes me so confusedly busy that I feel as if the back of my head would come out. Never mind; I am now, being just 29, insured against death, accident & disease—I shall get £500 if I lose both eyes or even both legs (but I am not sure about the legs.)

I don't feel bad about the 'excised breasts', for it was not a sin of carelessness. I think I am incapable of writing so out of carelessness. But evidently I miscalculated. That sentence was meant to be as when one says a thing with an affected ridiculous accent or with a grimace or mock solemnity, & it was meant to convey any not altogether good-humoured contempt for the 'religious instructor'. Also, I think the word 'excised' was 'odd' in the text.[1] To me the hard word still seems to suggest the hard act of taking away the breasts from the nymphs in the brake. So I am not to be despised this time, am I? Not yet.

Among my sufferings has been the necessity today amidst my proof reading to have to write an introduction suddenly to the big natural history thing.[2] The fact is I dislike the book; so I ran dry at once—had to steal from old articles & patch them up—& even then could not cover the space   which
finally
I covered
with the help of
a sonnet by De la Mare
and
a long sentence of prose by W. H. Hudson.
Oh Lord I am vain, because I go cold at the thought of what people worth considering will say of this introduction.

I don't think I shall ever write anything I want to write again, or even get the feeling of calm necessary to trying. So *The*

[1] I cannot trace this phrase in any signed reviews.
[2] *The Book of the Open Air.*

Bookman article is the melodious tear dropped upon the prose
poet's corpse.[1] Shall I send you the harticle?

I have just had the consolation of finding that in reviewing de
la Mare's 1st book years ago I quoted all of 'Lovelocks'.[2] Thank
God. Goodbye with our love to you all.

Yours ever Edward Thomas

66

27 March 1907   *Berryfield Cottage*

My dear Gordon,

Perhaps it is the Equinox, but in spite of this delicious weather
& the beautiful beeches & the happiness of the children & Helen I
have been having another bad time & am still in it. Away in
Wiltshire I enjoyed the Downs & Savernake Forest and the
winds very much & seemed well, but as soon as I took to my
chair & my reviewing down I went.[3] Still, I kept on reviewing &
must do & my beastly editing. I doubt though if I can write a
letter. So I will begin by answering your questions.

Garnett's play was not on Gunnar:[4] I can't remember who,
but nobody famous I think. Now his hopes are on a modern play
which is actually to have matinées at The Haymarket—
Granville Barker's success is having its influence—when, I
don't know.

There is to be a competition for prizes of guineas—to say how
$\frac{1}{2}$ an hour is 'best spent out of doors' in April & so on. Lord, I
wish I knew. Not gardening, at any rate, says my back. I fear
you can't compete, being a contributor.

You didn't enclose anything by Hudson.

Yes I review Wright's *Pater*,[5] an absolutely silly book, how
silly I was not well enough to say in my *Chronicle* laughter.
'Biographer of Orphans' is good.

[1] See Letter 63, note 1.
[2] See Letter 53, note 1.
[3] During April 5 reviews appeared in *DC*, 4 in *MP*, and 2 in *B*.
[4] Edward Garnett, *The Feud*, 1909.
[5] Thomas Wright, *The Life of Walter Pater*, reviewed 1 April. ('These two volumes, nominally about Walter Pater, author of *Imaginary Portraits* and *The
Renaissance*, reveal an unexpected and most welcome vein of humour.')

Yes, I did tell the *Electrician*[1] about 'The ship, the chariot, & the plough'—had to hold a knife at his throat to persuade him to put it in place of 2 pointless quotations of single sentences.

Doughty is great. I see his men & women whenever I see noble beeches, as in Savernake Forest, or tumuli or old encampments, or the line of the Downs like the backs of a train of elephants, or a few firs on a hilltop.

What do you think of the enclosed J. Marjoram?[2] He seems to me to think and compose verse sincerely, independently, & usually with subtle effects. He approaches Sturge Moore in some ways & may well be a good man disguised, but who? Rossetti will interest you, though he isn't important.

I am to see another publisher's reader soon to discuss a book. I am invited to make suggestions, but I don't seem pregnant yet. I dally with *The South Country* to include a bit of history— perhaps the history of England from the point of view of one parish or great house (a grand idea, but I am not learned or patient enough to do it)—not necessarily from the year 1 to 1907! It would turn out to be mostly people & houses & fine evenings I suspect. I shouldn't mind & I do want to work again. Then there is a book on English poetry in the manner of Belloc's 'Avril'—dealing with persons largely (largely me), say 12 of them, Chaucer(?), Sidney, Spenser, Drayton, Herrick, Traherne, Vaughan, Dryden(?), Gray (is he a person?), Cowper, Macpherson, Shelley, Keats, Wm Morris. But it would be very very hard & not quite my line. Then I do want to arrange my chiefly pathetic memories of the Suburbs—their grave charming old Annes now tumbling down at the feet of the villa-builder— their little bits of waste ground—my own special memories—a little girl, the first whose sex I dimly knew (when I was 7 or 8) —the quite new houses so difficult to like & yet to be liked.[3] But of course not 100 people want such a book.—What else is there?

---

[1] A. M. R. Ransome—a description of his galvanic energies. [*GB*]

[2] ET probably enclosed the first 4 volumes of a new shilling 'Contemporary Series' published by Alston Rivers: W. M. Rossetti, *Democratic Sonnets*, 2 vols.; W. H. Davies, *The Soul's Destroyer*; J. Marjoram, *Repose, and other Poems*, reviewed *B*, April, and *DC*, 24 June.

[3] This constant theme in ET's letters (cf. letter of 20 March 1907 to Jesse Berridge) finds expression in some of his books of essays and, ultimately, in *The Happy-Go-Lucky Morgans*, 1913.

Looking at that Evans' profile of me[1] a woman said: 'He looks as if he were going to fall off his stalk'. And a good coarse Broadsman omitted to send an invitation to rough it with him at night on the Broads because of that profile never having seen me & my pimples &c. It is not exhaustive, is it?

But I am tired. Goodbye. Our love to you & Emily & please send back *Pater* soon. (Let me keep Wilde until the new edition comes, not long hence I think.)

Yours ever Edward Thomas

67

22 April 1907   *Berryfield Cottage*

My dear Gordon,

I shall be very glad if you do dedicate a book to me. It is the one thing I should not mind collecting, I think,—dedications: & I shall do well to begin with you and William Davies. I hope the book will not be very long. Will you try Alston Rivers? or is it too long for that shilling series? Davies' *Soul's Destroyer* has already appeared in it.[2]

I should not have been so long before writing to you had I not been away a good deal—mainly interviews with a publisher—and then had a long visit from Freeman[3] (while Helen & the children were in town): so I got very much behind with my work; and also I have had two bad spells of languor and melancholy. Nor am I likely to be much good just now. For I am trying to give up smoking & apparently my work suffers—as might have been expected—by the sudden drop from 8 pipes a day to 2. It is like me to have started this attempt after Ernest Rhys saying that Swinburne & Dumas both gave up tobacco because it lowered their vitality. Well I know how little vitality I have to lose; yet I thought I might regain a little before it is too late. And I shall want all my energies & more if I am to do my next job well. Probably that will be a life & criticism of

---

[1] The portrait accompanying Ransome's article on ET in *The Bookman's Gallery*. It faces p. 59.

[2] See Letter 66, note 2.

[3] Martin Freeman.

Richard Jefferies. It ought to give me many opportunities. There have been two: Besant's excellent advertisement, called a *Eulogy* and Salt's vigorous but not exhaustive pamphlet.[1] In two years I might do something, knowing the man's native country & his books. Should you hear of any of his early & mostly bad novels—yellow backs—like *The Scarlet Shawl*, I wish you would let me know where. I must have everything here at hand especially as the Museum is closed. It is not quite settled yet, but Hutchinson's reader, Roger Ingpen, thinks I can have £100 in advance of royalties for not over 80,000; & such a book might become a useful property to me—just possibly.

One of my saddest jobs lately has been reviewing John Davidson's drama: *Triumph of Mammon*, with an epilogue.[2] I think his brain must be giving way. There is a lot of energy, as usual; but an unusual incoherence and much less beauty in detail. Of course I couldn't praise it yet I did not like having to say anything against this sad serious, very 'clever egoist'.

Speaking of reviews, thank you for Scott on me. Frankly, I did not much like it. I wonder does he always write so? or did my book corrupt him? I seem to be able to trace his 'womanly flesh of rivers' —which I think ridiculous—to my 'crystal flesh' which was barely pardonable where I was almost personifying a little river. I cannot think that he really cared for the book & tried to discover what originality it may have: at least it would be hard to learn from it what (if anything) made the book differ from all others or what effect (if any) it produced upon him which no other book could produce. I wonder what you think.

No. Marjoram is a young bank clerk—22 years old—at Norwich.

Thanks too for Hudson—a trifle & yet with something of his unique personality in it, a personality most dear to me. Rothen-stein has just painted him—badly—making him not an eagle in a palace court, but an eagle at the Zoo and contented to be there.

I have made friends with Walter de la Mare. You would like him—a subtle honest person—an accountant in the City (& a clever one, I hear) but rather willing to leave it if he saw a way

---

[1] Sir Walter Besant, *The Eulogy of Richard Jefferies*, 1888; Henry S. Salt, *The Faith of R. Jefferies*, 1906.
[2] Reviewed *DC*, 30 April.

that would not hurt his wife & 4 children—34 years old—handsome like young Dickens, but short & his eyes too small—finally
he has the foible of liking my reviews & (I fear) preferring them
to my landscapes & people who seem to him from a different
hand from the *Chronicle* reviewer's, which annoys me.

About Wright's *Pater*. I am told that Jackson is a liar & has
probably stuffed Wright with lies.[1] If the infatuation is rightly
reported, even so it is not sufficiently related to the *Pater* who
emerges to justify Wright's treatment of it. I confess I should
not be surprised if it were true, but I daresay Pater was physically not equal to his mental preferences. I get more & more dissatisfied with Pater. His work seems fatally external to him—a
very wonderful tour de force, but on a level with Greek or Latin
verses by a professor. It is often singularly beautiful but even
Denys falls short. Pater makes him do things—& how painfully
recalcitrant are those bishops kicking the ball in the Cathedral—
surely genius would not have allowed us to see the effort (that
fails after all) to produce these unusual effects? I wonder do you
know what I mean when I say that I do not see the necessity for
his work?—I see nothing in it which was beyond his control, no
divine agency in it at all. But I need not say that I am suppressing
admiration of a great many details & that I believe him to have
achieved everything which a purely self-conscious use of words
could achieve, more than any other Englishman.

I haven't time to oppose you thoroughly in the subject of my
fitness for writing about English poets. It would take too long
to explain how forced my criticism nearly always is—how often
I *think of things to say*—what a struggle it is to fill a column &
how impossible it seems to write at more length. Perhaps my
intense desire to say only things that come from the depths & to
get on to paper somehow the (perhaps few) passionate moments
of my reading life—perhaps this has given a quality to the writing which a friend will not distinguish from perfect sincerity &
independence of view.

I don't know Donne very well, but I will. Yes Collins would be
better than Gray & of course it was a slip when I forgot Blake.

---

[1] See the review (*DC*, 1 April). 'We must not omit to mention that with the life
of Pater is incorporated the life and eulogium of a Mr. Jackson, the original of
"Marcus the Epicurean", together with an incomplete list of his notices and
literary treasures.'

7 Edward Thomas, a sketch by John Wheatley, in 1916

8 Edward Thomas and Gordon Bottomley in 1916

I am glad of what you say about Suburban houses. I must look at Madox Brown's Work. Is there anything solid and dull about that period of architecture?

Yes, do a play about Gunnar. To give an excuse for hearing those words & seeing that woman on the stage would be true benevolence.

Balmer is in luck & I congratulate him.

Helen says we have room for some of those seedling larkspurs & I should like them.

Goodbye & our love to Emily & you.

Ever yours Edward Thomas

68

14 May 1907   *Berryfield Cottage*

My dear Gordon,

It is a beautiful still evening at 7 o'clock & I sit & look at the most luxuriant beechen hill & coombe in the world. I have no need to do any more work today, because I did 1,600 words of reviewing before 3.30,[1] after which I wasted 2 hours trying to pay calls with Helen but finding my victims out. Then I said 'don't' to the children many times, & finally to myself; then suddenly seeing how beautiful it was, I thought I ought to enjoy it & could not think how. I can't read for pleasure. I tried gardening: it annoyed me, and there was an end to it. It is no use walking, for I do nothing but feed my eyes when I walk, & it has at last occurred to me that is not enough,—a man in the country must be a naturalist, an historian, an agriculturist, or a philosopher, & I am none of them. I have no 'interests' at all, & I know that beauty can bore & even infuriate one who is seldom passionate. So I am writing to you which is obviously a poor thing to do as it simply clarifies my introspection a little but will not—I know well—lead it anywhere. Oh for a little money, to turn round for a year, to make sure whether there is

---

[1] F. Coutts, *The Romance of King Arthur*, reviewed *MP*, 20 May, and A. G. Bradley, *Wiltshire*, *MP*, 27 May; Rt. hon. Sir Herbert Maxwell, *Memoirs of the Months*, 4th series, reviewed *DC*, 28 May, and Ralph Hodgson, *The Last Blackbird, and other lines*, *DC*, 30 May.

anything I should want to do if I had not to do reviewing. I tried
to get my agent to help me out of reviewing.[1] But he could only
suggest fiction, which I can't even begin to think of yet. I
suggested a book on the Suburbs, but instead of my little 20,000
words he wanted an important work of 60,000 & I know what
that means, & he wants a syllabus & I don't know what that
means. The *Jefferies* has not been settled yet & I am afraid of it.
It is silly thing to do a bad life of a good man & I shall have no
leisure to try to do a good one. I wish I hadn't written this
because it is not clear enough to enable you to help, supposing
I can be helped. But I leave it, I think, just because I don't like
sending you a very short letter & I don't like keeping you waiting
very long. Oh, my self-consciousness, it grows & grows & is
almost constant now, & I fear perhaps it will reach the point of
excess without my knowing it. ——

I won't send you my Anthology until the 2nd impression
because it is full of misprints. I simply cannot concentrate my
mind on familiar poems so as to detect misprints.

What you say about 'a new movement of Naturalism—naturalism of feeling where Wordsworth's was no more than a naturalism of thought', I believe is well worth thinking about, & I
have meant to get conscious of it to some purpose (having long
thought vaguely as you do); but positively only reviews &
nature ever make me think at all & that in a way beyond my
control—things occur to me & I think for about the length of
a lyric & then down & blank & something new—if the old idea
returns it will not grow, but is only repeated. Perhaps we worry
less about conclusions, generalizations nowadays, in our anxiety
to get the facts & feelings down—just as science picks up a
million pebbles & can't arrange them or even play with them.
I am by the way going to plead for a little more playfulness &
imagination (if to be got) in archæology, topography & so on: the
way in which scientific people & their followers are satisfied with
data in appalling English disgusts me, & is moreover wrong.[2]

About Jefferies—I never read *The Scarlet Shawl*[3] but it is a

[1] C. F. Casenove. See Robert P. Eckert, *Edward Thomas*.
[2] A constant theme of ET and a key both to his poetry and his best prose: cf.
G. Saintsbury, *The Later Nineteenth Century*, reviewed *DC*, 29 October; H. Belloc,
The Historic Thames, *DC*, 18 June; and, more obliquely, A. G. Bradley, *Round
about Wiltshire*, *DC*, 6 June.
[3] Published 1874.

yellow back & said to be an entirely vain attempt to write an ordinary novel about lords. But I should like to look at it when I come down. By the way, as Helen is a daily schoolmistress from 9 till 10.30[1] she cannot get away until August & will then most likely go with the children.

I like the idea of blank verse for your Gunnar play,[2] but then also I should like to see how you would do prose to that extent.

I don't know why de la Mare should not like you, by the way.

Yes; I only smoke about $1\frac{1}{2}$ pipes of tobacco a day. Perhaps I am a little hungrier, but I am neither more joyful nor more wise.

It is past 8 & almost too dark & there is little more time.

I use a stylographic pen now—hence my handwriting.

I introduced Guthrie's landscape to a very clever acquaintance of mine who has money & spends it & most of his time in learning to draw. He liked Guthrie's feeling immensely but says he ought to try working with a fine fountain pen on smooth paper & give up his 'mezzy' methods! But I imagine Guthrie will have to be satisfied with his *results* now, won't he?

Our love to Emily & you.

Ever yours Edward Thomas

69

Early June, 1907 *Berryfield Cottage*

My dear Gordon,

My thanks for *Chambers of Imagery*[3] which I shall probably read on my way to you[4] for I am crammed with work[5] & Davies in the intervals. Oh, de la Mare likes your 'Dairymaids to Pan'.

[1] At the children's department of Bedales School.
[2] *The Riding to Lithend* (based on *Brennu-Njáls saga*) was dedicated to ET. For this, and another dedicatory poem, see *Poems of Thirty Years*, pp. 135–7.
[3] GB, *Chambers of Imagery*, first Series, 1907, in a limited edition of 500 copies.
[4] See a letter, dated 21 June 1907, to Jesse Berridge: 'Your letter reached me at Cartmel near Windermere where I was having a fortnight with Bottomley in the rain. I was walking and talking all day and had to work hard all the evening. I got back here yesterday and found the roses out and the hay harvest well begun and everyone well: Now I have to work at the *Jefferies*. Helen and I will probably take our short holiday at Corte where he was born and lived 30 years, though I have already known it 20 years myself.'
[5] During June and July the following reviews appeared: 8 in *DC*, 2 in *MP*, and 2 long multiple reviews in *B*, for June and July.

I will bring his *Brocken*,[1] but may I keep the Wildes because I can't finish with them until I have written my article, a thing I can't do till I must, which will be when the complete Wilde comes? But I shall not have Marteino's *London*, I fear. I am perhaps staying Wednesday night at Northampton & am asking my host there to tell me all about trains to Corte. When I hear I will let you know mine. If you write to give me leave to retain the Wilde, tell me what sort of weather is most likely & if I ought to be rainproof. The proofs & quotation all right.

Yours ever Edward Thomas

70

21 June 1907   *Berryfield Cottage*

My dear Gordon & Emily,

I did think of you on Wednesday night in London. I thought of you as the friends who had just given me a perfectly happy & calm holiday that weaned me from my usual fidgets & discomforts in the most surprising way. Helen would tell you now that in spite of the intervening day in London I am much nicer & cheerfuller than I was, & when I was able to enjoy finding the children awake last night as I arrived & roses in the garden & the hay in swathes in the fields around, it was because of you & your house. Can I thank you in a better way? How I wish you could have come to see the South as it is now, with all the roses & pinks & lupins & irises & the clematis over the hedgetops & the plums getting big. But the wind is restless & I don't think we have done with the rain.

The children were delighted with Miss Gordon's mugs & the picture of the Pied Piper. Wouldn't you like to hear a score of their school-fellows sing 'The Holm Bank Hunting Song'? They are learning it now.

Mrs. Jefferies has put me off & I am not to see her till next week.[2]

Bernard Shaw has written an amazing preface, says Davies,

---

[1] W. de la Mare, *Henry Brocken*, 1904.
[2] Widow of Richard Jefferies.

for his Autobiography, calling him the 'Supertramp'. And now Davies is to dictate his terms: it should be a proud brief moment for him. He asked to be 'remembered' to you, Gordon.

Goodbye now with Helen's love & mine.

Yours ever Edward Thomas

71

5 *July 1907*   *Berryfield Cottage*

My dear Gordon,

This is only to enclose Doughty's head & the words of '*Auprès de ma blonde*'. For I am in a great muddle with proofs, letters, carpentering, gardening, reading & an additional journey to town for a dinner with the celebrated

John Galsworthy
Nevinson
Garnett & Muirhead Bone
Masefield
Norreysconnell
L. Housman
Bullen
Jepson

& certain *Daily News* lights: but I had a continual headache & was glad to be back again though here the wind will not cease. But I got on with Bone a little & am to go to his house when I like to see his pictures. He spoke well of Guthrie & your Hay. And that reminds me that I have your friend Scott to thank for a very nice review of the *Pocket Book*.[1]

At last I have settled all with Hutchinson,[2] after consulting the Author's Society & making further amendments. I saw Mrs. Jefferies but she had callers & I didn't get ahead much. However she was friendly & I am to go again. I had a glorious walk back from her through Haslemere here, about 22 miles, ending at midnight.

[1] Dixon Scott. Hay is GB's friend, John Hamilton Hay: see Letter 62, note 4.
[2] Publisher of *Richard Jefferies*.

You would have liked to hear Bone talking about Shannon & Ricketts & John[1]—especially John with his long red beard, earrings, jersey, check suit, & standing six feet high, so that a cabman was once too nervous to drive him. But I can't talk a bit & I write now because I see solid masses of toil to be gone through before I can pretend to be at ease again. So we salute you & Emily and I slink down a side street & mess along.

Ever yours Edward Thomas

72

10 *August 1907*   *Berryfield Cottage*

My dear Gordon,

It is good to have two of your letters in a short time yet I am still ashamed of not writing to you before this. Helen & the children have been away 2 weeks & the maid part of the time, & Freeman has been with me, so what with cooking, washing up, walking, talking, & my life's work, I could not write after the daily dozen on Hodder & Stoughton's[2] or somebody else's business. And now Helen is back and I am packing up because I go to Jefferies country

c/o Miss Smith, Broome Farm, nr Swindon, Wiltshire

on Tuesday, stay till the end of the month, Helen joining me on Friday. I shall walk & mope and for one or two whole days fish, & come back, I know, not any the fitter for writing a life of Jefferies. For the damned blues are on me and will never go, I think. So I am just going to look through your letters & say what it is fairly easy to say.

I have forgotten to look for *The Dawn in Britain* at Thorpe's but will try to remember on Tuesday.[3]

Alberta V.

---

[1] Charles H. Shannon, R.A. and Charles Ricketts, R.A. collaborated in *The Dial* (1889–97), which influenced GB's early work. 'John' is Augustus John. Publishers of *The Book of the Open Air*.

[3] Thomas Thorpe, a London bookseller to whom ET sold his review copies, some of which were substantial series, e.g. the library edition of *William Morris's Collected Works* and the *Cambridge History of English Literature*.

Montgomery,
I do not envy thee.

Goodluck to *Gunnar*. But you do what you would like about a dedication & as to *Laodice & Danae* there is no reason why I should object & every reason—the one reason that it is a book by you—why I should be happy for it. Did you know Jefferies told the story of Laodice & Danae in his *Story of My Heart* to show how horrible is the fate of men on this earth?

Bathbone
Rathbun

is good.[1]

I wish I could remember the good things Freeman[2] told me of his cousin, but I only recall the least good—
Farquharson (as host) : 'Now do taste this shoulder of mutton. We got it very cheap. It was killed by lightning—the act of God and not of a certified slaughterer.'
He loves cripples because of the delicate artifice which upsets the stupid symmetry of Nature.

———

I am glad you did not mind my review,[3] truncated though it was & shorn of remarks on 'The Viaduct', compare it favourably with Chesterton's 'Euston', with quotations.

Elkin Matthews tells Davies that only 160 copies of *New Poems* are sold in spite of the Welsh & English papers.

You ought to do the Parish church. You have time. I have despair: and my egoism comes frightfully near to being complete—it must end in madness if it is left to itself & *I* cannot interrupt it.

'The Lost House', too, is good.
Here are 24 pennystamps for the *Cavendish*.[4]

[1] I had offered him Bath-bun as a rhyme to Rathbone. [*GB*] Clerihews were in fashion then.
[2] Martin Freeman.
[3] An unsigned 2-column review of *Chambers of Imagery*, together with volumes of verse by F. M. Hueffer, D. Radford, and Cyril Scott, in *DC*, 5 August. ('Mr. Bottomley's newest verses are difficult, we think, because they are not always wrought up to the condition of poetry, but seem to have been left in a raw state that can appeal to the intelligence only, except in a few places. . . . They seem to us to be in their present stage short of poetry, to demand the amplification of prose, and not the sensuous and elliptical forms of verse.')
[4] 'Cavendish', originally the pseudonym of Henry Jones, became the title (and

For a month now I haven't written a review even. I have 4 volumes of notes made since *The Heart of England*, & none of them used. *Jefferies* does not advance. I have few unpublished letters & none of interest yet. I am to see Mrs. Jefferies tomorrow & C. J. Longman on Tuesday—I have an offer of help from Henry S. Salt. Oh, you don't know that I have undertaken to write about Borrow in the course of the next 16 months.[1] If you know of articles in books or magazines do tell me. I am in a sleepy despondency.—I have suggested to Guthrie that he might do 2 drawings for the *Jefferies*, one of The Downs & one of The Forest. If the publisher won't buy them, I will.

Goodbye & with our love

I am yours & Emily's ever

Edward Thomas

73

22 September 1907   *Berryfield Cottage*

My dear Gordon,

I see it is a month since you wrote to me & I remember how glad I was in Wiltshire to get a letter from you. But down there I was nearly always out of doors & when indoors I was writing out my notes or writing to crowds of people who were supposed to be likely to help me to know Jefferies. The three weeks there passed quickly: I could do no ordinary work there, so that when I got home I was working from 9.30 a.m. to 1 a.m., reading & writing, & am still busy. My information comes in in scraps; often long letters & nothing said; & each letter gives a new address which I write to & get the same result. Still, I met one or two good people—one splendid old woman—in Wiltshire, & ploughed thro Parish Registers, & altogether I have a mass of trifles that are new & will have some effect. But I see that I must use Jefferies' books chiefly as my sources, & quote more

---

accepted colloquialism) for a series of *Guides*, *Rules*, and *Pocket Guides* to various games (e.g. tennis, whist, piquet, croquet etc.) published by T. De la Rue between 1863 and 1924.

[1] This offer (from Methuen) fell through. *George Borrow. The Man and his Books*, 1912, was published by Chapman and Hall.

than I like doing. 80,000 words will not be hard to write: the difficulty will be to use all the most relevant things. If possible I must all but finish it by May & then look at Borrow (which is for Methuen). And now Grant Richards wants me to do a book for the Spring dealing more or less definitely with the question of townsmen going out into the country to play, to work or to live. I can't accept unless I can get a good framework to build on, & I can't write a treatise. So I must refuse unless someone will give me a simple plot. Not a lot of ramifications, recognition scenes, &c, but just a progressive narrative that can help me to get out, first my knowledge of the Suburbs, then, for contrast, the country. Does anything occur to you & Emily? I have till the end of the week to decide.[1] I would refuse at once only I want to see how far I can 'live & live better by books instead of reviewing'. A Diary would be easy—too easy—& it is not a form I desire. Letters also I don't like & they would be hard (as you know). If I could be anonymous—which G.R.[2] won't allow—I could be frankly autobiographical. As it is, I can't put all, or even the main part, of my own experience into a book to be wildly advertised & obviously a publisher's book. Besides I should hurt a lot of people & I can't yet.[1]

Jefferies by the way only uses Danae to illustrate the cruelty of life.[3]

I have been reviewing Prior, Beddoes & a book about Arthur in the English Poets for the *Saturday* & Yeats & Jefferies for *Bookman* & other trifles.[4] But work that brings money at once

---

[1] See page 135, note 3. W. H. Hudson believed that 'most of the characters in the *Happy-etc.-Morgan* were autobiographical'. A close comparison of many sketches and short pieces in *The Heart of England, Rose Acre Papers, Rest and Unrest, Light and Twilight* and *The South Country* with *The Childhood of Edward Thomas* and Helen Thomas's *AIW* and *WWE* would show how totally ET drew on his own intimate experience for most of his 'personal' writing. His poems are an extension and refinement of the same intense desire to interpret his spiritual autobiography.

[2] Grant Richards.

[3] A reference to the tale of Laodice and Danae in *The Story of My Heart*. See Letter 72.

[4] 'Other trifles', ET's usual comment on his reviewing, disguises both his dedicated care as a critic and the perceptive awareness of the living stream of twentieth-century poetry, drama, and prose displayed in the following reviews in August and September (among 16 in *DC*, 5 in *MP*, 2 in *B*, and 3 in *SR*): *Poems of T. L. Beddoes*, edited by Ramsay Colles, *SR*, 9 August; Matthew Prior, *Dialogues of the Dead*, edited by A. R. Waller, *SR*, 28 September; Howard Maynadier, *The Arthur of the English Poets*, *SR*, 21 September; *Poems by Wordsworth*, selected by Stopford

does not abound, & Milne especially does not encourage me except by ⅓s of a column at a time.

If this weather lasts you ought to come here. What are your plans? Late October will very likely be fine here, tho it may be very misty in the mornings as it has been for two weeks (tho not dripping mists yet). We should like to see you here.

I like your account of Guthrie. I have not been able to see him yet, but I shall try this week.

I am not well, worried, hard at work, discontented with myself & everyone I see, but chiefly myself & I am troubled by a lot of sleepiness not only at night after 10 but even in the morning, tho I usually get 7 hours sleep at night. I begin to think that this kind of life can't go on for ever & yet there are old faces which contradict me. Why have I no energies like other men? I long for some hatred or indignation or even sharp despair, since love is impossible, to send me out on the road that leads over the hills & among the stars sometimes. Till then I must grind everything out, conscious at every moment of what the result is & so always dissatisfied. I was told the other day that I seemed a calm dispassionate observer with no opinions. I hope I am more. I have no opinions, I know. But cannot the passive temperament do something, a little? For I have impressions of men & places & books. They often overawe me as a tree or a crowd does the sensitized paper; & is that nothing or as good as nothing? The men I admire most seem to say it is nothing. Yet think of the pain going on living & not being able to do anything but eat & drink & earn a living for 5 people. Would anyone do it that was aware of what he did? And will not the doing of it be a most sharp martyrdom to which no church allows any honour?

Yours & Emily's ever Edward Thomas

Brooke, and *Poems by Keats*, selected by A. Symons, *MP*, 19 August; Richard Crashaw, *Steps to the Temple etc.*, edited by A. R. Waller, *DC*, 20 August; *Poetical Works of Keats*, edited by H. B. Forman, *DC*, 26 August; 'Some new singers' (including Osmaston, Dillon, and James Joyce), *DC*, 31 August; Laurence Housman and H. G. Barker, *Prunella*, *DC*, 9 September; C. Le Fanu, *Reflections of a Frivolous Philosopher*, *MP*, 29 August; J. M. Synge, *The Playboy of the Western World*, *B*, August, and *DC*, 13 September; W. B. Yeats, *Deirdre*, *DC*, 28 September, and *B*, October.

74

11 October 1907   *Berryfield Cottage*

My dear Gordon,

Thank you for your suggestions about Back to the Land.[1] I ought not to have troubled you, for it was so very unlikely that I could at short notice give any vitality to another man's form, however good, & that is what I find. So I have told G.R. I can't do it yet at any rate.[2]

But I was glad to hear you have been working so well at *Gunnar*. You must show it to me when it has got into shape.

I should like to see you on Oct. 23 or 24 in London, but you will be in a hurry & have lots to do, so that I won't come up especially for that, tho if I do happen to be in town I will let you know. So you will come here in December. I hope it will be a hard, clear December for your sake. It will be very pleasant having you & Emily here & Guthrie too. Give us time if you can to make everything ready for you—so that I need not be having to work. I am very busy. Scores of books from the *Morning Post*[3] which I dare not refuse,—and not enough from Milne. It is only in the *Chronicle* that I feel quite at ease & do my best when any best is possible. But he has new men & feels my innate hostility to him. Arthur Waugh pleases him & commands his respect.[4]

I rather like Machen's thing. Do you recognize 'Paradise' in the Welsh forms *Paradwys, Mharadwys* ?[5]

Thanks for *Brocken*.[6] You would like de la Mare himself, & I

---

[1] Probably a title for a book suggested by ET to the publisher Grant Richards.

[2] Grant Richards.

[3] *MP* frequently allowed ET $1\frac{1}{2}$ columns or more for his reviews, most of which were unsigned. During October, November, and December, *MP* published 11 reviews including Arthur Ransome, *Bohemia in London*, 3 October; *An English Prose Miscellany*, selected by John Masefield, 2 December; Francis B. Gummere, *The Popular Ballad*, 23 December; and Stopford Brooke, *Studies in Poetry*, 28 December.

[4] Too much should not be made of this comment on Milne and *DC*. It is true that Arthur Waugh became *DC*'s principal and most constant reviewer, while slightly fewer of ET's reviews were signed than in 1904–6, but most of ET's reviews in 1908 and 1909 were longer than a single column. His comment to GB is a temporary annoyance based on a series of 3/4 column reviews from July to October 1907.

[5] Arthur Machen, *The Hill of Dreams*, reviewed *B*, September.

[6] See page 142, note 1.

will try to get him down here for a day while you are here or at
Harting. But he is tied to an office & has to be there at 9 on
Mondays even, so that week ends are impossible. He has a nice
wife & 3 children & I believe they are often very happy. They
are almost poor.

Fame has found me. A letter to Edward Thomas, Petersfield
(from Yarmouth) reached me without delay.

But it is not the natural pride in this that makes me stop so
soon. I am weary in my fingers with reviewing & in my head
with reading & trying to skim bad books. One of my works has
been a muddled column on various means of producing visual
effects by words—very muddled.[1] But what a fine history the
growth of the power & the wish to produce such effects w^d make!
I have a mind to fill a note book with illustrative passages &
string them together in the next world. Tell me what you think.
You are not a reviewer. You can think things out.

Well now I have to read for the *Bookman*:[2]

Lady Gregory's *Saints & Wonders*
Mrs. M. L. Woods' *Poems Old & New*
Wild Life in a Norfolk Estuary
Trees in Nature & Myth & Art

Read & review them in 48 hours & also copy out 2 columns, &
saw some wood & get some fresh air. Goodbye. Our love to
Emily & you, & good luck to *Gunnar*.

Ever yours Edward Thomas

75

2 November 1907   *Berryfield Cottage*

My dear Gordon,

On Monday I go to London for a fortnight of the British
Museum & I am working to get rid of all reviewing up to date,

---

[1] *Hampshire Vignettes*, by the author of *Mademoiselle Ixe*, reviewed *DC*, 2 November.
[2] ET's name is included among the list of contributions to *B* for January to July
1908, but there are no reviews signed by him. *Saints and Wonders* is reviewed,
with Alfred Noyes, *Forty Singing Seamen*, in *B*, January; Margaret L. Woods,
Poems Old and New and Arthur H. Patterson, *Wild Life*, etc., in *B*, June; Ernest
Phythian, *Trees in Nature*, etc., with John Galsworthy, *A Commentary*, in *B*, July.

also at an impudent introduction to George Herbert for Every-man in the Street.[1] So I cannot take more than a minute or two to congratulate you on drafting *Gunnar* and finding Eileen Raven.[2] It is a good name, different from Helen Alexander which I noticed lately, also a good name. I will look at *Bronwen*[3] some day & see.

Deirdre is perhaps the most *perfect* thing Yeats has done, but I don't like it most, perhaps because I resent more & more his giving drugs to all the Irish heroes in turn. Margaret Woods doesn't interest me, not a bit.[4]

Will you tell me as definitely as you can soon when you could come here, because I want to be sure before I arrange for another short visit to Wiltshire & a long one to a cottage on the sea near Dunwich where I hope to write my *Jefferies*.[5]

I could give you a Margaret Woods if you liked when you come here.

With our love to you both

Ever yours Edward Thomas

76

26 December 1907   *Berryfield Cottage*

My dear Gordon,

I don't know when I shall next get a chance to write to you & even now it nears dinner time, I expect Guthrie, & I have still to pack, for tomorrow I leave here for

Minsmere, nr Dunwich, Suffolk.

where I hope to write about Jefferies. I brim over with little things but have no notion of a good movement & sweep yet. Could you send me the Wilde books there as I understand the new edition is coming early in the year?

---

[1] George Herbert's *Temple*, with an Introduction by ET (Everyman's Library), 1908.

[2] Gunnar, the hero of *Riding to Lithend*. Eileen Raven is the name of a character in the play.

[3] In the Mabinogion. [*GB*]

[4] See page 150, note 2, and reviews of her work in *DC*, 28 September, and *B*, October.

[5] The cottage was found for ET by his friend Harry Hooton who lived at Dunwich.

Isn't Nietzsche magnificent? & so necessary these days? Yet he damns me to deeper perdition than I had yet bestowed myself.

I am glad to hear I was enjoying life.[1] Perhaps my melancholy is a delusion of the surface, a term mistakenly applied by one who is after all only a $\frac{1}{2}$d. critic. I did enjoy yesterday though because Bronwen excelled herself in joy & expressions of joy & even Merfyn was never peevish. We did not over eat, touched no alcohol & I actually laughed as I was getting to bed. The other night I went into the children's room, by the way, & awakened Bronwen by accident—she burst out laughing and fell asleep again. Fancy laughing in bed & at night & on just waking up. I ought to bend all my efforts to live up to her as the Superman.

I was sorry Emily ran off so gaily, but it was all a hurry & it does not rankle.

You are right about Yeats & I felt the same even when I praised *Deirdre* but if he does it again I shall administer an emetic for the laudanum with which he is always drugging big hearty people. But it was so perfect in its kind I couldn't throw stones, though glass houses are really meant for stones. Trench[2] has a better spirit in his *Deirdre* & the ravishment of Naois is well done; there is a most beautiful comparison in it (I forget where now) of Deirdre's astonishment at sight of Naois—to the astonishment of a man who comes suddenly out of woods upon a vast quiet estuary & his horse's hoofs startle the seafowl that were glassed—with sky & cloud—in the ebb. Oh, glorious. Yet I know I like it because with great good luck I might have done it myself.

Adieu Sylvanus with love to Sylvana from your loving

Urbanus

Have you any book that touches well on the mystic trance—its origin—typical visions &c.? I ain't a mystic myself & I want to know what is possible before coming to *The Story of my Heart*

---

[1] I have omitted five brief notes (dated 15, 18, 20, 21, and 30 of November) which refer to GB's plans to come south and to his visit to Berryfield Cottage between 29 November and 3 December; also to a back-log of reviewing and a payment to GB for his *Open Air* articles.

[2] 'I will keep Mrs. [F. L.] Woods for you and I shall have two volumes of [F.] Herbert Trench for you to look at.' (Omitted letter, 18 November.) W. B. Yeats, *Deirdre*, reviewed *DC*, 28 September, and *B*, October. I cannot trace reviews of *Deirdre Wed, and other poems* (1901), *New Poems* (1907), or *Lyrics and Narrative Poems* (1911), all by Trench.

in which there are some trance-visions or experiences. I know Inge's *Christian Mysticism* & Carpenter's chapters in *Adam's Peak to Elephants*.[1]

77

15 January 1908   *Minsmere, nr Dunwich, Suffolk*

My dear Gordon,

Forgive me for not writing before. You will when you know I have been writing hard at Jefferies all day & every day since the 5th, so hard that with the large incidental quotations of letters &c. (not yet copied out) I must have done fully 40,000 words, & the book need only be 80,000 (but will probably be 100,000). And now I have made myself weary with it all. I came here straight from a specialist who messed me about, commanded abstinence from alcohol & sugar & almost abstinence from tobacco, & gave me a wonderfully compounded medicine (bismuth, bromide &c) & small green tabloids—a specialist in neurasthenia. Then I got here with bad toothache & acquired a stiff neck & was tired with travel. But the medicine & the air & the lively company of the Aldis family who live in the other coastguard's cottage next door soon made me rotund in spirit if still lean in body: & I settled down to work in the midst of a patchwork of notes, references &c without much ceremony & lo! got into the thing fast. The first chapter at present is a long[,] too poetical (where it isn't too dull) chapter on Jefferies' Wiltshire. Then genealogical stuff & ancestors. Then the farmhouse & parents & childhood. Then the big boy & country journalist writing about stories & very competent journalistic articles on agriculture &c.[2]

There are prodigiously dull blocks in the thing, because you see nobody has done the thing completely or attempted it, & the scale asked for made completeness necessary. So I give the main points of even the 2nd rate stuff. A lot of the earlier work & even up to his 32nd year (he died at 38) is just competent vivid fluent

[1] W. R. Inge, *Christian Mysticism* [The Bampton Lectures], 1899, and Edward Carpenter, *From Adam's Peak to Elephants*: sketches in Ceylon and India, 1892, revised 1903. (Chapters 8–11, *A Visit to a Ghani*, printed separately 1911.) These books, like the works of Nietzsche, were read in preparation for *Richard Jefferies*.

[2] A precise description of the first six chapters of his *Jefferies*.

(for the period uncommonly good & well informed) & straight from the soil criticism of the position of farmers & labourers when labourers began to form unions & demand higher wages. Better journalism couldn't be & it is usually fair minded & illuminating, but as it isn't first rate thro being either encyclopaedic, or entirely fresh & important, or of an artistic completeness, I have announced that it does not concern me in my book except as it shows the growth of his mind. Is this right, should you think? I simply ignore Besant,[1] tho my chances of controverting him with security, of pointing out his indolence his incompetence his incompleteness & his inaccuracy are many; not to speak of his pervasive vulgarity.

Alas! it is impossible to knead all this together into something satisfying in every part. And even when I get to the good books I shall have to quote a lot. I have got some things I like in but I shall have to prune away a few scores of charming metaphors I foresee. I wish you had some of his books & could send me your views now & then so that I might stir mine up. It is a big thing to do in solitude & the mind can't always glance about but is fond of sliding into a groove.

Nietzsche will have to come in later. *The Genealogy of Morals* is a very great book.[2] But I kick at his too completely aristocratic view.

Oh Dunwich is beautiful. I am on a heaving moor of heather & close gorse up & down & ending in a sandy cliff about 80 feet perpendicular & the black, peat strewn fine sand below. On the edge of this $1\frac{1}{2}$ miles away is the ruined church that has half fallen over already. Four arches & a broken tower, pale & airy. Just beyond that the higher moor dips to quite flat marsh with gentlest rises inland with masses of trees compact & dark & a perfect huge curve of foamy coast up to the red light at Southwold northward. In the other direction, just behind us, the moor dips to more marshes with black cattle dim & far off under white sun, & three faint windmills that work a sluice & then trees—inland more gentle rises with pines. No hills (unless you lie down in

[1] Sir Walter Besant is mentioned once in ET's book (p. 323). See page 137, note 1.
[2] *The Genealogy of Morals*, vol. 13 of *The Complete Works of Nietzsche* in translation, edited by Oscar Levy, appeared in 1910. ET, like his father, read German but he probably refers here to *The Works of F. T. Nietzsche*, edited by A. Tiller, 1899 and later. Unsigned reviews of the Levy edition are preserved in ET's newspaper-cuttings. See *B*, June 1909, p. 86.

a dip of the moor & fancy the moorland as part of a Welsh
'black mountain'.) I get my firewood, kindling & logs, from the
beach, where we pick up champagne corks, sailors' hats, Antwerp
beer bottles, fish boxes, oranges, lemons, onions, banana stems,
waterworm timber and the most exquisite flat & round pebbles,
black, white, dove grey, veined, wheat coloured. Why does
Nature make these beautiful things so carelessly & then one
wonders whether all beautiful things are not of this careless
inevitableness and yet long wrought out too & then one has to
earn one's living. May that funny spirit bless *Gunnar* for you.
Tell me how it goes.

I will try to remember Mr. Murdoch.

Accept this hurry & good intention. It is late & I am tired &
bad in the back.

Yours & Emily's ever Edward Thomas

78

7 February 1908   *Minsmere*

My dear Gordon,

I have seemed just a machine lately for turning out lengths of
Jefferies almost every day—some days I had to give up to reviewing, tho alas! I fear the brave days when I could make a bare living out of the *Chronicle* alone are gone: for 6 or 8 months I have
had less than $\frac{1}{2}$ my old amount of reviewing printed & ∴ less
than $\frac{1}{2}$ my old earnings. Milne is (unintentionally I firmly
believe) so neglectful & rude that I have several times vowed to
throw them over before they throw me, & see what I can make
by books alone or almost alone.[1] But I fear quantities of books
would soon reduce such quality as I have. So I hang about the
skirt of the $\frac{1}{2}$d Press. I have got to do *Borrow* after all: (there

[1] See Letter 74, note 4. James Milne's references to ET in Chapter XI, *The
Memoirs of A Bookman*, 1934, support the 'unintentionally'. Milne appreciated
ET's quality and continued to use him as a specialist reviewer—especially of
modern poetry—until 1914. Milne firmly believed that the 'general reader'
wished for 'simple directness' in the book notices. (See his *A Window in Fleet
Street*, 1931, pp. 293–311.) He never imagined that ET, 'a most likeable man
and gentleman, both sensitive and modest', relied so much on general reviewing
as a means of livelihood.

was a doubt) : & that must be a bad book unless I get really well
& incredibly exuberant.

I don't know a bit what *Jefferies* will be like. I have had to
quote so much in order to make my special claims for him quite
clear & I shall be buried under the load of his good things &
produce only an untidy anthology.

My health keeps good in this bracing air with few worries &
a useful medicine. But I believe my specialist is lazy with me:
I am too docile a patient & too schoolboyish & unquestioning
with him; as soon as I get into his room I relapse & expect him
to discover everything—So I shan't go often again even if I
couldn't afford it. Among few disturbances here I got very fond
of a girl of 17 with two long plaits of dark brown hair & the
richest grey eyes, very wild & shy, to whom I could not say 10
words, nor she to me.[1] She used to milk the 2 cows her father
owned, but has now gone away to school. She is a clever child
who has begun to write verse. But I liked her for her perfect
wild youthfulness & remoteness from myself & now I think of
her every day in vain acquiescent dissatisfaction, & shall perhaps
never see her again, & shall be sad to hear she ever likes anyone
else even tho she will never like me. Which reminds me that
Garnett has been praising *The Heart of England*—'The Brook',
'A Winter Morning', 'First Daffodils', 'Fox Hunt' &c. & says
I am a poet & says my self-consciousness is akin to my sensitive-
ness & both due to my *youthfulness*. I suppose I am youthful to
like a girl in this way. Yet you have said I am older than the
eagle cock that blinks & blinks. Which is right? Both? I used to
think him a good & invariably unbiassed critic, but now he praises
me I doubt him!

By the way, I have just had a long letter from an Oxford
undergraduate aged 24 saying I have been for 4 years one of the
three great influences in his life—the others—guess!—Wagner
& Beethoven! I am trying to write a letter neither conceited nor
ironical. Fancy my corrupting the academic youth.

I was at Walberswick today, pestered by inane pretty houses,
paintable bits & an elderly aesthetic lady with youthful ankles &
neat old cottage furniture. But the dreary intersected marshes &
invisible sounding sea in twilight mists repaid me a little—with

[1] Cf. *WWE*, pp. 123–5, and 'The Fountain' in *Rest and Unrest*, pp. 138–43, where
this girl is described.

a hump of woods just visible as culmination of the mist. I met a good name over a shop at Southwold BOGGIS, also several others including ADNAMS. Our combination here of wavering moorland & marshes beats all Walberswick. You should have seen Southwold in mist, an almost wholly new town on the top of a gentle hill, with an old flint-towered church, & approached by a sheep bitten slope with gorse & on the gorse whitest linen strewn.

I come home daily with pockets full of the smooth pebbles, often pearshaped (flattish), rosy or primrose coloured & transparent nearly, & in the fresh moistness wonderfully beautiful: others white & round or oval: some split & with grain like chestnuts: not one but makes me think or rather draws out a part of me beyond my thinking. How unprofitable so many of our most genuine likings are, pebbles and seventeen years old, for example. Why was I not an artist to make them abide instead of being a sleeper who greets the old sun stirring his fingers idly & frowning & now & then kicking out & muttering—disturbing a bedfellow, no more? Why? Yet am I Yours & Emily's ever

Edward Thomas

I expect to leave here about the 25th with the first draft in my pocket.

79

26 February 1908   *Minsmere*
11.30 p.m. Wednesday

My dear Gordon,

I very much wanted to write to you the day—Monday—your letter came, but something naughtily prevented; & now I daresay this will suffer for my disobedience to the little will that is in me. I was reading Abercrombie's book at the time.[1] It cost me two whole days though I was not allowed to do a long review, & as it is I have wasted some space. He is good there is no doubt. He reminded me a little of you[.] If he can get finer without losing his energy he will pass Sturge Moore. But he is already fine, has his own vocabulary & a wonderful variety in his blank

[1] Lascelles Abercrombie, *Interludes and Poems*, reviewed in *DC*, 27 February.

verse, has certainly his own vision of things, is perhaps too metaphysical.—But though I have written a review of the book I have not made up my mind about it except that it is the sincere work of an artist. I wonder what he is like & envy you your chance of knowing him. I have lately enjoyed Mary Coleridge's poems & Michael Field's new book,[1] also above all Doughty's *Wanderings in Arabia*—Before I forget it, thanks for the two '*Saturday* articles', tho I haven't yet read the one you mistook for me. I am always glad to see Hudson's work. I love the man, tho I don't mistake that particular piece on 'Furze' for great literature when I say it gives me extraordinary pleasure—The tenderness & wildness of it—the mention of those hard big hands of his—the modesty, ease & serenity of it give me more than some better work. But of course it is nothing like his finest work except in its candour. Except William Morris there is no other man whom I would sometimes like to have been, no other writing man. William Morris' *Message of the March Wind*,[2] though nothing like Hudson, reminds me of Hudson, & isn't it a noble piece of humanity? There is nothing of the 'masterly superb describer' about Hudson.

I laughed at your trying to find what Wagner & Beethoven might have, out of their abundance, in common with me. But my admirer, tho not a great intellect, did not link us except as 'influences' on him. I wish I believed you when you say I can touch natural things 'with a large simple emotion'; but I can't, knowing how I go about the world with a worried heart & a note book. Garnett's phrases were so incurious that I am inclined to think them a concession to our acquaintanceship, & the only phrase that might commit him—'considerable poet'—is relative (to I know not what). I believe you are right in preferring your own aim & method to that of Conrad & others, simply because you use verse, & hitherto prose has practically never been capable of transmuting matter, though it can help the mind of the reader to transmutations (as in De Quincey, Meredith & I forget). My mind at any rate refuses to be illuded by anything but verse—excepting a few short passages of prose. Poetry in verse is at one

[1] Mary E. Coleridge, *Poems*, edited by Henry Newbolt, reviewed in *B*, February; Michael Field, *Wild Honey from Various Thyme*, in *MP*, 5 March; C. M. Doughty, *Wanderings in Arabia*, in *MP*, 6 February.
[2] See 'Poems by the Way', *Collected Works of William Morris*, vol. IX, and ET's full-scale treatment of William Morris in *B*, February 1911.

with the tides and the pulse; prose is chaos cut up into beds & borders & fountains & rusticwork like a garden. A merely great intellect can produce great prose, but not poetry, not one line. As you know! Forgive the commonplaces as of a $\frac{1}{2}$d paper. Yes, Milne must have evolved the Meredith article. —By the way I have only lately realized that Wilde was but 26 when he wrote *The Duchess of Padua* in which case it is his most astonishing work, I should think. I was less than just & Milne curtailed me so that it was not clear how the two died at last.[1]

I will try to remember *The Breaking Point*.[2]

I am trying to finish the draft of *Jefferies* by Friday when Helen comes for the week end to recover from nursing the children through measles. The book is not, cannot be organic. It may have a lot of small lights, but no light on the whole man. Trying to mingle biography, criticism & mere exposition of his matter, I have made confusion. When done it is to lie by for some months. Meantime I must think about Borrow, & I may also have a smaller book (without pictures) like *The Heart of England* to do, & as it must very likely be the last of its kind for me I want to make an effort. Helen & I leave here on Monday or Tuesday next. As I have told you I don't like the country on the whole, only the two or three miles of moor, sandy cliff, flat marsh & sea visible from here, & even that is a remembered dream now that the child I told you of has become a phantom face & a kind but moderate letter-writer. Isn't it absurd that while she was here I dared not speak & walk with her, & now that she is gone I put her to the unjust test of letters? What girl of 17 or 18 could express anything in letters to one wholly unknown & not loved? She is infinitely kind (and mildly wondering), yet her letters can barely kindle a response from my very ready pen & ink: so that self-deceiver and denier of what is though I may be, I dimly foresee a guttering candle, a flicker, another flicker, a smell & an awakening to find the fire as well as the light gone out, the house cold & dark & still & the one thing possible a shivering undressing & so to bed & the usual dull torment before I dare to rise & begin another day—more than a whole hour do I lie in the morning twilight daily,

---

[1] *The Duchess of Padua*, a Play by Oscar Wilde, reviewed *DC*, 13 February.
[2] A play by Edward Garnett. [*GB*] *A Censored Play. The Breaking Point*, with preface and letter to the censor by Edward Garnett, 1907.

struggling to sleep & put away worthless thoughts & images but vainly until at last my regular habit compels me to rise to light my fire &c. at 7.15; no doctor can cure me of that.[1] Yet you are partly right when you propose the consolation of an unassailable vision of her. That, I dread to think, will be a possession after she is gone right away below the horizon, while I (I know it is possible) may remain quite a kindly reality to her.

I can't think just now when perhaps Helen & I could come to you. It is always hard to arrange for someone to have the children for more than a week-end. But you could help me to a decision perhaps if you told me what times I should best choose from.

Give my love to Emily and to your father & mother & Aunt Sarah.—You & your house are among the few things that exist in this head & will remain till it resembles those of dead leaf browns which tumble out of Dunwich church onto the sands.

Yours ever Edward Thomas

80

30 March 1908   *Berryfield Cottage*

My dear Gordon,

I haven't forgotten the dear letter you sent me just as I reached home from Suffolk. But I have really been thinking that I should never write back again. An east wind or a wind from underground has swept over everything. Friends, Nature, books are like London pavements when an east wind has made them dry and harsh & pitiless. There is no joy in them. They are more dead than if they were in a Museum correctly labelled. And this is true not only this morning, but every morning, every afternoon & every night. I am now uniformly low spirited, listless, almost unable to work, & physically incapable. I have no idea what it means, but I crawl along on the very edge of life, wondering why I don't get over the edge. The change from the strong east winds off the sea, the regular, uninterrupted life at Minsmere, to this milder place full of 'little' responsibilities, the garden

---

[1] At this time ET had consulted a number of specialist doctors and continued to do so at intervals—and to follow their frequently contrary diets and counsels—until 1914.

bedraggled after a sodden winter, meant something. Also the night before I left Minsmere I was pedantically asked not to go on writing to the girl who was away at school. Off my guard, I promised simply to obey: she is reputed to be obedient to the point of self indulgence. So there is a more unhappy raw truncation, & tho one heals like a dockroot it does not feel easy or simple.[1] But I suppose there is more than the change of air & the loss of this new outlet for my egoism, to explain my numbness. Neither I nor the doctor knows what. Or rather, I think I do, but it is so many things that at one moment I recognize at a flash that I am incurable & might as well go to the Salvation Army & be 'born again', & at another I idiotically propose to let the Doctor spend a year or two at my bowels, a year or two at my kidneys, then revise the bowels & so on, forgetful of time like any lover.—Nor is it consoling to think that if I ever do get out of this tangle it will be by accident & I shall be no wiser than before.

Well, then, forgive me if this letter is only an acknowledgement of my debt to you.

You won't get the old *Arabia Deserta* for a very long time. The London library is full of demands for it. Garnett's abridgment leaves it a fine book.[2]

Thanks for the wholly imaginary Shiel & the real Gray.

About Wilde, at first Methuens were for sending only *The Duchess of Padua* to papers. Now they have decided to send 10 full sets & the *Chronicle* gets one & it comes to me.[3] But as I have done a column on *The Duchess of Padua* I am only allowed a perfunctory notice of the rest: besides all my notes refer to other editions & were made so long ago that I can make little use of them.

I can't promise to come to you. I believe I shall have no holiday this year. *Jefferies* still needs a lot of work as well as copying. *Borrow* is all before me. Also I shall if necessary undertake to do a book suggested by Dent (no pictures: on 'The South Country') also within this year.[4] This looks wanton. But I feel so wretched & unable that I thought heaping responsibilities

[1] See page 156, note 1.
[2] *Wanderings in Arabia*, being an abridgement of *Arabia Deserta*, arranged with Introduction by Edward Garnett, 2 vols., reviewed in *MP*, 6 February.
[3] *The Works of Oscar Wilde*, complete in 13 vols., reviewed in *DC*, 13 April.
[4] Published in 1909.

on myself the only way to make myself work. At present I feel as if I could let all work slide and find entertainment in the mess.

Guthrie thinks of making a plunge into town work & society. It is probably a good thing. He wants me to join him, but I doubt if it can be or will be managed. It would be costly & I may want all the money I can get to buy this house. It is to be sold & if I don't buy it, it may mean going right away, as there are so few houses near. Of course I have no money, but I can borrow and be careful for a year or two.

Mind, I should like to come to you & so would Helen, but at present it looks impossible.

Could you send us a little Bergamot? The Old Man's beard looks well, & so did the Rosemary but it was weeded away by someone, & I daresay you haven't another little piece of that.[1]

The children are very well. Helen usually gets a share of my depression, & in fact has done so for so many years now that she is always too near the edge, has lost her buoyancy & is thin & often poor-spirited: but she still has a lot of courage & whenever I let her, gets hopeful again.

Ever yours Edward Thomas

Keep Garnett's play as long as you want to.

81

21 May 1908   *Berryfield Cottage*

My dear Gordon,

Thank you for the Bergamot. It has survived frost, sun, rain, wind & weeding & therefore may be supposed to think well of us as we of it. I think of sunny rain & the whiteness of Well Knowe whenever I see it. But I ought to have said this long ago. Your letter was written on the 23rd of last month. Since then I have been reviewing hard,[2] writing the last chapter of *Jefferies* or

[1] Slips of herbs had been brought to Berryfield Cottage from Cartmel.

[2] The 'Red Book' (a red bound index of all the longer reviews preserved by ET which Helen Thomas kindly gave to me on extended loan in 1966) indicates the following reviews published May to July: 19 in *DC*, 13 in *MP*, 5 in *B*, and 4 in *SR*. Some books were reviewed twice but each separate review expands the criticism.

at least sketching it, & walking for a week about Sussex Surrey & Kent. This last was because I am doing a book on the South Country for Dent & he wants a solid-looking framework, so I am collecting place-names so as to pretend to be a writer of guide books gone wrong. This has to be done in 4 or 5 months, & during that time I have to turn out a large book on Borrow. It looks impossible & will in fact be a testimony to my phlegm & British pluck if it is ever done. *Jefferies* too is still nearly all to copy. What a priceless privilege then I am bestowing on you in sending you a letter. But indeed it is hard to get the time & peace for the imagination one wants in writing a letter not wholly polite. This particular letter I am writing, by the way, partly because it is only eleven at night & I vow not to sleep till after 12; yet as soon as I try to read I nod.

Walking you will perhaps see suits me. Really I am never so well as when I am rid of the postman & all company walking 20 or 30 miles a day. I was as well as ever I hope to be in my week's walk, & its effect has lasted over another week. I get as depressed & irritable as ever but seem to recover faster. Five months purgation of course has something to do with it. —On the other hadn I can't say I feel any 'mad pride of intellectuality', tho a feeling of extreme virtue after 5 months teetotalism & almost abstinence from tobacco is hard to avoid. But seriously I wonder whether for a person like myself whose most intense moments were those of depression a cure that destroys the depression may not destroy the intensity—a *desperate* remedy?

You are mistaken in thinking of a famer's daughter.[1] Her father is a retired Anglo-Indian who kept two cows to nourish his sapless frame. I have had a new interest in life since I heard that my letters to her have been shown to quite a number of amateur psychologists & detectors of vice. It is understood that she was just saved. Here I see my egoism has a value. Indignation & wounded vanity are covering up the other sore.

Titterton's verses disappointed me.[2] The violent man thinks himself a strong man. He is said to be coming out as the universal sympathizer with the outcast & downtrodden, the self-tortured &c, this time in prose.

No there is no 2 volume Doughty. What will you pay for

[1] See page 156, note 1, and *JM*, pp. 152–3.
[2] W. R. Titterton, *Studies in Solitary Life*, 1908.

volumes of the original & only edition? There are several, perhaps a set at Thorpe's,[1] which I could probably get for 2/6 a
volume (instead of 4/6 net) perhaps less. Here I send the *Adam
Cast Forth.*[2]

Davies has a Shakespeare, thank you. His book is praised
everywhere, but I do hope it will bring him cash.[3]

You agree with me about *The Breaking Point* & I agree with
you. He supplies a number of excellent opportunities for a
divine actress to exert all her skill in making the most of
colourless words. I would have plays that do not depend upon a
divine actress. The monotony is true & almost devilish. I think a
break of hysterical joy or joy simulated to deceive the lover into
hopefulness would have been an easy & sufficient way of breaking
up the monotony.

I haven't seen much of Guthrie lately but hope his way is
clearing. He gets far too little & far too unvaried company for a
man with his liking for talk & for talking rather lazily about
himself & trivial things. I am no corrective. In town he would run
up against other kinds of intelligence in a useful way unless his
quiet assurance is blind as well, which I don't believe. How he
lives at all is marvellous to me, his range is so narrow. That too,
intercourse—he really is a social animal—might cure.

No we haven't bought our house yet & don't know what it
will cost. There is just a chance of having one built for us by a
friend close by,[4] but that is too uncertain to boast of yet, though
secretly it is a delight to ruminate on. Really I cannot see how to
get to you. Helen can't come till the end of the term when the
children might be stowed away, & then I shall be at my busiest.
And if I travel at all it ought to be in the South, for time is very
short & so is my purse. But could you not come here for a little
time from town,[5] if you reach there? A simple journey of $1\frac{1}{2}$
hours from Waterloo, weekend tickets 5/9. I don't see how you
can refuse, so don't. But first of all, are you coming to town?

Helen's love & mine to you & Emily.

Ever yours Edward Thomas

[1] See page 144, note 3.
[2] By C. M. Doughty, reviewed *DC*, 9 April, and *SR*, 23 May.
[3] *Autobiography of a Super-tramp*, reviewed *MP*, 14 May.
[4] Geoffrey Lupton, an Old Bedalian, who owned 30 acres of land on the high hill
behind Berryfield. See *JM*, pp. 160–6.
[5] ET did not visit them at Holland Park. An omitted note (dated 17 June 1908)

82

19 July 1908   *Berryfield Cottage*

My dear Gordon,

I took your letter to town with me thinking to find the leisure there that doesn't dwell here, but I left my letter unwritten & seem to have lost yours. I am sorry to have lost it & hope I haven't. Yet that need not be my excuse—every letter I write to you does need one. The fact is I have just finished *Jefferies* (all but index & preface), & have today & yesterday compiled a monstrous bibliography for those who come after me. Life is not long enough to tell you how I have enjoyed copying out—being unable to amend and too poor to destroy—innumerable rants, vaguenesses &c. I wonder could you help me, would you, with the proofs? So far you have made all the books that have passed through your hands perfect in that way. And with the Index to rack my colossal intellect & true English endurance I should be, unaided, worse than ever. Think of it. And now comes *The South Country* & *Borrow*. I shall do *The South Country* first (both have to be finished by Christmas) because I want to make it the better book; the other must be bad. Yet so far I have no scheme, no frame on which to hang my landscapes &c, & I have promised Dent to make one & also to scatter *real place names* plentifully. Is it going to be done? If only my Physician had remade me instead of just unmaking me. Physic being in vain, I am reduced to $\frac{1}{4}$ hour of dumbbells, 2 hrs steady walking, daily, & the old abstinences from alcohol, butcher's meat, sugar & tobacco. If that does not help there are to be heroic methods.

Cornwall is a long way behind me now. I had five whole days[1] —from 5 a.m. to 9 p.m.—of sunlight & sea wind walking down the coast from Tintagel to St. Ives & round Land's End to Penzance; all meals out of doors, cream & fruit & little else; no books; in fact nothing but breathing & seeing, I think. Then two days in London robbed me of most of the results except my

---

announced the end of copying the *Jefferies* and looked forward rather ironically towards *The South Country* and *Borrow*. 'Can I do both in 6 months and review also and take medicine and walk and dig in the garden and abstain from beating my children?'

[1] Probably 20–25 June.

note book.—Almost the finest things I saw were the water over green rock & purple weed in a cove near Zennor where I bathed & the little circle of upright stones at Boscawen Inn where Welsh legend says the bards used to meet—they were in a quiet little remote field of long grass & no cattle or any intruder & they looked as if nobody ever went to look at them close & had been there all that time quite oblivious & unaffected, so that their antiquity was a most extraordinary thing, like a real destruction of time (unaided in my case by any historical knowledge or archæological surmise).

Monday

You will forgive me for posting this with even the apology incomplete when I say I began *The South Country* today & am tired. I haven't got a scheme for it yet, but only wrote a long passage that will have to be fitted in. There are to be more characters than ever, I think, & I have one or two women in view.[1] Do send me some advice or warning on vaticination.—I fear Helen can't reach you this Summer, & I dare arrange for nothing until my work is well in hand, again. With Helen's love & mine to you both.   Ever yours Edward Thomas

83

9 August 1908   *Berryfield Cottage*

My dear Gordon,

Your letter deserves to be answered at a better hour (for letters) than midnight, but I cannot choose. I am so pressed by work & time. For I am now deep in my South Country book trying to force forward the first draft while there is not much

[1] In her 1932 Introduction to *The South Country* Helen Thomas describes the book as 'one of the happiest of the prose works of ET written at a period of comparative ease and tranquillity—for his own pleasure' and 'very characteristic of the author at his best'. ET acknowledged that many short passages in it had appeared in *SR*, *N*, *New Age*, *DC*, and *Daily News*. Its loose framework reflects a natural year beginning with 'The end of winter' and passing through spring and summer to 'The end of summer'. There are many slices of disguised autobiography (e.g. Chapter VI, 'A return to nature', pp. 77–97) and a gallery of portraits of, and re-corded conversations with, humble people ET met on his travels. Much of the book not only resembles his volumes of short essays, but also contains material that later appeared in his rapidly composed poems.

reviewing to be done.[1] I have in fact got thro nearly half of it & a curious artificial thing it is as a result of trying to make it continuous instead of ejaculatory. I force myself at it every day now, with desperation increased by my appointment as Assistant Secretary to a Royal Commission on Welsh Monuments (prehistoric &c).[2] What the work will be I don't yet know, but it certainly means much of London & I dread lest it means daily office hours. If it does I must chuck it soon. How I can do *Borrow* &c. in evenings in London I can't see. So more than ever do I thank you for offering to read the *Jefferies* proofs. I have sent in the M.S. & they will soon begin to arrive now. But I am very sorry you are ill again & pray that this renewed blessed weather has put you right. Tell me if it has. I enjoyed the rain of the interval almost as much as the heat itself.—Oh you should be out on our hill in the full moon when the crickets sing & the owls hoot & the glow worms glow & there is no wind even, let alone a man.—Still if you have time dont be afraid of any 'objectionable particularity' about *Jefferies*. By the way did you see my review of *Old England* & did you care about the Cornish ending?[3] Thanks for your suggestions about *The South Country* & I will remember Palmer[4]—I wish I had some of his work by me to inspire & warn. But I have nothing better than Cotman, Cox & De Wint.[5] Oh Lord, my dipping into 15 closely written note books for solid details to support my soarings & flutterings about the South Country! I have dragged Cornwall in, as I dragged Wales into *The Heart of England* (at the end).

[1] The 'Red Book' records the following reviews for August–October: 20 in *DC*, 17 in *MP*, 4 in *B*, and 2 in *SR*.

[2] ET's father was a minor Civil Servant and had always wished his son to become one. Philip Thomas probably used his London-Welsh Liberal connections (*via* Thomas Jones, C.H., secretary to Lloyd George, then Chancellor of the Exchequer). See *WWE*, pp. 134–5, and *JM*, pp. 155–7.

[3] *Old England*, text by W. Shaw Sparrow, pictures by J. Orrock, R.I., reviewed *DC*, 1 August. The last half column is a significant statement of ET's view of history that reveals his study of Jefferies and helps to explain his intuitive realization of D. H. Lawrence's potential as a writer. ('But because we are imperfectly versed in history, we are not therefore blind to the past. The eye that sees the things today, and the ear that hears, the mind that contemplates or dreams, is itself an instrument of antiquity equal to whatever it is called upon to apprehend. We are not merely twentieth-century Londoners or Kentishmen or Welshman . . .')

[4] W. T. Palmer.

[5] The early nineteenth-century landscape painters, John Sell Cotman, David Cox, and Peter de Wint.

Your bergamot flourishes here. Don't forget to give me a piece of rosemary when you can. But we don't know yet whether we shall long be able to stay here. A friend may build a house & let it to us on the hilltop ½ a mile away & 400 feet above us, just not in sight of the sea & Isle of Wight—but rather far for Merfyn's school.

Helen has just gone to Cornwall. I can hardly get another walk in before I go to London, I am afraid, but shall try. I had been asked to go to Long Melford (Borrow's & Isobel Berner's Long Melford) in Suffolk for mid-September. Now it seems impossible.

Goodbye. My love to you all.   Edward Thomas

84

ROYAL COMMISSION ON ANCIENT MONUMENTS
IN WALES AND MONMOUTHSHIRE,
36, GREAT GEORGE STREET,
WESTMINSTER, S.W.

16 September 1908   *Rogate, Worple Rd., Wimbledon SW*

My dear Gordon,

Thanks for proofs II,[1] & before I forget it—I don't know about Chesterton. I did hear the rumour & it would not surprise many if true. On the other hand I have not heard it from, or spoken of by, any who know him. That *Daily News* article was good. A. G. Gardner the Editor is a delightful man quite unspoilt by London journalism, like Nevinson & very few others. What is Trevelyan like? I lent his *Polyphemus*[2] to W. H. Hudson who liked 'The Bat' very much. It was for that I sent it: a friend of his—now Mrs. C. F. G. Masterman (a Lyttleton)— wanted a bat poem for an anthology! I have adopted all or nearly all your suggestions in the proofs. Sometimes it is curious how you have made the very suggestion which I—looking at my copy of the proof—have also made. I misunderstood 2 of your

---

[1] Two omitted notes from Worple Road (dated 9 and 15 September 1908) make clear that these were proofs of his *Jefferies*.

[2] GB had stayed at R. C. Trevelyan's house on Leigh Hill. Trevelyan, *Polyphemus and Other Poems*, see page 43, note 1; his early book was *Mallow and Asphodel* (Poems), 1898.

first corrections when you said 'Delete, after thatched' I thought you meant cut out the adjectives or pendant note book stuff that followed 'thatch'!

'Sarsen' is said to be the same as 'Saracen' : it means a foreign stone, i.e. one brought by glacial movement to a country where, lying on the surface, (e.g. sandstone on the chalk downs) it is obviously strange. There are myriads on the Downs by Avebury & elsewhere, & in groups they are often called 'grey wethers'. The largest have often been used in making cromlechs &c. Avebury temple is made of Sarsens which happen to resemble (ever so roughly) pillars or bits of wall. A Winterbourne is a river running only in the winter. They are common in the chalk. All the Summer you can walk over their grassy beds & under their bridges, as a rule. They give part of the names of many villages in Dorset & Wiltshire.

I should like to see Trevelyan's early book someday, but Lord how busy I am. I work from 10 a.m. to 12 midnight or later every day. The town work is poor because of the air. The evening work is poor because I am half done. Still, I shall stick at it if possible for the sake of the years of Welsh walking or driving. I don't know yet how to travel. Walking will not always be possible as I must carry a $\frac{1}{2}$ plate camera & a measuring rod & tape. Cycling I hate & it is no quicker on mountains.[1] I don't know how the Treasury will like paying £1 a day for a pony & trap. Goodbye.

Yours ever Edward Thomas

85

ROYAL COMMISSION ON ANCIENT MONUMENTS
IN WALES AND MONMOUTHSHIRE,
36, GREAT GEORGE STREET,
WESTMINSTER, S.W.

24 September 1908
Thursday

My dear Gordon,
    Thanks, thanks. I was rather alarmed by what you say of my

---

[1] Later ET cycled a great deal, particularly with his son, Merfyn.

not giving a more organic account of the progress of affairs in Jefferies family &c. I know nothing about them, except that the farm was sold & his father became a gardener in Bath where he & the mother lived until they died. It was not even possible to say that R.J. was a good husband & father with any certainty. But the exact extent of my insufficiency you will not see just yet. I had hoped that I had done away—pretty well—with the need or expectation of much more by suggesting that he was just a poorish, isolated writing man living & content to live with his family & occasionally meeting old friends—. What do you think? But there, the thing is done now: nor in any case could it have been much bettered except by more discretion or cunning.

About the owls,[1] there is no sort of doubt that they do no harm worth speaking of in comparison with the good in destroying rats mice & voles. Their destruction has been proved responsible for a plague of voles. But of course they are known to kill young pheasants or partridges, though rarely. A landowner like Sir Herbert Maxwell, also a Christian & Darwinist, & a real naturalist, makes the point clear in one of his books.[2] Hudson's experience tells the same way.

Well, I don't like London. I am sick of working in bad air & until after midnight & getting no exercise & therefore getting moody & doing work badly. So I shall leave this place in a week or so. It was as well to have learnt what such work means. I am elated at the prospect of getting back, especially as in the Spring a friend who has bought 20 or 30 acres at the top of the hill[3] (and built himself a house & a workshop—he is an old Bedales boy & makes furniture) is going to build us a house up there according to our needs, including a study for me right away from the house at the edge of a wood. We shall be nearly 800 feet up & have a mighty view. Up there you can come to see us I do hope. Goodbye.

Yours ever Edward Thomas

[1] Referring to a perpetual conflict of mine with a neighbouring keeper. [GB]

[2] Probably *The Living Animals of the World*, 1901.

[3] See Letter 81, note 4. A stone to ET's memory was unveiled there in October 1937.

86

1 October 1908   *76 Worple Road, Wimbledon, SW*

My dear Gordon,

Aren't these quotations from *The Dewy Morn* good?[1] Don't they express a love of beauty that never was excelled, though as to the expression I see its limitations? But I wonder what people will say of a biographer who allows his subject to hold the field so.

Many thanks for your latest suggestions. Some of them were quite inevitable, though they had escaped my hasty eye (I am impatient of this stage & weary of the book too). I wish I felt sure you do think the book an excusable compilation. As to his friends I could only give a few names, no conversations, virtually no letters, & absolutely nothing essential or suggesting the essential.

My leaving has been postponed owing to the necessity of considering the Chancellor of the Exchequer's[2] secretary who recommended me. I am to stay till Christmas but to go very easily meantime & take weekends from Friday to Tuesday! Also I am to have some days—tomorrow & Friday first—for finishing my Museum work for *Borrow*. I could be enormously busy if I wished. The *Saturday* gives me work & would give more, lately. I only wish a decent magazine would give me a chance to do something, not criticism of course.

The South Country is—not finished—but brought to an end. It has about a dozen characters & tales & several interludes about Nature-study, poetry & personality, &c which I hope may have got me nearer to a real book form. Yet it is made up of separable parts. My mind is lyrical or if you like jerky & spasmodic. Now I have to copy *The South Country* which is returning to one's vomit, a cultivated taste I have not achieved.

Yours ever Edward Thomas

---

[1] Jefferies, *Dewy Morn*; ET's discussion (Chap. XV, pp. 232–62) consists largely of quotations from it. In an omitted note (dated 5 October 1908) ET is pleased 'to hear you praise Jefferies' Felise [Goring, the heroine of *Dewy Morn*], so much have I been in love with her.'

[2] Lloyd George, cf. Letter 83, note 2.

87

October 1908   *13 Rusham R^d., Balham SW*

My dear Gordon,

Of course artists don't 'write about' anything. I know. Jefferies wrote loosely & he didn't really mean that they do. I admit he sometimes does, often does, but not that he is not an artist. I think many of his essays & *Dewy Morn* & *Amaryllis* creative. But surely an artist must at times be weary of the competition with God & inclined to be content with his really very great works?

I've just heard from Guthrie. He seems pleased but of course —low coast, always Autumn, especially such an Autumn would be pleasing. I am glad to see *Gunnar* is getting ready. Oh Lord, I have not yet written a little note for Guthrie to stick at the beginning of an Album he is publishing.[1] I work day and night & can't get at my impressions of his work at all.

Congratulate me. I believe I have escaped from *Borrow*. Of course it means losing some weeks of solid work but then to add to my laurels as a man who *has not* written on so & so & so & so think it worth while. The world does not know of these things. They—including some nice people—sneer at me for doing so much & think me brazenfaced & unaware of my limitations. I am a passive artist if you like & if it were not for the blank necessity of keeping a house & household going I would have nothing to do with books, certainly not reading & reviewing them. I wonder are stocks & shares & cheap furniture as defiling to those who deal in them. I think perhaps not just as often fornication is far less evil than marriage because its evil does not continually encrust the soul.

Yours ever Edward Thomas

de la Mare has chucked his oil millionaire & taken to literature.[2] Friends are helping & he has got some reviewing for *The Times*.

[1] Probably J. J. Guthrie, *A Second Book of Drawings*, 1908.
[2] De la Mare had worked in the London office of the Anglo-American Oil Co. since 1890. In 1908, on the advice of Henry Newbolt, he received an annual grant from the Privy Purse in order to devote his time to writing.

88

October 1908   *13 Rusham Rd.*

My dear Gordon,

If you are commissioned to wring the neck of eloquence here is a hundred headed beast suited to your task.[1] Alas! But here is an end at any rate. Only the bibliography & note of introduction remain. You are excellent. I adopt your suggestions shamelessly & with no intention of announcing to the world that you wrote the book. Seriously I don't feel as if I could publicly 'thank Mr. Gordon Bottomley for his &c.' or shall I? I didn't say fornication was good & marriage bad. Only among sensualists there is something worse more steadily deadening in marriage than in fornication. That's all. Goodbye! I kiss Rachel's hands & am

Yours & Emily's ever Edward Thomas

Thank God I have sneaked out of *Borrow*. Being bound (in honour) to offer a substitute I have suggested a history of English literature (or only poetry) and the element of Nature in it. I want a large space & time & think it might be a good thing to do.

89

ROYAL COMMISSION ON ANCIENT MONUMENTS
IN WALES AND MONMOUTHSHIRE,
36, GREAT GEORGE STREET,
WESTMINSTER, S.W.

6 November 1908   *13 Rusham Rd.*

My dear Gordon,

Try to forgive me for not writing again until it was almost necessary. Reviewing is thrust upon me, while work here & living in London & copying *The South Country* reduces my working power so that I don't get any time. I get cleaned out weekly with long late hours & look forward eagerly to my deliverance.

---

[1] The final chapter of *Jefferies*. There are no clues to the argument about fornication and marriage, except, of course, in *Jefferies*.

Last week end I walked over to Guthrie's & back & but for my blisters I enjoyed the walk. They seem to like their new place but as a matter of fact it has many serious faults (not simply from my point of view either) & I should not be surprised if they had a bad winter. Guthrie is as cheerful as ever but it is a terribly depressing house with those measled children with sores & spots. Mrs. Guthrie is not looking as well as she was & her nerves are so bad that she is terrified if left alone after dark. But with it all I quite see that it is a better household than mine because they are often happy.

Guthrie says you are probably well again. I hope so & out of bed too to see the end of this beautiful season.

The book on Poetry & Nature is off. Methuen is afraid, & I am casting about for another subject tho I have no heart to think of a book yet. I suggest the Severn & the Welsh Coast (with Guthrie to illustrate), but Lord! I want to be quiet, but they won't 'let me be', as the Matthew Arnold's phrase is.

I will try to remember to read Noyes' 40 *Singing Seamen* if I have got it.[1]

My *Jefferies* is postponed till early next year, by the way.

How I hate London; no exercise, no air, & continual bellyache & head ache & discomfort all over. Also I waste time seeing people. It is not good for me to see people as I listen to so much that I don't understand—politics, art & so on—& pretend to take an interest & say (& for the moment think I mean) foolish things. I have a feeling of returning with difficulty to myself after these histrionic bouts. People despise me too—with reservations on account of my superficial amiability & profile. When I saw on a newspaper placard that a Railway Porter had just had £17,000 left him, I was quite seriously thinking how I should like to have that much or a little less so as to be able to stay somewhere alone & not have to work—in fact I hurried back to my lodgings with a sort of flushed expectation of I don't know exactly what, not £17,000 perhaps. I didn't find anything.

How nice it would be to be dead if only we could know we were dead. That is what I hate, the not being able to turn round in the grave & to say It is over. With me I suppose it is vanity:

[1] Alfred Noyes, *Forty Singing Seamen and other Poems*, reviewed *MP*, 30 January 1908.

I don't want to do so difficult a thing as dying without any chance
of applause after having done it.

Yours ever Edward Thomas

90

14 November 1908 *Swansea*

My dear Gordon,

Thank you for the Bibliography. It was noble of you to
discover those omissions & inconsistencies. I should never have
done so. It is this lack of attention that makes my prose the dull,
long, pendant stuff it has now become—still it is more real than
the airs & graces of *Horae.*—I envy you letters & translations
from Sturge Moore. I hear he is doing a book on Flaubert.[1] By
the way *Melusine* by George Ernle is a lovely narrative poem
lately published.[2] Fancy Binyon troubling to republish *London
Visions* (which are better than my prose but very like it in
observation, feeling & lack of unifying impluse & of style).[3]

Muirhead Bone offers to let me reproduce some of his Sussex
drawings for my *South Country*—& Dent hesitates & says my
work is best without illustration. I wonder what you'll think of
The South Country with 2 or 3 women in it & long studies of men
& (of course) the Suburbs & also London & the unemployed.
Why won't some one pay me 3 times as much so that I may
write $\frac{1}{3}$ as much? I know so well when I am writing muck but I
have to leave it in with the (several) things which are pretty
well done.

I shall see *Mariamne* soon.[4] The authors keep their secret well
& so do you.

Swansea is a magnificent place, huge almost entirely new
thrown together anyhow but amongst mountains, some green
some copper-poisoned brown, & at the edge of the sea. It is
quite big & labyrinthine & yet easily seen by the eye, as well as
the mind, as a whole. It has a centre of large gaudy electric

[1] See page 200, note 2.
[2] Reviewed *DC*, 1 September.
[3] Laurence Binyon, *London Visions*, reviewed *MP*, 7 January 1909.
[4] T. Sturge Moore, *Mariamne*.

lighted shops & then a ruined castle & then filthy or brand new warrens up & down, always in sight of the mountains.

But I have a headache from the bad air, the bad light of this room & a slight continual fret of loneliness (being with nice kind people whom I don't really know & who don't know me, in an almost intolerable house—but with a nice brassy kitchen, innumerable jugs & 2 clocks ticking like little birds together). So I won't write any more. Nor will I, intentionally, die just yet, as I want to see my Castle among the sandhills tomorrow & my lake among the moutains soon after. I return to town in a week. This was a suddenly arranged Expedition & it was only when I had settled it that I thought I could perhaps have gone to Gordon's. Forgive me, & perhaps I couldn't have gone either.

Yours ever Edward Thomas

91

I should like *Melusine* back soon, but keep Storer.[1]

3 January 1909   *Berryfield Cottage*

My dear Gordon,

We were very glad to hear from you, Christmas or not & only felt sorry we should have unwittingly added to the responsibilities of the festive season. It seemed a long time since I heard from you or of you: I was glad to know you had not been ill.

I was in Swansea when I wrote last, wasn't I? Well I saw my lake in the mountains & Penard Castle & Careg Cenen Castle (reputed Uther's), & then I got back to the office if not the work of the Commission. I reviewed & I saw people & I visited a doctor—who has made some extraordinary cures by suggestion (without hypnotism)—almost daily. Now I have finally left the Commission & temporarily the doctor—who has convinced me I suffer not from my stomach but from myself. He hopes to cure me of the elaborate self consciousness which he says is at the root of everything wrong in me. I am not to worry

---

[1] Edward Storer, *Mirrors of Illusion*, reviewed *DC*, 25 May.

about what I eat & so on. I am sure he can cure me & when I am regularly with him I feel that he is curing me. I wish I had £100 to go daily for a couple of months. N.B. Don't discuss this doctor & his methods with me. It is bad for me to think about the subject.

Dent is an ass but I am afraid I can't convert him. Bone[1] was so good, too—had half a dozen admirable simple strong things, mainly from Sussex, that I could use. Of course they would not have appealed at once to the *thousands* whom Dent fondly believes he is going to persuade to read E.T. Will you read the proofs of my *South Country* for me in a month or so? The Guthrie preface is extracted from it, though the greater part was of course written definitely about him in the first place.[2]

Here is *Melusine* & what do you think of the polite M[r] Storer? I think he has a good deal in him unless he has some literary source which I am unacquainted with.

I was very sorry indeed to miss Trevelyan's poem.[3] It went to some one, I don't know whom. But I may see it yet—the *Saturday* sends verse, much belated sometimes.

I envy you meeting Abercrombie,[4] but doubtless he will find his way to London.

We are not up the hill yet. The house won't begin until March. So far only the garden is touched. I only wish my work house was ready—you know I am to have a little thatched room a hundred yards from the dwelling, at the edge of the Hanger. You will like it. I hope you will be in it sometime before next Winter.

Bronwen is to be bridesmaid at an Oxford friend's wedding this week & all but me are going to town. I hope to start a story in the hours of solitude. I have two or three goodish schemes for stories or episodes.—Can you suggest a subject for a book? I owe Methuen a book.

When I walk next I hope I shall arrive at Cartmel. Goodbye & our love to Emily and you.

Ever yours Edward Thomas

[1] Muirhead Bone.
[2] Untraced among the numerous pamphlets published by Guthrie. See Letter 87, note 1.
[3] Possibly R. C. Trevelyan, *Sisyphus*, 1908.
[4] Lascelles Abercrombie who succeeded Dixon Scott as leading critic on the *Liverpool Daily Courier* and the *Daily Post*, 1907–9.

92

13 February 1909   *Berryfield Cottage*

My dear Gordon,

When I tell you I have delayed writing to you because I have been writing not reviews, not commissioned books, not landscapes, but character sketches stories &c., I believe you will forgive me. Since the beginning of the year I have had an extraordinary energy in writing & have done nothing else & only been to town for one day. But I have come in this afternoon a little before tea so I can send you a word. I don't know what these sketches will turn out to be. For I have been too busy to copy them, except one or two that are short. Most are unfit for the papers & magazines by being too unpleasant, or too fanciful, or too quiet.[1] So it seems to me I shall have an empty belly (I haven't earned anything yet this year). But I shall make up for that by a swelled head. Garnett tells me he likes the *Jefferies* very much & his praise means a great deal as I feel his ideas have ramified through me until there is little else, at least when I am writing of books. Then *The Times* had a favourable & long notice. Salt wrote saying he thought my work good, too.[2] But really it is my improved health & selfcontrol (due to my new doctor) that makes me so cheerful now. I work, I walk & I sleep & I hardly ever make people miserable. All I want now is my house & study on the top of the hill & they are just at the foundations now & the traction engine is always panting up the long road round the coombe with bricks.

Before I forget Arthur Symons will shortly be dead of General Paralysis of the Insane. The usual cause you probably know, but they say it did not exist in his case & they talk about overwork. I hear his latest essays to be printed soon in a book on the Romantic Movement are very good.[3]—I am glad you liked Storer & above all that you liked *Melusine*. I did hear the author's name but forgot it. He is an old Winchester boy, aged about 35 who has been in India 15 years or nearly, I believe. Isn't it odd.

---

[1] Collected in *Rest and Unrest*, 1911.

[2] H. S. Salt, *The Faith of Richard Jefferies*.

[3] Arthur Symons, *The Romantic Movement in English Poetry*, reviewed *DC*, 7 October 1909, and *MP*, 20 January 1910. Symons lived until 1945.

Haynes was married some years ago. Bronwen was brides-maid to an Oxford contemporary named MacAlister,[1] now secretary to the R.I.B.A. after W. J. Locke.

My fingers are getting numbed by the N.E. wind.

I sold my Wildes[2] or I would gladly lend you the Poems.

Thank you for suggesting Barnes but he would hardly bear turning into the big book Methuen want.[3] I have done with 'country books' so-called now, though of course my sketches are full of landscape.

Yes that is a child's hand on the back of the *Venus Accroupe*.

O yes isn't Davies fine now? I was terribly excited over the new book.[4] It was almost incredibly good. Yeats wants him to 'cultivate his instrument' more. But Davies wouldn't know what the phrase meant.

I have not come round to your view of Poe, but am glad to admit I feel the essence of 'Annabel Lee' e.g. to be perhaps as fine as that of any lyric in the world. When I found fault—& the faults are most unpleasant—I was still in the stage when one wants all women's noses to be straight or else perfect curves (like what the *Strand* used to call 'types of English beauty'). However you & Garnett have slowly cured me. Only I will never *read* Poe again. What he has enabled me to feel is so much beyond his words even to my purified eyes.

Goodbye & excuse my cold hands. This is the 2nd day of continuous N.E. wind, hard & grey under foot & soft milky blue overhead.

Yours ever & Emily's Edward Thomas

Guthrie's landscape is the finest he has done. It belongs to me in a sort of way & I treasure it but have to lend it for an exhibition that G. hopes for.

Let me know in good time about *Gunnar* please.

[1] Sir Ian MacAlister; Haynes, another Oxford friend, is E. S. P. Haynes. (See *JM*)
[2] *The Works of Oscar Wilde*. See Letter 80, note 3.
[3] Prompted by the perceptive review of *Select Poems of William Barnes*, edited by Thomas Hardy, in *DC*, 28 November.
[4] *Nature Poems*, reviewed *MP*, 31 December.

93

15 March 1909   *Berryfield Cottage*

My dear Gordon,

I was afraid you were not well as you were silent rather longer than usual & am sorry to know I was right. But I think perhaps you are feeling not uneasy as you are making such big & charming plans for Spring. Don't worry another second about *The South Country*. Dent wants to delay. He says the season is very bad for his trade; but I think the fact is he wants to organize & advertise a series in which my book shall appear. When the proofs do come, be sure I shall very gladly ask you to look at them. I have very little else to tell you about myself. Here is nearly ¼ of the year gone & I seem to have been sitting close up to the fire all the time writing all sorts of things which you shall see some day only I don't like to trouble you with M.S. & the typescript is being thrust upon editors. I have done a great deal at first under a real impulse but latterly (the long frost having quite undermined me) by force of daily custom as much as anything. I can do almost anything if once I can start doing it every day at a certain hour. And as reviewing has been scarce I have had few interruptions.[1] I feel sure it is better work or in a better direction than all but the best of the old but it is even less profitable & quite impossible to palm off on a publisher as part of a guinea guide book. A difficulty will soon arise unless *Jefferies* brings me offers of work—which it has failed to do except from the Editor of a new magazine who asked me for a short 'semi-poetical' article on 'why I love an out of door life'! I don't live an out of door life & can't be semi-poetical to order so I asked a prohibitive price & so got out of it. Meantime I get articles returned on every hand. *The New Age* printed a thing last week.[2] Did you see it? But it was written a year ago nearly. — Evidently I am developed into a worse kind of bore at any rate. Put it down to the big fires which I have to sit close up to in this weather.

---

[1] The 'Red Book' notes the following reviews published January–March 1909: 13 in *DC*, 5 in *MP*, 1 each in *SR* and *B*. This was normally a busy reviewing season.
[2] Untraced.

I am very glad *Gunnar* is soon coming. If I were sending out review copies I should not go beyond *Times, Chronicle, Daily News, Telegraph, Manchester Guardian, Saturday, Outlook, Nation, Bookman* &, perhaps, *English Review* (tho they review very little). I don't know if I can decently review a book dedicated to me but I will do it indecently, if not.

The English Review may perhaps help me if it lives.[1]

I wish I could talk to you about Edward Garnett. (I shall doubtless; & by the way it seems likely I shall be walking out of Yorkshire into the Lake country in June or thereabouts, & if so I should like to stay a day or two with you, if you are at home & free.) Certainly his talk is far better than his writing. I hardly know a poorer writer of any ability at all. I don't know which Turgenev preface you mean but there again I should like to talk about naturalism—writing would weary me—I've had a day of it & woodchopping & reading to children (who have chickenpox; Helen being away) & walking &c. I don't know anybody who seems to see literature & life as a whole so well as he, judging from his talk. But nevertheless I think that my respect for his opinion *of my own work* is possibly exaggerated by feeling that he was at one time reluctant to like it & even perhaps antipathetic to me & it; so that I had something to break down before reaching him & to succeed in that would always please my vanity. He is like the one sinner who repenteth. The man who readily sympathizes with my work & says he likes it I am with insistent cursedness, inclined to suspect, on the other hand. There's a grand fire now & my legs are burning.

Tell me why you frown on the later Symons? I suppose you detect in his broadening out also a thinning down. But I should have said that, allowing bulk to count, he hardly had a superior living as a critic combining instinct & scholarship. I don't think he had any originality, but then that is true of his other work too. But I thought a few of the later poems[2] as good as anything he had done before, tho not better than (of their kind) the earliest. I imagine he could never be what I should call quite sincere, that is why he had not style; but in the later attitude all

---

[1] *The English Review* survived 1908–37 and printed six articles by ET. I think it is possible to detect his work among the unsigned reviews from April 1909 until November 1914.

[2] *The Fool of the World, and other Poems*, 1906.

the flimsy avoidable insincerity had gone. But I don't possess *London Nights* & I am writing on the strength of perhaps very early impressions.[1]

Then we kiss again with tears over Poe. Hawthorne I know little of. I have read some very indifferent creepy stuff of his tho it didn't produce a creep.

Arthur Ransome is married, I hear, & is coming to try to live for the Summer near here. I met his lady. She belongs to the higher orders & no connection of hers has ever been in trade. She paints herself. She has many rings. But she is pretty & spirited & clever but not clever enough to do her own hair. Unfortunately I never venture to limn the higher orders in my sketches. . . .

It is 10. I must read about the Zeno of the London Celts. You haven't got to—please when you are well write again a long letter. I can't. You can: also you have, at least perhaps you have, more time. Please do.

Yours ever Edward Thomas

94

POSTCARD

Undated   *Petersfield*

Thank you for the M.S. & two notes. My note enclosing the proofs has no doubt reached you now. I sent it, addressed to Well Knowe, on Tuesday morning. It reached me (forwarded to London) on Saturday, the 17th, & I can remember no sign that it had been open. I am still busy making up for time lost in Wales & can't write except to say I am very glad to have the M.S. I shall send you soon a very interesting book of verse called *Personæ of Ezra Pound*.[2] Have you seen it or Hewlett's *Artemision*?[3] ET

[1] *London Nights*, 1895, revised 1897.
[2] Reviewed *DC*, 7 June.
[3] Maurice Hewlett, *Artemision, Idylls, and Songs*, reviewed *MP*, 26 April.

95

28 April 1909   *My new study at the top of Ashford Hanger*

My dear Gordon,

I am afraid I must seem ungrateful, ungracious, undutiful, leaving your long letter & your gifts almost unnoticed. I think I told you I was in Wales for ten days from Good Friday on with Mervyn. There I could not write. I had no time whatever alone. Either I was out with the boy or I was indoors with many people I was glad to see for a little while. When I got back to London— I could not get home easily in a day—I went & saw Davies & then was suddenly called home to do some work for the *Morning Post* which was hard up for copy & wanted me to manufacture it as they know me for a punctual bloke.[1] And getting home (a week ago) I felt suddenly very weak & sad & could do nothing but turn out the work asked for & then stare in the fire & wonder why I should be like this, physically weak, purposeless, hopeless, & then set about thinking it must be due to my poor fare (of bacon & tea chiefly) in Wales, & so on. And I read mechanically at dullish review books & got up here & lit a fire & sat down & looked at the Downs & read & got home tired, day after day. And if I had written then it would have been a worse letter than this.

Later

It does no good writing like this. But when I am not working or out of doors it is all I can think of. So you see my wonderful doctor was not wonderful enough. I am giving me up. All he did, I see now, was to convince me that I could be cured, but he left me to find out that after all I had to cure myself.

Perhaps we shall not meet this Summer after all. I shall most likely give up my Yorkshire walk as it will cost money & I am earning very little. Also I have been invited to spend 10 days at Looe in Cornwall & I want to accept, & it will cost me nothing.

[1] The following were reviewed in *MP* in May: L. Cranmer-Byng, *A Lute of Jade*, 3 May; Basil de Selincourt, *William Blake* and E. Garnett, *The Feud. A play*, 13 May; Henry Murray, *A Stepson of Fortune*, 20 May; W. R. Titterton, *River Music and Other Poems* (with other volumes of verse) and August Goll, *Criminal Types in Shakespeare*, 24 May; Price Collier, *England and the English*, 27 May.

And if I do I can hardly spare the time for Yorkshire as well, & even [if] I did you would not be at home, I gather. I do hope this holiday of yours will be a good one. Weather favours you, if you have our sun & south west wind. When are you to be in town? And I wonder could you get here for a time? Don't forget to answer these questions.

My one regret about *Gunnar* is that I shall hardly be able to review it. The poem to me makes it impossible to *ask* for it.[1] But the *D.C.* may not notice that.

_____

1 May

I had better finish this. You would rather have it now than never, I am confident. So I will just look at your letter of April 8 that reached me in Wales & see if there are things I ought to answer in it.

I am glad you liked the Morris. . . . Did you know Dixon Scott was doing a book on Morris?[2] I know nothing more than that. And by the way I may be doing one on Maeterlinck if I can bring myself to accept very bad terms from Methuen.

The Ransomes are $\frac{1}{2}$ a mile away & have been there 5 weeks or so but to tell the truth . . . well, it is hard. We see little of them. Arthur is a little uncomfortable in his new glory, I think.

About Blake, I wonder have you seen a book on him by a not very sympathetic but also not at all fashionable outsider named Basil de Selincourt? He is a clever man of the 'no nonsense' kind & while I don't think he has got very far, he has so challenged the supporters of Blake that they will have to think what they are at before answering. Since Swinburne nobody except Ellis & Yeats has really faced the difficulties & Ellis & Yeats have not explained them by seeming to overcome them.[3]

_____

[1] GB, *Riding to Lithend* has a dedicatory poem to ET.

[2] W. Dixon Scott, *The First Morris*, 1912. Two omitted notes (dated 25 September and 1 October 1908), written when ET was at the Royal Commission of Ancient Monuments, refer to his meetings with Dixon Scott who had reviewed ET's work favourably in *The Liverpool Daily Post*. See *The Letters of W. D. Scott*, edited by M. MacCrossan, 1932, where Scott agrees to review a book by ET: 'Yes, I'll do it gladly. I admire Thomas and am sorry for him; he's a fine delicate subtle creature grossly misused and overworried; and I'd like to intervene, if I can't do more, between him and young Rhadamanthe like L.A. [Lascelles Abercrombie]—whose lusty derision of ET's *Swinburne* made me feel sad.' [To Allan Monkhouse, 3 October 1913.]

[3] *Poems of Blake*, edited by W. B. Yeats (The Muses Library), 1893 and 1905. *Poetical Works of Blake*, edited and annotated by Edwin J. Ellis, 2 vols., 1906.

Yes I know Blaikie Murdoch on Symons.[1] Dixon Scott strikes a similar note at times.

In answer to Emily I should say emphatically that Ransome is living with his wife—decidedly.

I haven't a duplicate of Dixon & my only copy being from *The Morning Post* has to go back.[2] But here is Ezra Pound & I think he has very great things in him & the love poems & the 'Famam librosque'—in fact nearly all—are extraordinary achievements.[3] I know nothing about him but have an idea he has come from America.

Yours & Emily's ever & having patience

Edward Thomas

96

4 June 1909   *Berryfield Cottage*

My dear Gordon,

Are you better now? I am sorry I did not come to see you on that Thursday when I was in London. I could have done so but— well I can't explain easily; also I was not sure if you would like me to come when you were ill & perhaps not able to talk. Please thank Emily for writing, though as she says her handwriting is now ominous. Well, I did get to Cornwall & had eight days there walking & sailing, taking notes & reading the *Apocrypha*, arriving at the hotel usually too sleepy to write, & I was Haynes' guest & he is a persistent (& a good) talker.[4] So I could not write. And now there is the usual stack of work in arrear, & I am artless enough to try to lure you into another letter by sending you a copy of the last *English Review* of which I have 2 copies because the Editor sends one to each contributor.[5] I have no news. The Maeterlinck job is still uncertain. The Complete

---

[1] W. G. Blaikie Murdoch, *Memories of Swinburne, with other essays*, 1910.

[2] The Rev. Richard Watson Dixon, *Poems*, reviewed *MP*, 5 April.

[3] *Personae of Ezra Pound*, reviewed *DC*, 7 June.

[4] E. S. P. Haynes. See his portrait of ET in *Personalia*, 1917 and 1927, pp. 2–18. 'His talk was incomparable. . . . But he was as reticent as he was responsive.' [Although they reviewed each other's early work dutifully] 'we always frankly expressed a decided preference for each other's conversation. . . . His melancholy would instantaneously disappear in congenial company on a holiday'.

[5] The June number of *ER* contained a review of 'Two Poets' (i.e. Pound and Hewlett).

Jefferies I was to have edited seems likely to fall through. Nor is
there anything much to tell even of the Electrician.[1] Perhaps you
caught the smell of burning in the startled air—for I hear he was
at Coniston. We see little of one another, as the Two rise for
breakfast (when they do rise) between 1 & 5 p.m. while we are
bourgeois in such matters. Although he is a lightning author &
transformationist there are not yet any small Electricians that I
know of. —It is now a strange twilight, very cold, very misty &
full of dropping water though it is not raining, & the thrushes
are singing with the blackbirds among the tossing trees. I wish
you would play & shut out these things or rather let them pour as
pure spirits into my brain. When shall I hear you play again? In
the evenings at Looe I had the same wish & the same question.
Goodbye. I am ever yours   Edward Thomas

97

12 June 1909   *13 Rusham Rd.*

My dear Gordon,
    I am in town a day or two & must send you a word thanking
you for your letter & also saying I think the beginning of July
would be a good time for *Gunnar* but after that not till September. I hope it will be July though. Guthrie is unfortunate but he
stands it better than some do fortune. Garnett's play I ought also
to tell you is out & I have read it.[2] It's a very fine heroic shape
to hang good voices & dresses on. In fact Helen & I came up
chiefly to see it played & a good deal of it was excellent. Thanks
for the *Guardian*. I suspect the critic—Montague—was too kind
to the players whom doubtless he wishes to encourage, for when
I saw them all but 3 or 4 were fearfully stagey & even the
beautiful heroine, Moira Limerick, didn't know when to let her
voice go easy. I had read the play, of course, & I thought nearly
all of it carried well. The end, a scene where the heroine cuts the
bonds of her family's enemy —— a powerful man whom she
wholly hates & half loves, & puts out the torch of the prison to

---

[1] Arthur Ransome.
[2] *The Feud*. See Letter 95, note 1. Like *Riding to Lithend*, Garnett's play was based
on an Old Icelandic saga.

give herself up to him, was extraordinarily hard to do. To act as
the thing would have occurred was impossible perhaps, & the
symbols chosen were faulty. The thing does not interfere with
Gunnar in any way. Perhaps they would be glad to use the dresses
etc. of *The Feud* for your play?

Oh I do humble myself over Ezra Pound. He is not & cannot
ever be very good. Certainly he is not what I mesmerized myself
—out of pure love of praising the new poetry!—into saying he
was & I am very much ashamed & only hope I shall never meet
the man. My greatest humiliation is due to regret for cheapening
praise & using the same words about such a man as about, say,
Sturge Moore, though of course I did indicate the chaos of the
work.

What a good time you had in London notwithstanding. You
are lucky to see just the people you like & admire.

The Yorkshire tour is impossible now, I expect.

Now Helen & I are taking my mother to *The Playboy of the
Western World*. Synge's *Riders to the Sea* is wonderful & equal to
the Greeks, isn't it?

I hope Emily & you are well again now & fit to play your
next hazard in London.

Yours ever Edward Thomas

98

1909[1]   *Berryfield Cottage*

My dear Gordon,

I am only just back from 10 days in Wales with Mervyn & I
am perplexed in the extreme by work & letters. So I only have
time to look through your proof & to say that I like the poem to
Edward Thomas very much in both ways, as a poem & as an
expression of friendship.[2] The play itself I had to read in the
train but I got the impression that it was an admirable entity
with many good things in it & none superfluous. I feel no doubt
that it justifies itself & I felt the thing all over again & not merely
as a memory out of *Burnt Njal*. But I must not go on writing:

[1] The date is by GB.
[2] The dedicatory poem 'To Edward Thomas' in *The Riding to Lithend*.

as you can see, I am thinking about something else.—-Helen likes the poem to me.

As to the proof I found no mistake but I thought that perhaps the punctuation at the top of 9 (first 2 lines) was wrong & that you speak of Gunnar as 'tender of Iceland's fame . . .'

Now I must go to other things & post this hoping it is not too long delayed already.

Thank you for your letter

I am ever yours Edward Thomas

99

16 July 1909   *Berryfield Cottage*

My dear Gordon,

Thank you for your letter. I ought to have said it before & would have done had I known I was to glide into such a languid desperate condition as I am in now. Yet I ought to have known for by referring to diaries I have at last found out what I suspected before that I get periods of depression particularly once a month for a week or so. But this is enough of the natural history of ET for the present.

I have seen the Book and it looks very well & fitting.[1] The printing is not 1st class & the house at Lithend has come out rather badly, but the pictures are very good—I like the horse's head at the beginning. It is good of you to promise me a Pullman edition & I quite understand how that may be delayed. Mrs Guthrie seems worse than ever & was to undergo an operation this or next week if no better. I haven't seen them for months, perhaps not this year, though Helen has. I don't like going into the house where there is so much disease & pain, especially as the house seems to suffer too.

If only you were here now you would see de la Mare. He is staying fairly near & we see him & his family often. You would like his singularly (sometimes comically) restless & curious & innocent mind. Our other neighbours are scarce ever so. They

---

[1] *The Riding to Lithend*, with drawings by James Guthrie, was printed at Guthrie's Pear Tree Press and limited to 120 copies, twenty of which contained an extra plate and were hand-coloured. The latter formed the 'Pullman edition'.

frequent Petersfield & other pubs enlivening the countryside with song. We like the 'painted lady' less & less & call her the Unicorn because she has a small ivory horn in the midst of her forehead. We feel very bourgeois beside them but deferentially expect *Bohemia in Froxfield*.

What do you think of Arthur Wor now after his review in the *D.C.*?[1] Do you think he is not altogether fool. Still you won't care, after Sturge Moore's opinion which I am glad to hear.

We have seen Garnett's play acted.[2] The middle was slow & was full of the smell of old skins which the family was beating while awaiting the warriors' return. But the beginning was good & the last act very fine. He had a lovely dark girl as Helga. Here I send it. *Deirdre* is an exquisite whole on the stage. But I want to know how *Yeats* came to use the phrase 'Libyan heel'. It isn't Yeats at all, is it? But *The Playboy*. Have you read and seen it? I daresay it is the greatest play of modern times. Of course I don't know. But I felt it to be utterly new & altogether fine. Goodbye now. In a hurry and I hope you are well again now. Write & tell me. I am Emily's & yours ever

Edward Thomas

100

1 September 1909 *Berryfield Cottage*

My dear Gordon,

I have just given up reading because I could read no more & it is midnight. But as I vowed this morning I would write to you today so I do. You are the victim of my lofty principles therefore. Please execrate the principles & forgive me. I have been very restless lately. I have had practically no work,[3] & I have had several disappointments—a chance of a book offered, then apparently dropped; & now the hope of publishing a fair collection of my recent sketches & tales dwindles to a little volume uniform

---

[1] In *DC*, 14 July 1909—a review which shows Waugh's complete ignorance both of the famous Icelandic saga and of GB's intention in writing the play.

[2] *The Feud*. Presumably Helen and ET saw Yeats's *Deirdre* as well as plays by Garnett and Synge.

[3] This 'idle period' did not last. The 'Red Book' contains the following published reviews for September–December: 19 in *DC*, 12 in *MP*, 2 each in *SR* and *B*.

with *Horæ Solitariæ*[1] & *The Roadmender* & designed to depend on its superficial resemblance to that work for its success with the Tooting public. However it is a little better than nothing to have got my stories into print & so far outside me as to be judged with equanimity (by myself). They may be out this year. Will you help me with the proofs? *The South Country* long delayed is now being prepared & if you are fit & still willing to do so I shall ask you to help me with that also. I am to make nothing out of the stories, I fear. In fact, save reviews, I have nothing profitable to do except edit a volume of unpublished & un-collated essays by Jefferies.[2] Dare I ask you to read that also? My only prospect of other work is in a guide to Wiltshire. The chief charm of that is that it will mean 2 or 3 months (off & on) out of doors. It is not to be quite the driest kind of guide but in any case it will be a pretty severe task for me, as you can imagine. However it is far from settled & I should be as much pleased if I did not get it as if I did—being afraid. I have been giving way for I think the first time to some very useless annoyance that my position is so bad & insecure & unimproved, though wiseacres told me my *Jefferies* would help. This is no news & there is no other.

I daresay you are right about *The Feud*.[3] I am no critic. I saw a fine intention & a fine outline & words passable: add to this my knowledge of Garnett's character & singularity & you will see the way of my error, if such it is. But I can't discuss it. In any case I should never have thought of saying it proved Garnett's powers. You have to see & hear him to know them & I am con-vinced he can never write anything worthy of them. He knows himself this weakness in literary expression & though he must feel my inferiority to him as a nature & a mind he says quite honestly with a smiling admiration that I have a natural talent for writing which he has not.

Have you seen Synge's poems?[4] They are raw poetry &

---

[1] When *Rest and Unrest* appeared in 1911, 3 other volumes were advertised opposite the title page as 'Uniform with this Volume': *The Road Mender* and *The Grey Brethren*, by Michael Fields, and *A Modern Mystic's Way* (dedicated to Michael Fields).

[2] R. Jefferies, *The Hills and the Vales*, with an Introduction by ET, 1909.

[3] See Letter 97.

[4] *Poems and Translations*, Cuala Press, Churchtown, Dundrum, reviewed *DC*, 26 July.

something more—wonderfully lean & bare & yet compelling us to clothe them in the warm & radiant life which they disdain. . . .[1]

My feet are cold now. What a year! I have now learnt that I cannot enjoy everything the weather does so long as I remain attached to my bones—which are rheumaticky. I hope you got well again in that spell of fine weather which I know really did visit us but was utterly forgotten in twenty-four hours of rain & cold that followed. Tell me, & accept this as an apology for not writing before. I should like to come to you but expect that if I can get away again this year it must be somewhere close at hand—Wiltshire, I hope.

We are all well except Mervyn who has a 'rheumatic throat' for the time being which keeps him to bed & other luxuries. We send our love to Emily & you.

Ever yours Edward Thomas

101

Berryfield Cottage

15 September 1909

Dear Emily,

Thank you for your letter.[2] I was afraid Gordon must be ill. For I confess I was anxiously expecting to have a word. But the delay did not matter at all, so far as I know. The proofs came in two big lumps & the publisher could not expect them back at once. I was really anxious, partly because I was uncertain what might be wrong & partly because I thought my envelopes might have broken in the post, or one of them. So please do not think anything more about the delay. But is Gordon really fit to look at the rest of the proofs? If you think not please do not let them trouble him. As usual his corrections are most valuable. He sees actual errors which I had overlooked & also makes suggestions for improvements which I nearly always adopt. So if he can go on with them I shall be very glad indeed & I expect he can finish them by the beginning of next week. The book must be a great

[1] 195 words omitted.
[2] I have omitted 3 short notes (early September, 9 September, and 11 October) accompanying the complete proofs of *The South Country*.

trial to him, I know. However, he will have some satisfaction in knowing it the last of its tribe. For he always foresaw that there was to be a last & knew moreover that there ought to be.[1] I will not trouble him with the Jefferies[2]—except perhaps my introduction to it (in a few week's time)—but perhaps when my book of stories & sketches is ready Gordon will be quite well & he will look at the proofs.[3] I hope so. It is a thousand pities he could not see The Michael Fields (why not simply Michael Field, a collective substantive?), for they is (or he are) a wonderful persons, I know, apart from its beautiful work.[4]—I glanced at *The Bookman* review of *Gunnar*, & thought I detected the reticent personality of an admirer of Ransomes, named Ashley Gibson,[5] a very nice but not highly gifted man who is unable to earn a living at anything but literature & not at that just now. I think it is possible however that he achieved that guarded omniscience without any *direct* inspiration from Above, though of course if his is the 3rd generation its quality is in no need of any other explanation

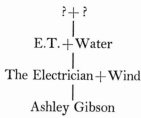

But I refrain: I might be lured into the mysteries of the Trinity.

Please thank Gordon for his comments on *The Book of Friendship* &c.[6] It was composed in collaboration with the Ivory-horned, with the help of their own library and about 12 books of mine, in the intervals of more pleasing if less productive labours. It is a massive bantling of over 500 pages & costs a lot. Have you seen any of his introductions to the selections of short stories he

[1] ET was compelled to write other country books.
[2] See page 190, note 2.
[3] *Rest and Unrest*.
[4] See page 190, note 1.
[5] See *B*, September p. 278. Is this another ET pseudonym?
[6] *The Book of Friendship*: essays, poems, maxims and prose passages, arranged by Arthur Ransome, 1909. 'Ivory-horned'—the Thomases referred privately to Mrs. Ransome as 'the unicorn'.

edits? They are very carefully done & the writing has a kind of merit tho I am not clever enough to define what. I could give a genealogical line. But it would look monstrous.

Helen's love & mine to you both & we hope Gordon will soon be well & quite well—

Edward Thomas

102

29 September 1909 *Berryfield Cottage*

My dear Gordon,

I am very glad to guess by your postcards that you are better, & I am sending you the proofs.[1] They have just begun to come more quickly & I have had to send off some to the printers. So I would like you to return to me first—as soon as you can—pp. 97–160; the rest you can read at leisure, & if your corrections (but do not trouble to make any) include any that I ought to have made I will use them in the final proofs. I do hope you will like some of them after *The South Country*.

The turtle dove is very much smaller than the woodpigeon & flies low as a rule & very lightly.[2] Its voice is a soft purring, sounding as if half buried & very warm and luxurious, far softer & less articulated than the woodpigeon's 'Take two cows Taffy'. The stockdove is a third species, about the same size as the woodpigeon but not ringed round the neck & with a coo that is more of a grunt as a rule than the woodpigeon's, a soft grunt, but it has other very pretty notes which I can't describe. But 'the voice of the turtle is heard in the land' refers to this Spring immigration.

I shall look out for Noguchi certainly.[3]

With our love to Emily & you.

Ever yours Edward Thomas

[1] 2 notes (dated 19 and 25 September), accompanying proofs of *Rest and Unrest*, are omitted.

[2] In an omitted note ET points out 'that turtle-doves do go away and return in May'.

[3] Yone Noguchi, *The Pilgrimage*, reviewed *DC*, 31 May.

103

12 October 1909   *Berryfield Cottage*

My dear Gordon,

Thank you for your two letters & two lots of proofs.[1] I hope your handwriting though in pencil means you are decidedly better. For Helen saw Mrs Guthrie last week & got at second or third hand (I gathered) a very bad account of you, which I hope applies to a remote period. Mrs Guthrie—perhaps you know—is now recovering from an operation for which she stayed three weeks at a hospital. Guthrie has had a very poor time, chiefly with the children, but writes this morning a long very cheerful brave letter to try to cheer me—but I am proof against such things.

I am glad you found things to like in the little book. It is too small a selection from the things I have been doing to be quite fair to me. Also it is my own selection & various bad reasons led me to include several—one of which was 'The Fountain', a glimpse of a girl by the sea sand,[2]—I wonder did you like it at all? I think I agree with your preferences—also in what you say of note books. But I shall not burn them I expect. Only I shall certainly use them less & less as I get more of an eye for subjects. Among my bad habits was that of looking through old note books of scenery &c. in order to get a subject or mood suggested to me. I now use the note books more & more exclusively for the details of things conceived independently. Also I am casting about for subjects which will compel me to depend simply upon what I am—memory included but in a due subsidiary place. I think of Welsh legends. As to modern subjects I can do little with more than one character & that one is sure either to be a ghost (of a pretty woman or nice old man) or else myself. So far the best things I have done have been about houses. I have quite a long series—I discover, tho I did not design it. The house in 'Sand & Snow' is one.[3]

[1] The proofs of *Rest and Unrest* and the Introduction to *The Hills and the Vales*; (mentioned in 2 omitted notes dated 5 September and 6 October).

[2] See Letters 78 and 79 and *Rest and Unrest* pp. 138–43. I think, too, that this girl is remembered in *The South Country*, Chapter VI.

[3] In *Rest and Unrest* the house is called 'Snow and Sand' as also in an article in *ER*, March 1910, pp. 393–8, which precedes a sketch, 'Goose Fair', by D. H. Lawrence.

Nobody wants me to do a book now, alas (for my purse)! So I have to do all the reviewing I can get. How I hate it. How much does Abercrombie do? I imagine he is a pretty robust young man with a strong spirit,—and he writes very well & very rightly about *Gunnar*,—but how long can he stand it, especially if he comes to town? I should like to see him in town, but feel inclined to hope he won't go. I have to give it up more & more. I have had to give up dining in London altogether—bad hot city air, smoke, smell of food & alcohol &c. makes me bad for a week after these few hours.

Have you seen Masefield's 3 plays?[1] He is a wonderful man. It is beautiful natural prose dialogue & full of poetry—also I believe thoroughly sound for stage purposes; in fact even Shaw says he is the best of the young men.

Another anthology by E. V. Lucas.[2] I get sick of geniality & odd charming characters all extracted from their context as if you should spread jam over toffee & eat it with honey.

Goodbye for a little while. And I hope you and Emily are better.

Helen & I are ever yours Edward Thomas

104

14 December 1909   *Week Green, Petersfield*

My dear Gordon,

This is the new address. The rhythm of it is quite modern at any rate, though Garnett puts the house down to the period of King Stephen. We move in on Saturday & I have just packed all my books & take the children to town tomorrow to be rid of them for the move. We are in a pickle. I am dirty & my hands are all chipped & scraped & stiff. So I doubt if I can write. But I want to send you Masefield's book. I think *Nan* a very fine thing & so do you.

I was glad to have some news of you though it was bad. I guessed it would be. This must have been a deadly year for you.

---

[1] *The Tragedy of Nan and other plays* [i.e. *Mrs. Harrison* and *The Campden Wonder*], reviewed *MP*, 14 October, and *B*, November.
[2] Probably *Good Company: a Rally of Men*, edited by E. V. Lucas, 1909.

It has been a great weight to bear continuously & I hope for a crisp winter to clean the earth & help you. For two months nearly I have been better, chiefly because I have had to work hard & regularly in the new garden clay. I don't really care about it, but it had to be done & I kept at it day after day & it did me good almost against my will.[1] I got a hard hand and my fatigues were more purely physical than usual. I had to do my reviewing badly & to do very little else. Still, one or two stories I worked at did not turn out badly. I used some old Welsh fragments of legends. You shall see them some day.[2] I always feel that when I treat these *external* things my approach is very literal & matter of fact, but I hope not. Perhaps I am not quite just to myself in finding myself very much on an everyday ordinary level except when in a mood of exaltation usually connected with nature & solitude. By comparison with others that I know—like de la Mare—I seem essentially like the other men in the train & I should like not to be. This is quite genuinely naïve & will amuse you. It may be only because I am inarticulate & that I can usually only meet others on ground where I have no real interest—as politics, social & current literary affairs.

I am perhaps about to begin a book on poets & women. Originally it was to have been the influence of women on English poets.[3] But that is too difficult: so it will be mainly the attitude of poets to individual women & the idea of women & so on. Please send suggestions, warnings &c. as they come to your mind. I have been dangling after publishers with all sorts of proposals but could not come to terms. This looked bad & I was willing to accept anything especially as our move means an increased expenditure & Helen talks of having another baby.[4] In fact I have consented to do a guide—pure guide—to Hampshire & Wiltshire, but it is not settled & I shall cry off if I possibly can, though my expenses will be paid to cover some fine country & I should get much material by the way. I am not sure that I could do it. The General Election will postpone my little book of

[1] See *WWE*, pp. 131–4.
[2] See 'The Island', 'Winter Music', and 'The Castle of Lostormellyn' in *Light and Twilight*, 1911. Possibly, too, a few stories in the posthumous collection *Cloud Castle and Other Papers*, 1922, belong to this period.
[3] *Feminine Influence on the Poets*, 1910.
[4] His second daughter, Myfanwy.

sketches.[1] I am trying to cozen Dent into letting me do a country book with houses—cottages, farms &c.—as centres, & dealing more than ever with people. If he will let me—& let me bring in Wales as well—I could make a good book of my kind. I hope *The South Country* at its best was beyond *The Heart of England*. It had no structure & its joins were execrable, but I felt some of it was the truest I had achieved.[2]

Ezra Pound's second book[3] was a miserable thing & I was guilty of a savage recantation after meeting the man at a dinner. It was very treacherous & my severity was due to self-contempt as much as to dislike of his work.

Goodbye. I must go to bed out of this empty room.

> Yours & Emily's ever Edward Thomas

105

3 January 1910   *Week Green*

My dear Gordon,

I am so plagued with the necessity for writing Christmas polite letters that I think I must include you in this industry. Thank you for *Danae*.[4] I am too stupid to say more. We are just settled now & Davies is staying with us. Helen has been unwell & in bed during the move & now there is something the matter with Bronwen. And I have accepted the dirty job of writing the text of a book on Windsor Castle this month.[5] After your usual custom please tell me something about Windsor. I shall have to give a list of celebrated or wealthy visitors. Were you ever there? It all has to be discovered, read about & the book written & copied in these 4 weeks. So I do not feel amiable at losing the first week completely owing to visitors whom I can not put off early enough.

---

[1] *Rest and Unrest.*
[2] See page 166, note 1.
[3] *Exultations of Ezra Pound*, reviewed *DC*, 23 November.
[4] GB's play *Laodice and Danaë*, 1909. Reprinted in *King Lear's Wife and other Plays*, 1920.
[5] *Windsor Castle*, described by ET, pictured by E. W. Haslehurst. 'Dirty' is ET's usual word for a piece of writing he was forced to do cheaply; in this instance the adjective—but not the book—is tinged with his inherited dislike of the monarchy.

I am very glad to hear *The Riding to Lithend* may be played.[1] Tell me as soon as it is certain. How beastly my handwriting is. It is the new house. We like it very much, but it is new. We can see our old one nearby from the windows, & could run down to it straight through the woods in 3 minutes if we did not break our necks. We are in a new parish called Froxfield, a much pleasanter address, but it might lead to my letters &c going to a notorious debtor of my name—Edward Thomas—who uses that address. The bailiffs & young men with summonses &c. have already been troubling us. 'Week Green' is the name of a small district with about 4 houses in it. It is our briefest possible address, though it does resemble Peak Freen.

I wish I could come to Well Knowe this year. 1909 was a devil. This has begun to take after it. I hope it will be broken of the habit. Goodbye & our best wishes to you & Emily & your father & mother & Aunt Sarah.

Yours ever Edward Thomas

106

My dear Gordon,

It is more than a month since you wrote your letter to me. I am sorry I did not send a word before especially as I have no more to say than I should have done a fortnight ago. Things are in an unpleasant uncertainty. Publishers will not go on giving me money for books except that they now offer the usual hack's terms for books to suit *them*—guides & works on celebrated statesmen &c. The only pleasure I get out of these revelations is refusing the offers—I wrote 4 sentences to Fisher Unwin which is my masterpiece of prose. *Windsor* I have done, a dirty job & it has left me dirty. I went to see it & (to my regret) into the Castle. —But really I am in a quandary.

Before I forget it, Davies is now at 11 High Street, Sevenoaks.

I am sorry for this beastly paper. It did not look so beastly when I ordered some reams to be stamped.

[1] It was first produced by Terence Gray at the Cambridge Festival Theatre in 1928. See C. C. Abbott, Introduction to GB, *Poems and Plays*, p. 15.

How are you now, & Emily too? Are you pretty well? This damp & frost, damp & frost, can't suit you. It doesn't suit me except for lyrical moments.

Here is the new book at any rate.[1] So unnecessary. Its chief distinction will be that it is the only book I haven't & shall not ever have, made a penny out of, during the past 8 years.

Yours Ever Edward Thomas

107

(These I now learn are the local spellings: 'Week' is merely an Ordnance Map offence)

15 March 1910   *Wick or Wyke Green*

My dear Gordon,

Thank you for your letter & the *Morning Post* cutting. I am writing now very largely because I want to beg your help yet again. I have undertaken—very rashly but yet necessarily—to produce three books in the next 12 months. One is practically written. It is a sort of country book but is really about a dozen studies of houses & their people. I am trying to get the publisher to take drawings for it from Guthrie. The idiot refused to pay Bone the very modest price he was asking for 6 drawings done especially for me![2] The other two books are (1) on Maeterlinck[3] & (2) on Women & Poets—i.e. on the influence of women on English poets & on the position of women in their poetry, the attitude of the poets towards the ideal & the real woman etc. Please give me any pregnant suggestions that occur to you & mention any books & passages to be consulted—Furthermore Duckworth is reissuing *Horæ Solitariæ* with some omissions & with the addition of the last two papers from *Rose Acre Papers*.[4]

---

[1] *Rest and Unrest.*

[2] Muirhead Bone. This particular book was not written. See Letter 110.

[3] *Maurice Maeterlinck*, 1911.

[4] *Rose Acre Papers, including essays from 'Horae Solitariae'*, 1910. The author's note reads: 'Most of the chapters in this book are reprinted from my "H.S.", first published in 1902. "An Autumn House" and "Rain" formed part of a little book entitled *Rose Acre Papers* [No. 2, The Lanthorn Series, 1904]. All were written between 1898 and 1901.'

Do you recall any corrections that must or ought to be made in either, whether of misprints or of exceptional fatuities?

In spite of all this before me I have been thinking of you in this fine weather & hoping you can enjoy it. You ought to be here. Our brick terrace all along the south wall would please you very much in the sun. It is the new house which was building all last year. It has no name, but the district which includes two or three farms & cottages & two other new houses is called Wick Green. I wish you could come to it with Emily before your American reputation makes you too big for our house.[1] Until then I shall continue to be glad of it. What are you working at now?

I have been reading Sturge Moore's *Art & Life* & tho I have a most complete admiration for his knowledge seriousness & original thinking I do find his power of expression very uncertain.[2] The book was very hard to read & I put it down not merely to my own stupidity but partly to his style which is (1) too elliptical and (2) either too elaborate or not elaborate enough, for it is patchy & uneven & has no pervading quality.

I still hope for the grand edition of *Lithend*. Meantime I hope Guthrie is growing rich. In spite of my dying conscience etc. I am not.

We are very well & want to know that you and Emily are. We send our love.

Yours Ever Edward Thomas

108

6 April 1910   *Wick Green*

My dear Gordon,

This can only be a word as I am falling asleep (not in Jesus)

---

[1] *GB*'s *A Vision of Giorgione* was published by T. B. Mosher (Portland, Maine, U.S.A.) in 1910.

[2] *Art and Life*, reviewed *DC*, 30 March. This book consisted of a long study of Flaubert and a shorter one of Blake. ET criticizes the book's construction and style. ['Even where his writing is certainly clear and good, we seem to detect too laborious (or not sufficiently laborious) a use of words after Pater's manner. The words too often have a mechanical, but not a living, value.']

& tomorrow & tomorrow & tomorrow will be packed with dirty work. But I want to tell you that you are not to lose *Rose Acre Papers*.[1] On the contrary the whole new book is to be yours & the venerable but unfriendly Edwards is to be left to discover it. So there.

Thank you for the suggested books for Maeterlinck. I do not know Charles van Lerberghe.[2] If you can & will lend me any books bearing on Maeterlinck's origins I shall be very grateful— but no hurry, as I can do little until I have got through most of my reading for the book on women & poets. This is troublous. I am trying to carve out such a portion of the subject as I can attack without indecent temerity in so short a time. The basis of the book is to be—or was to be—'the influence of women on English poets'. But there is not enough material except what relates to recent poets, so I must extend this description so as to include something of the relation of women & the idea of woman to poetry. Tell me some fractions of the subject that I can fasten on to.

It may have been haste that prevented me from understanding Sturge Moore, but I don't think so. I have a great admiration for him & I read very carefully & humbly. What do you say to his use of 'dancing' in 'dancing Spring'—where Flaubert goes to Rome in the first chapter? Is it not an undigested, unabsorbed word? Otherwise what a brilliant chapter that is.[3]

I have been gardening hard in the early mornings of these fine days. The work is endless & my strength is not. The Old Man or Lad's Love you gave me is now a beautiful great bush at my study door. The Bergamot is multiplied & sweetens three corners of the garden. The Rosemary disappeared. Have you any seedlings of it—or of anything that specially belongs to you & Emily & your garden—that you could send us? If so, please do.

Ever yours (in sleep as awake)

Edward Thomas

P.S. Who wrote *The Romance of Poetry* which you speak of?[4]

[1] *Horae Solitariae* was dedicated to O. M. Edwards and *Rose Acre Papers*, 1904, to GB. The new *Rose Acre Papers* was dedicated 'To Gordon Bottomley/Poet'.
[2] I have not been able to trace this reference.
[3] See page 200, note 2.
[4] *The Romance of Poetry*, compiled by a Medical Muser, 1901.

109

22 April 1910   **Wick Green**

My dear Gordon,

Thank you for answering a question that must have looked inept & rather like that of a *Daily Mail* special correspondent.[1] I really wanted to have my own surmises strengthened or shattered. You have strengthened them especially by your remark that 'all poems are love poems' which is almost exactly what I had hit upon myself in one of my cloudy cogitations on the whole vast vague question. I shall keep your letter by me & reproduce it consciously or unconsciously, literally or in digested form. Thank you. Where does W. M. Rossetti speak of his brother's method?

I am still without plans & of course difficulties increase. I have been examining the poems & letters &c. of Keats, Landor, Wordsworth & Donne. I don't know yet if I can dare touch the Provencal & Italian poets. Is there any translation of Petrarch that is like poetry or like Petrarch?

I have still to thank you for an earlier letter chiefly about Maeterlinck. Your suggestion that I should look at Sharp's *Vistas* is a likely one.[2] I read the book once & forgot it. I believe it might provoke something.

It would take too long—time is money for an illpaid author!— to bring up all the possible forces against '*dancing* Spring'. It is merely that in its context 'dancing' has no effect upon my mind save as a conspicuous word which I can only connect with 'Spring' by such an effort as would destroy any aesthetic value in it. I don't think that Moore proves that if he had stood over Blake with a birch he would have made a better artist of him though he might have made a less troublesome one.[3]

Thank you for a promise of Rosemary &c. We would like some

---

[1] Refers to a request in an omitted note (dated 14 April 1910): 'Now do you feel able to make in prose a statement as to the condition under which any particular [love] poem of your own was written.' There is a similar request in the letters to Jesse Berridge. The replies were included in *Feminine Influence on the Poets*, Chapter II, pp. 18–48.

[2] William Sharp ('Fiona Macleod'), *Vistas*, 1894.

[3] See Letter 107.

Peruvian Lily & Larkspur seed. The Larkspur is easy to get but I should like some of yours & Cartmel's.

Ever your hurried & harried prose man Edward Thomas

Thank you for the cutting about the old huntsman—I wish the photograph were clearer. May the otters be at peace now.

110

24 July 1910   *Wick Green*

My dear Gordon,

I was very glad to see a letter from you at last. Your silence made me think you must be very ill or else had at last found it impossible to reply to my languid letters. *The Riding to Lithend* is worth waiting for. It makes altogether I think the best modern book I have and to open it & see that blue is like a big natural effect. I am proud & grateful to have it. I must send my subscription copy to de la Mare.[1] He is doing very good work now, some of it very happy childish rhyming, most delicate & new. He is coming to Harting for a month at the end of the week & I wish you could see him there. I am a little too busy & getting anxious as Helen is within only a few days of her time. She is still very well though. I gave about 3 months to hard reading for my Women & Poets & allowed myself, or was allowed, 2 months to write. It was not enough so I have really been bent on finishing anyhow & satisfaction at producing *something* by the end of a weary day has nearly overcome my disgust at what it really was. The result is I have worked—in a kind of suppressed panic—much faster than I need, & the thing is now nearly at an end, with all August still at my disposal if necessary. I am sick at having to do it but I believe I am justified in not doing as well as possible a piece of work I never could do really well with my powers. That is provided I do not harm my ability to do other things more natural to me. The slightest of these you have seen in the *Nation* etc.[2] How did you like 'Lostormellyn' & 'A Group

---

[1] See Letter 99, note 1.

[2] All three sketches are in *Light and Twilight*. (See 'Author's Note'.) 'Olwen' is a recreation of his Welsh travels with a pronounced Lawrentian flavour. I believe much of ET's work is buried anonymously in *The Nation*—a weekly sympathetic to his interests.

of Statuary'? That Welsh girl Olwen was very barbarously bowdlerized so as to spoil its point altogether. Do I mature or only get old? How can I tell? I only know I am still very childish & inexperienced. Your criticism is just I believe, but I thought it could not be applied to my recent work so much. You would be kind if you sent me anything of mine with the inharmonious notebook stuff *marked*.

I was very much taken with the 'Gifted Friend'. But you do seem to have got hold of people with *Gunnar* & I am hoping to see you responding in the of course to me unimaginable ways your nature secretes. What is it to be? Are you for plays or narratives?

Poor Sturge Moore! It must be wretched to suffer like that from publisher's parsimony. I am not sure if I agree with you about separating the 'temporal & spurious part' of Blake. It is not like Wordsworth's, Wordsworth being at bottom normal & suffering from facility, so that a great deal of him could be safely destroyed. But Blake had no mere facility. Wordsworth's bad is clear as water, Blake's good & bad is always more or less turbid with good things in imperfect solution.

I haven't either of those books, but can assure you Way's *Sophocles* is likely to be extraordinarily bad if anything like his *Euripides*.[1]

You are lucky to have Trevelyan. I have missed his last book if not two & am sorry for it.

Dent is asking me for another book so either his brain is softening or my sales have much improved. In any case I am glad as I have a lot by me which I can probably use. I want to do a book on houses & people for him. Did I tell you an imbecile publisher rejected such a book by Muirhead Bone & me in the Spring?[2] And now Bone is too busy to collaborate.

Have you Skeat's *Chatterton* or any sound text? I have a new *True Chatterton*[3] & some of the quotations are extremely different from the text I have in the Muses Library. If you have

---

[1] Arthur S. Way, *Euripides in English Verse*, 1894, and *Sophocles in English Verse*, 1909.

[2] See Letter 107, note 2.

[3] John H. Ingram, *The True Chatterton*, reviewed *DC*, 3 August, and *MP*, 29 August. This brief insight into ET's scholarly approach to reviewing is fully supported by the reviews themselves, and, of course, by the testimony of those of his colleagues best able to judge. According to the 'Red Book', the following reviews were published between January and August 1910: 47 in *DC*, 40 in *MP*, 5 in *B*, 4 in *SR*, and 1 in *N*.

a really good edition & can send it at once I shall be very glad.

Suppose I could get away for 10 days from about August 20, would you take me & Bronwen in? She would give no trouble & I believe you would like her. She would sleep with me. It is only just a chance, so do not put yourself out to make it possible.

Yours & Emily's ever with our love Edward Thomas

111

6 August 1910   *Wick Green*

My dear Gordon,

I was very glad to read your letter & there was nothing here for it to jar with. Helen is perfectly well but still double & expectant, she regrets to say. I agree with you about Skeat. He really thinks it is only a matter of what Lewis Hind calls 'j—jolly old w—words', whereas it is a matter of music & also of construction &c. Chatterton's whole attitude somehow changed when he was writing as Rowley. So I return him at once, especially as I have had the loan of the 1777 edition.

I wish I had been at or near Well Knowe on July 4th! Thank you ever so much for suggesting a date in September, but I doubt if either Bronwen or I can accept it. She will be going to school not very late in that month & I may be compelled to take whatever holiday I can get very soon. Mervyn & I are going down to Conrad's about the 20th & walking along the Pilgrim's Road on our way for a day or two before. Then I must get away alone. After all this muddled & hurried reading & writing I feel as if I ought to walk day & night for weeks if I am ever to get rid of the effects.[1] To have done the book is bad enough, but I don't want to be always the man that wrote Women & Poets. Did I tell you Dent says he wants another book? But it has got to be less 'nebulous'. Tell me how this is to be done. Can I be a sort of an A. G. Bradley and E.T. at the same time?[2] It is asking a lot of a poor perplexed journalist, it seems to me.

I hope you are right in foreseeing Ransome on the Academic

[1] See Letter 110.
[2] Occasioned by his sharp review of A. G. Bradley, *The Avon and Shakespeare's Country* in *DC*, 1 September.

Committee. He is sparing of his autobiography to me now, though he threatened to return to these parts. Goodbye. As usual I am hurried & the hour is late. If I can come to Well Knowe—perhaps walking—be sure I will. With our love to you both & to your father & mother & Aunt Sarah

Yours ever Edward Thomas

112

26 August 1910   *Wick Green*

My dear Gordon,

I wish I were with you now or could come at once. I am back again with the intolerable swishing of the trees in rain & wind which I have had ever since I came here last Christmas.[1] It makes me want to hear music, & I have never enjoyed music anywhere as much as yours at Well Knowe. However. I don't think I can come. I have just had a couple of days on the Pilgrims Way in Kent & a couple with Conrad but I was not well at least except when alone & out of doors. Now I am expecting every day to go to Wales but am dependent on a travelling companion. Since I finished the beastly book I have been unable to work or rest, so I hope it will not be long. Proofs have begun to arrive & perhaps I will send you the first batch now. It does look horrible in small bits. Please send them back as quick as ever you can. Or shall I only send you the page proofs. That would be kinder. Or I will send you duplicates of the slips & use your suggestions in the page proofs.[2]

I am sending 'July'.[3] It is one of those crude mixtures of experience & invention which prove me no artist. Damn it. I am only just beginning to discover it.

We haven't given the baby her names yet. We think of Olwen Margaret Elizabeth or even Mevanwy (Myfanwy) Margaret Elizabeth, because Olwen is too like Bronwen.[4] Helen is getting

---

[1] See *WWE*, p. 133 for a description of the exposed position of the new house.
[2] Proofs of *Feminine Influence on the Poets*.
[3] 'July' (in *Light and Twilight*, pp. 96–116) closely parallels *AIW*, pp. 39–41.
[4] In the next omitted note from Swansea (undated) ET writes, 'The baby's name is probably to be Helen Elizabeth Mevanwy (Myfanwy is the Welsh spelling but impossible in England). I like Olwen best, but it is too near Bronwen.'

on very well & sends her love to you & Emily. (This is vile paper).

I am too stupid to tell about Conrad, except that he looks something like Sir Richard Burton in the head, black hair, & moustache & beard & a jutting out face, & pale thin lips extraordinarily mobile among the black hair, flashing eyes and astonishing eyebrows, and a way of throwing his head right back to laugh which he often does at things which tickle him—such as Hueffer's[1] 'harsh & oppressive' treatment of the National Liberal Club porter. But I was uneasy with Conrad—though he is very friendly to me—and kept saying things I neither meant nor wished it to be supposed I meant. Alas! if only I could live in solitude complete.

Ever yours Edward Thomas

113

25 November 1910   *Wick Green*

My dear Gordon,

I sent you my book a few days ago & hope you did not think it was in reply to your letter—which I was very glad indeed to get. It is so long since you have been able to write & of course I have succumbed to the temptation not to write myself, I know. I often wonder what I should do if I could be quite free. For example what should I write? Not books entitled by publishers *Feminine Influence on the Poets* & the like. It is a wretched wretched book but full of material you may like to have gathered together.— Yes you did thank me for the *Horæ*, I feel sure.[2] At least I never missed anything I expected. There is little news. Ransome's *Poe* is very poor stuff.[3] But he is to do a Wilde for the same little few (trained in the House of Eveleigh Nash).[4] He wants me to do another, but there is little inducement. I am just setting about *Maeterlinck* with a sorry heart—can you help?— and have undertaken to do a book, like Belloc's *Old Road*, on the

[1] Ford Madox Hueffer (later, Ford).

[2] Probably the new edition of *Rose Acre Papers*. See Letter 107, note 4.

[3] Arthur Ransome, *Edgar Allan Poe*, reviewed *MP*, 13 October, and *N*, 15 October.

[4] James Eveleigh Nash, the publisher, sustained two cheap series: 'Nash's Shilling Novels' and 'Nash's Summer Library'.

Icknield Way which runs from Norfolk through Cambridgeshire, Buckinghamshire, Berkshire & Wiltshire into Dorset. . . .[1]

We are all well but do not like the cold coming as it seems too soon after the long lovely Autumn. Helen is herself again & the baby goes on as well as possible.

I saw Guthrie lately & he seemed better & cheerfuller though Mrs Guthrie is the same I believe. He has done some very good things for Osmaston's book. I see a good deal now of Ralph Hodgson. You would like him, such a vigorous & simple nature, careless generous & in some ways unfortunate—did you read his 'To deck a woman' in the *Saturday*?[2] I thought it his best: monotonous & of a Tennysonian finish perhaps, but most intensely wrought.—Forgive me ending with the sheet. As usual I write at midnight to save myself from falling asleep. With Helen's love to you both with mine

Ever yours Edward Thomas

114

16 January 1911   *Wick Green*

My dear Gordon,

I have been thinking of you every day since Christmas & wondering how you are. We did not hear from you. Was it a slip of the post or are you ill or are you simply like everyone else too modern now for Christmas cards? I only hope you are not ill, & it is to ask you to say you are not that I write. I am taking 3 days holiday with some friends after getting to the end of the beastly *Maeterlinck*. I reached it on Friday last. It is merely a chronological series of reviews of each of his books with a Conclusion & a semi-biographical introduction. His early plays are his best works. That is my firm opinion & I expect you will agree. Now I am going to arrange a volume like *Rest & Unrest* for Duckworth's.[3] It will be no better I expect. De la Mare's *Mulla Mulgars* was a wonderful book that grew out of a story told to

---

[1] *The Icknield Way*, published by Constable, 1913.
[2] See 'To Deck a Woman (Harold Hodge Remembered)', in Ralph Hodgson, *Collected Poems*, 1958, pp. 111–26.
[3] *Light and Twilight*.

his children.[1] He is doing many good poems. Davies has revived again[2] & he has done some wonderful chapters about women he has known—which no publisher probably will ever take. They are chastely expressed but they are true.[2] Send me a bulletin on a postcard please & give our love to Emily.

Yours ever Edward Thomas

115

23 February 1911   *Wick   Green*

My dear Gordon,
    How are you? I wish it were you that were writing this windy night & that I should be having a letter from you by Sunday's post. It would be a better letter. I confess I am only writing after my wrist failed me at copying a paper lately written on an old hunting song. I am very busy. *Maeterlinck* somehow—I know how—got finished last month. Proofs will soon be coming. Can you look at them? I am correcting proofs of another collection like *Rest & Unrest*? Then I have three books in hand. One on the Icknield Way (running S.W. across England from near Norwich to nobody knows where). One, a short one on Hearn.[3] A third a collection of Celtic Tales rewritten (more or less) for schools & to be published by the Oxford Press.[4] Can you advise me where to go for Highland *heroic* tales? All this does not mean wealth, but in each case poorer pay than for reviewing. Reviewing is failing me a little, tho I now do some for *The Nation*.[5] I am sick of it & do not do my best at it I fear.

1 *The Three Mulla-Mulgars*, reviewed *MP*, 8 December, *DC*, 14 December, and *B*, December (as part of his portrait of de la Mare for 'The Bookman Gallery'). ET also reviewed *Songs of Childhood* and *Poems* in a similarly detailed, but not repetitive, article for *ER* in December.

2 A reference to W. H. Davies, *Farewell to Poesy*, reviewed *MP*, February 1910, and *DC*, 28 March 1910. The 'wonderful chapters' form part of *A Weak Woman*, 1911, and *The True Traveller*, 1912—both published by Duckworth, whose reader was Edward Garnett.

3 *Lafcadio Hearn*, 1912.

4 *Celtic Stories*, 1911, contained 7 Irish and 6 Welsh tales.

5 ET's last reviews in *MP* appeared on 9 January. Between January and June, 20 reviews appeared in *DC*, 3 in *B* (including a large supplement on 'William Morris'), 5 in *SR*. There are 8 unidentified reviews in the 'Red Book', possibly from the *Daily News*. *The Nation* rarely published a signed review and never one

Guthrie may be going to illustrate my *Icknield Way*.[1] I saw
him for an hour in London lately & he promises to come here
now that he has a sister-in-law housekeeping for him. He looks
better than he was & talks cheerfully. He is again planning a
magazine. Have you seen *The Open Window* at all?[2] They might
like a poem of yours I should think. I hope you are working
again now & want to know what at. I must come to you to get a
talk now that I *am* an incorrigibly bad letter writer. I don't know
quite when it can be. If I could fly it should be now, especially as
I am capable of little else. I am at the end of a second week of
extraordinary weakness, unable to work in the garden or to
walk, & considerably dejected therefore, but not quite so frantic
as I should have been a few years ago in such a case. I am older,
several years older than the Eagle Cock. I shan't see 50 again by
the look of it. I creep & slink about the earth doing small
immediate things—forcing myself to work just to prove I live.
Since Christmas I (& the rest of us) have been a strict vegetarian,
but I am not a new man yet. Perhaps I am in the pangs of labour.
One of my jobs lately has been working with Garnett at a
petition to get W H Davies a pension.[3] We have got a strong list
& Gosse's help & considerable hope. I forget if you saw
Farewell to Poesy.[4] He is now getting ready a new book with
some very good things in it.[4] I now see a chance of his growing.
I feared he knew all he ever would know. He has done some wonderful but unpublishable prose sketches of women.

Ransome has been appearing & disappearing. He has been
hobnobbing with Paul Fort in Paris, getting remarks about the
later Wilde & supporting his vitality in beer & hardboiled eggs.
He also will have to think about vegetarianism one of these days.

---

by ET; after February 1911 it began to devote increased space to 'Poetry', 'The
World of Books', 'Reviews', and 'Books in Brief'. My view is that ET's work
found a ready outlet in all four columns. In fairness to James Milne it should be
stressed that the *DC* continued to use ET regularly after July 1911. See Letter 78,
note 1.

[1] The task was eventually given to A. L. Collins. Guthrie's standards and methods
would certainly have proved too exacting for commercial publishers.

[2] *The Open Window*, published by V. Locke Ellis, vol. 1 (October 1910–March
1911), vol. 2 (April–September 1911).

[3] Garnett and ET helped to obtain a grant for Davies from the Royal Literary Fund
and both were made joint trustees of that grant. Davies also received his Civil
List Pension. See Letter 116.

[4] See Letter 115, note 2.

With his wife's help he has a pretty good time, I fancy. They may be coming here again to live if her people will buy the house. The landlord won't let it to them as they used to bathe in champagne & never wiped up what they spilt. Heigh Ho the Holly!

Have you any sprigs of rosemary to spare? So far we have only snowdrops in bloom. The garden improves but the clay breaks first the back & then the heart.

Helen & I send our love to you & Emily & all.

Yours ever Edward Thomas

116

14 April 1911   *Wick Green*

My dear Gordon,

Thank you for your letter & Emily for hers. I wasn't at all hurt by not getting a letter, but was silent only because for sometime I have been in one of my worst moods & in fact seem hardly likely to get out of it. By the way don't put it down to vegetarianism, (which I have complicated by much reducing the size & number of my meals). I don't think it would be risky for you. Fruit, vegetables (steamed if possible), good bread & butter & nuts & cream, seem sufficient whether in simple or elaborate dishes: in fact I enjoy the taste of my food much more now than ever. But I can't advocate anything I practise just now: I am in such a poor way. I only hope I am still suffering from the transition out of youth, and that someday I shall laugh at having taken myself so tragically—as many people say they have laughed. I am beginning to see myself a little clearly & to see what things are probable & what improbable in my life. But I don't think I had better go into this & I apologize for merely telling you enough to trouble you a little without perhaps seeing what is up—which of course I do not quite know. It is connected with my work too, the unpleasant tendency being the necessity of producing many books instead of a few & much reviewing. The *Chronicle* & *Morning Post* are taking away my reviewing.[1]

---

[1] See Letter 115, note 5. Between 1903 and 1911 the 'Red Book' preserves an annual average of 120 signed or full-scale reviews. In the second half of 1911 it

The books are mostly not worth telling you about. One—a collection of Celtic tales retold for schools—I have lately finished. The *Maeterlinck*, by the way, ought to be in proof soon & I shall be very glad if you are able to correct the proofs. Thank you for promising. When they come I will send them. Then there is the *Icknield Way* but so far I have only done book work on it.

I am very glad to have your news, especially that you like Criccieth & the country & the sea round about. I hope it is really doing you good. I should like to be there, but my travels for some time must be chiefly in connection with work, especially the Icknield Way (from East Anglia S.W. into Dorset).

I can't remember when I wrote last. But did I tell you Garnett & I were trying to get a small pension for Davies? You have perhaps heard Yeats & Conrad were to have pensions. Davies is not certain yet. We got an interesting lot of signatures, including Bridges. Gosse is helping to get something from the Royal Literary Fund.

I saw Ransome in town. They are thinking of a Chelsea house now, & I suppose they are pretty well off. But I find myself remote from them now, especially from him. I heard about Tabitha & the little Abercrombie. Did you see *Mary & the Bramble*?[1] Rather loose & eloquent, with nice feeling, I thought.

I am falling asleep after a lot of gardening in these warm lovely days. How are they with you? The garden is very crude, but the terrace & the flowers are already pretty. We have some rose-mary—at least I have by my study window. But we hope for a sprig of yours. You should see my wallflowers, the yellow & the darker than blood. We are waiting for the cuckoo. When I see you next I have a Welsh cuckoo song to hum you. I hope that will not be far ahead. By the way, Guthrie was here a month ago. He & I hit it off less, I think. Except in his art he is inarticulate but not silent. We are all well & glad of the new weather I assure you. Goodbye. Give our love to Emily & thank her for writing & ask her to forgive my not writing back. She would not have thanked me had I done so when I ought.

Yours ever Edward Thomas

---

records 34 reviews and only 40 for the whole of 1912, the majority of them from *DC*.

[1] By Lascelles Abercrombie, reviewed (with 5 other volumes of verse) *DC*, 9 August.

117

August 1911   *Wick Green*

My dear Gordon,

Many many thanks.[1] You may be older but you correct proofs
with your youthful perfection. I think I have adopted all your
corrections & suggestions also. I think you will see that I agree
with you about the superiority of the earlier Maeterlinck as you
get on. But I am very sorry to see how much I have allowed my
intense disgust with the later work to give a carping & irritable
tone to what I say about the earlier. I ought to have rewritten it
all but was unaware until too late. But I am more & more oppressed by necessity & *the consciousness of it* & unless I meet some
good fortune things are likely to get even worse. Apparently I
shall have to increase my income yet submit to a decrease in the
price of my work. The only chance is that in the haste & pressure
of much work I may stumble upon myself again & a stronger
self.

Yours ever ET

118

4 August 1911   *Wick Green*

My dear Gordon,

God bless you and I wish I could persuade him to do something
really substantial, such as pay your fare here & keep you well
while you were here. You were mostly right about the French.
—The reason I did not mention *Axël* is that I had not read it. I
tried last year to get a copy without doing the obvious thing—
ordering it at Hachette's & so I did not get it. But the fact is my
knowledge of French literature is all so sketchy—especially
later 19th century—that I couldn't have filled up the gaps by any
conceivable effort for this occasion. So I treat him as if he were an
English author. By the way Sturge Moore's *Mariamne* is about
his best play.[2] He will soon be doing one in prose—I should

---

[1] An omitted brief note (dated 20 July) gives instructions for marking the proofs
of *Maurice Maeterlinck* and mentions that it would be published that autumn along
with *Lafcadio Hearn, Celtic Tales,* and *Isle of Wight.*
[2] Reviewed in *N,* July, and *DC,* 4 September.

think this would be perfect on the stage. No damned poetry about it & yet a very wonderful piece of art.

I look forward to Abercrombie's poem but not to its dedication.[1]

By the way, have you got *Mariamne* because if not you shall have it?

I am writing away furiously at my *Icknield Way*. Half archæology & history. Half guide book. The other half diluted me.[2]

Yours ever & Emily's ET

119

19 September 1911   *'Dolau Cothi Arms', Caermarthenshire*[3]

My dear Gordon,

When I am at Swansea I always get a letter from you & I am sorry I didn't answer it from there last week. But I wrote off at once to Thorpe[4] about the Welsh folklore. I left home nearly 3 weeks ago in rather a worse state than usual.[5] I have been trying to rest but can only do so upright. So I am learning to saunter instead of swinging along as I used to even when tired: It is all the easier because I am so weak. I suppose it is continual slight worry & the accumulation of sins and years that has done it. A breakdown would be far better because it would make rest inevitable.

I wish I knew what 'Welsh metrics amount to'. There is I believe a good deal that Welsh is the only key to: many tales of the princes & their women, for example, in the 'chronicles of the princes'. *The Mabinogion*[6] is the only readable translation of Welsh & even the unreadable—like the *Four Ancient Books of Wales* are few.[7] Shall I send you Marie Trevelyan's collection of

---

[1] Probably *Emblems of Love*, reviewed *DC*, 28 December.
[2] *The Icknield Way* contains a great deal of essay writing in ET's later style. See pp. 100–3, 189–98, 238–48, and 255–63.
[3] The dedication of *The Icknield Way*, to Harry Hooton, was written at this inn.
[4] See page 144, note 3.
[5] *JM*, pp. 171–5 gives a detailed account of this 'breakdown'. E. S. P. Haynes provided the money for ET's much needed holiday.
[6] By Lady Charlotte Guest.
[7] W. F. Skene, *The Four Ancient Books of Wales*, 2 vols., Edinburgh, 1868.

Glamorgan folk stories?[1] These are crude at times but usually quite literal & unpretending. If I hear of the other book of course you would like that first. Probably I shall be home in a week & will call at Thorpe's on my way.

Perhaps I did say something inaccurate about Sturge Moore. Very likely. But I hope I did not imply that poetry could not be naked. I think it can & it was not because it approached nakedness that I thought *Mariamne* near prose. It was only because I found no effect in it which was not the sum of its parts,—I was going to say its words. But how do I know? I have thought & said many fuddled things in this late hurry & worry of many books & a big garden. We are thinking of a cottage & a village school (or an Intermediate school) as a solution—to reduce the necessity for more overproduction.[2] But we are likely to leave it to fate to *compel* us to something in the end.

I have been staying first at Swansea looking at the smoke the chimneys the mountains & the sea & then in a big village with the bard Gwili.[3] I can't imagine what his poetry is like but it might be good. He is in many ways a coarse barbarian outwardly but with a real fineness of spirit as well as a crust of English culture. Oxford in 3 years didn't even teach him to eat silently. It taught him a little Greek & to take his own boots off which his mother or some other woman always used to do. He is 39 & a boy, but fat & scant of breath. I only understand half he says because he laughs continually. He is not the bard in *Rest & Unrest* tho the bard's mother & sister are his mother & sister.[3] It was like my stupidity not to make the thing above his suspicion. He hasn't seen it yet. I wish he had & had ignored or forgiven it.

It is being discussed whether I shall do books on Pater *and* Swinburne *and* Borrow *and* De Quincey. Laugh & then pity me. I both laugh & pity myself. I am also offering to do a book on Wales again, 'not verse now, only prose', i.e. with an honest

[1] Marie Trevelyan, *Folk-Lore and Folk-Stories of Wales*, introduced by E. S. Hartland, 1909, reviewed *DC*, 15 August 1909.
[2] See *WWE*, pp. 143–4.
[3] 'Gwili'—The Rev. John Jenkins (1872–1936), the most distinguished Welsh poet, man of letters, and theologian of his day, was born at Hendy, Pontardulais, and at this time taught at the Gwynfryn School, Ammanford. ET had relations in both places; his friendship with Gwili began in 1897. Cf. *Rest and Unrest*, pp. 49–92 and E. Cefni Jones, *Gwili, Cofiant a Phregethau*, Llandysul, 1937.

topographical basis. My *Icknield Way* has been the stepping stone to this possibility. More than half of it is quite literal & open to everyone to check.[1] *Eheu! fugaces*, Gordon, my Gordon, —but that is only half sincere. I am really beginning to see myself. I suppose it is a good thing. Will mystery or the light of common day succeed to the mist that used to seem mystery?

My love to you & Emily ET

Don't write here. I am walking about while the fine weather lasts, with nothing but comb, toothbrush, maps, & Shakespeare's *Histories*.

120

30 October 1911   *Wick Green*

My dear Emily,

I was not glad to see your handwriting because I guessed (as it turns out, rightly) that Gordon could not write. But thank you for writing & putting everything so full & clear. I think if you had been quite in favour of Wall Nook[2] I sh^d have come but as it is I think I shall go to Wales. I wish I c^d have seen a lot of you & Gordon but from your account I might have been grieviously disappointed for sometime. So as I say I don't think I will come. Probably I shall go down to a tiny seaside town I visited in August in Caermarthenshire called Laugharne (& pronounced Larne) & see what I can find there. I hope I shan't regret your nice farm people too much. I know I sh^d be well looked after where you recommended me but it is a plunge I don't like into a strange Welsh (half Welsh) town on a rainy November afternoon looking very lean & cold & very much like the teetotaller & non-smoker I have become. I am glad Gordon is so brave. I never c^d pity him he will be glad to hear, & please don't you think me unkind to say it. You have pitied me before this I dare say. Goodbye & I will write again when I have got settled into my book & my lodgings.

[1] Its basic conception is that of a ten-day bicycle journey with a careful description of places along the route.

[2] In an omitted note (dated 26 October 1911) ET had asked about the possibility of spending a recuperative holiday near GB at a farm called 'Wall Nook'.

With love from Helen & me to you both (I paused, almost changing my mind)

Yours ever Edward Thomas

P.S. On 2nd or 22nd thoughts I am so much tempted that if I positively knew I could come to that farm you speak of on Wednesday or Thursday I believe I would. But will you get this tomorrow (Tuesday)? If you do & c^d telegraph 'Yes' I should most likely come. I am so hesitating that I shan't expect you to do this but shall hope. I will reply, *if I am coming*, on Wednesday morning by wire & tell you my train. Don't you trouble in any case to say *No*. You might in your telegram say 'Yes Wednesday' (or 'Thursday').[1]

121

4 November 1911   c/o *Mrs. Wilkins, Victoria St., Llaugharne,*
                                                    Caermarthenshire

Dear Emily,

Thank you very much for your letter. It made me wish again that I had not been in such a hurry. But the fact is I meant to begin my book *before* the end of October.[2] Then came the offer which made it possible to get away & I was itching to begin— not from love of the thing but from a simple desire to prove to myself once more that I could begin a long task. Well I have begun & my wrist is sore with it after 3 days. I got lodgings here on Thursday & am quite satisfied. The woman is kind & not too inquisitive. She gets the freshest of fish & I have perfect silence & the estuary on which Llaugharne & its castle stand is very noble, guarded by two wooded cliffy headlands & far away south east is the mountainous outline of Gower & Worms Head. I don't know anybody here. But I get out for 2 or 3 hours a day & try not to overwork. I should have been wretched company for Gordon at present. I have not a spark of life except what gets into my fountain pen. Still, if only I could look in. If I get on well with my work & feel that a change would not upset it I may come near you yet: or if not before Christmas—when I shall

---

[1] An omitted note from London (dated 31 October) shows that he decided to go to Wales.

[2] *George Borrow*, 1912; ET's first book for Chapman and Hall.

probably go home—then afterwards. I hope Gordon will be getting through his stages as easily & quickly as possible. It is a pity he is not better fitted for the world & the world not better fitted for me. Ask him when he is better please to tell me *something* to say about Borrow. Please! Goodbye & blame or thank my wrist for giving way so soon.

Yours ever Edward Thomas

122

Christmas 1911   *Wick Green*

My dear Gordon,

I am sorry to be sending you the greeting today that ought already to have reached you, especially as William Davies who is spending Christmas here was speaking of you as very ill. We hope his news is very old: it came through Guthrie. Of course I owed you & Emily one when I was at Laugharne. I was away 7 weeks & when I was not working at Borrow I was out—chiefly in rain. I kept quiet & free from the blacks except when one of Helen's letter days passed letterless. Also I finished or brought to an end the book on Borrow. Then I couldn't rest any longer in the place where I had been writing the whole of the time I was indoors & so I came home on Tuesday, & am now watching & being watched to see how much better I am. I am a skeleton light bronzed in appearance.

But how are you? I am half glad there is no letter from you today for the childish reason that it seems to excuse *me*; but more than half sorry because it may mean you are ill. Guthrie says nothing but sends me a print of someone weeping.

Have you heard of the *Poetry Review* edited by Harold Monro —a nice fellow in sympathy with advanced thought & has publi- shed a book of verse?[1] They are asking for an article by me on Davies gratis.[2] The usual thing. It will die at the 5th or 6th

---

[1] Harold Monro and Arundel del Re, joint editors of *Poetry Review*, were among the group called together by Edward Marsh on 20 September 1911 which led to the publication of *Georgian Poetry 1911–12*. See Christopher Hassall, *A Biography of Edward Marsh*, 1959, and Richard Stonesifer, *W. H. Davies, A Critical Biography*, 1963.

[2] *Poetry Review*, February 1912, has an unsigned review of Davies's poetry.

number unregretted except by Poets whose circulation was guaranteed by the Poetry Society to reach 1,000. A home for incurables, I feel sure, but it gives Monro employment, a sense of usefulness, the use of a typewriter & possibly some pocket money, but I should think not.

I have just offered to write for Methuen[1] a book on the Court Life of Charles II. Don't betray the subject in case of rivalry. I shall be equally sorry whether he accepts the offer or not. I have vainly offered books on Milton & others & am hesitating about one on Our Lord whose birthday we are celebrating today.

How good the *Sicilian Idyll* & *Judith* are,[2] almost Miltonic but with no Miltonism except in the learned building of the line.

Give me some subjects, please. I have exhausted the *Dictionary of National Biography* almost. Suggest some person not literary whom I might make something of.

I shall send you my *Hearn* but the *Maeterlinck* was not worth while. M himself wrote me a comically extravagant complimentary letter. The man is nothing but wind. His command of language is dreadful.

Helen & I send you our love—Emily & you—& wish we could sometimes walk over the hills to you. I may yet come your way to do my book on Pater.[3] I should like to contest it chapter by chapter with you.

I am yours ever Edward Thomas

123

22 March 1912   *Stow on the Wold, Gloucestershire*

My dear Gordon,

I was very glad indeed when your letter caught me up just as I was starting on a short walk. I had been thinking of you daily wondering whether to write, knowing well you must be ill. It didn't seem worth while as I was always either busy at Pater & good for nothing else or contending with my usual devils. I

---

[1] The publisher of *Maurice Maeterlinck*.
[2] T. Sturge Moore, *A Sicilian Idyll and Judith*, reviewed *SR*, 20 January 1912, and *DC*, (along with Rupert Brooke, *Poems*) 9 April 1912.
[3] *Walter Pater*, 1913.

was not reborn in Wales. Work is the only thing though when I am at it I don't invariably realize it especially as it's always in a hurry. I roughly finished a book on Pater last Sunday: am keeping it by me to tone it down for a few weeks. I am going to write on Swinburne.[1] Probably I told you. I brought away *Songs before Sunrise* but at the end of a day's walking can make nothing of it. I am travelling from Cirencester along the Fosse Way to Stratford Warwick & Coventry, where I am to spend a day or two. I did think of rushing up to see you, but the strike & increasing irregularity of trains seems to forbid it. If I don't come I will send you some of my works but they are very numerous now. I have just corrected proofs of *Norse Tales*.[2] *Borrow, Hearn* & *Icknield Way* impend. *Celtic Tales* please Mervyn & Bronwen. They are exercises in English, only. I am only just learning how ill my notes have been making me write by all but destroying such natural rhythm as I have in me. Criticising Pater has helped the discovery.[3] But it is too late now, in these anxious & busy times, to set about trying to write better than perhaps I was born to. You have some advantages over me after all. Fancy being able to write those verses for music. I think they have the just nakedness for words to be sung, & I wish I could hear them. Tell me who was the foundress. Now if I had any *time*. No, I will say what I might—but should not—do if I had time, which is impossible. However, when I have exhausted the books which publishers & I can seem to agree on,—& that will not be very far hence,—I may find myself with Time. Stow on the Wold is perfectly silent after a day of wind & rain, except the choir practising in the church over the way. It is a little stone town on a slope & summit of the Cotswolds & looks far away east over floods & red ploughland. I wish I were not so tired. I will keep this over another day's walking. Goodnight.

Chance has brought me to Stratford upon Avon where it is evident Shakespeare once lived & is not alive now. I shall leave it to the tradespeople tho I am too tired to walk beyond it tonight. I wonder what a man would do here who was not afflicted by the spectacle of trade? It has been a beautiful warm

[1] *A. C. Swinburne, a Critical Study*, 1912.

[2] *Norse Tales*, 1912.

[3] ET's changing attitude to prose rhythms—a clear anticipation of his own poetry long before he had met Robert Frost—is shown quite clearly in *Walter Pater*, p. 109 ff. and p. 219.

day but I have been walking on my nerves all the time & am fit
for bed and not letterwriting.

'Glory to Man in the Highest! for Man is the master of things!'

says Swinburne. I shall have to discover what that amounts to.
Can you recommend me to some sane admirer on whom I can
sharpen my wits? Somehow I have fallen into a habit of abusing
literature for not being what it was never meant to be, & it won't
do me or the public any good I expect, especially as it probably
originates in personal disgusts of an irrelevant kind which I
ought to be getting over in silence & not in print.[1] Coining
everything into hasty words is I suppose the punishment as well
as the living of a journalist. Is it lifelong, too?

I wish I had been listening to Rathbone & not a cheap & outworn gramophone. It would have been worth *my* money, Emily.

Goodbye, and please write as soon as you can. I am yours &
Emily's ever

Edward Thomas

124

18 April 1912   *Manor House*

My dear Gordon,

Thank you for your book.[2] It has reached me at a Manor
House on the Somerset border where I am staying with Clifford
Bax and a doctor, a friend of his.[3] This doctor is working magic
with my disordered intellects & in a few hours I shall be better
able to enjoy *Chambers of Imagery II* than ever before. I shall have
something like your own courage—I hope it is not painful to you
to be reminded of this at a time when you have needed it all so
long. But there is such a continuous flow of talk here & of outdoor adventures to Bath &c. that I cant read anything. I leave on
Saturday & shall take the book with me home. Soon I shall be

---

[1] A reference to Wilfrid Wilson Gibson, *Fires*, Book I, reviewed *DC*, 9 March, and
The Second Book of the Poets' Club, *DC*, 19 April.

[2] GB, *Chambers of Imagery*, Second Series.

[3] The doctor was Godwin Baynes. See *JM*, pp. 181-2 and Eleanor Farjeon,
Edward Thomas: The Last Four Years, pp. 3-4.

hard at work on *Swinburne* but when it is over I may quite possibly get up to you. If anything occurs to you about Swinburne & your hand will hold a pen—do let me know. Goodbye. I hope the Spring will be as kind to you as to me. Here it has been perfect for a week. Give my love to Emily. I am ever yours & hers

Edward Thomas

125

1 September 1912   *Wick Green*

My dear Gordon,

Thank you for your letter. I didn't mean it to wear out a month in my pocket hither & thither before I wrote back. But first I went to Clifford Bax's & pretended to play cricket with 10 others for a week, nice people & moderate cricketers. Then Mervyn & I went bicycling through Sussex & Kent & saw de la Mare & W. H. Davies & V. Locke Ellis[1] (don't you like his poem in *Root & Branch*?) Since then I have been typing a little book on *The Country*[2] I have done for a new series & expecting work which never comes. Now I am going to look for it in London & then spend 5 or 6 days in Swansea collecting more impressions for an essay on the town which *The English Review* will be good enough to look at.[3] I suppose the Winter will come as usual & that something will have happened by then or will seem like happening. I am at present only wondering what will happen. Evidently I can't get a living by writing, unless I content myself with far less than I have got used to. Personally I could, but the children's schooling &c. makes a great change hard until it is compulsory. Well & I don't know what to think of apart from writing. I occasionally allow my mind to wonder towards some such thing as canvassing for advertisements & similar occupations for superfluous people, but not quite seriously yet. Now & then I remember that I am 34 & ought to stand alone, help myself & keep silent, but I really still feel as I did 12 years ago that people ought to help or might help me to solve my difficulties although I have no claims (has anyone?) &

[1] Vivian Locke Ellis, *The Venturers and other Poems*, reviewed *ER*, May 1913.
[2] *The Country*, 1913.
[3] Reprinted in *The Last Sheaf*, 1928, pp. 151–66.

although I know that it is really impossible to help the helpless except by a substantial legacy.

However, will the Winter bring you near Dorking? If so I shall come over & try to persuade you to come to us. I look forward to it, so does Helen. Tell us when you are coming & where you are to be found. If I cycle to town as I do now when it is fine I can take Dorking on my way.

With our love to you & Emily

Yours ever Edward Thomas

126

31 October 1912   *Wick Green*

My dear Gordon,

Thank you for Emily's letter. Helen & I were thinking of you and Holmbury just now so I must send you a word. The month has not been good for letters because I have always been either busy or anxious.[1] Now, however, things are a little better & for the moment I see that I can keep going. We have nearly settled to move in the Spring—into a new labourer's cottage that will just hold us with half our furniture. I may keep my hilltop study but the chances are I shall fix myself alone in London for about half the year. It seems necessary partly to ensure work & partly to give Helen peace, since I am a mere nuisance & a considerable one when I am working & rather worse when I have no work to do. Just now I have got some reviewing again.[2] What is more I have started a fiction! It is a loose affair held together if at all by an oldish suburban home, half memory, half fancy, and a Welsh family (mostly memory) inhabiting it & collecting a number of men & boys including some I knew when I was from ten to fifteen. The scheme allows me to use all memories up to

---

[1] In a brief omitted note (dated 25 September 1912) he writes: 'I am up and down between here and London looking for work and doing the little I can get.'

[2] Despite his earlier fears about his chance of work in the much altered literary pages of *DC*, ET continued as a regular (almost weekly) reviewer, principally of nature books and modern verse. I have been unable to detect any unsigned reviews by him in *The New Age*, which was generally critical of ET's books, but there are many short unsigned articles by him in *N* and *ER*. At this time, too, *DN* began to employ him as a critic of modern poetry.

the age of 20 & so far I have indulged myself freely.[1] I feel
however that it will be better than isolated essays & sketches,
each helping the other, & the same characters reappearing; & more
honest than the other pseudo-continuous books I have written.
I hope it will get finished or drafted before the year is out.

I look forward eagerly to hearing that you are at Holmbury.
I recall the turnings out of the Portsmouth Road to Ockley & try
to invent a place for you among the pine trees. De la Mare
stayed once at Ockley I remember. He is a too busy man now,
reading for Heinemann & reviewing multifariously & never
quite unpuckering in our scanty meetings. I shall try to get you
& him to meet though, & you would like Locke Ellis too,[2] who
has a nice young rich wife & an old house near East Grinstead
now & is amusing himself with a picture shop in the Adelphi.
Clifford Bax is 100 miles away near Bath but just off to Siena.[3]
He is a local magnet, cricketer, theosophist, and an amusing
talker who knows poetry because he likes it. He will probably
never write any. He edits an occultish quarterly—*Orpheus*—
which Cecil French contributes to, & also his brother Arnold
Bax, a most excellent pianist & composer, who writes verse &
stories under the name of Dermot O'Byrne.

Goodbye & I hope to hear good news of you before long. You
must have enjoyed the good parts of September & October. I
only watched them. With our love to you & Emily

Ever yours Edward Thomas

*   *   *

*After a worse breakdown than usual in April 1909, I had been ill
again and again, haemorrhages every few months, until there seemed
no end to it all. Especially, I seemed to be laid up all Winter: we
all felt something had to be done, and the only thing feasible at the
time seemed to be to try Wintering in the South.*

*Our friends Mr. and Mrs. Robert Trevelyan, hearing this, sug-
gested we should use their house on Leith Hill in Surrey, which would
otherwise be nearly empty, as Mr. Trevelyan was going to the Far
East, and Mrs. Trevelyan was to be abroad too. So we trans-*

---

[1] *The Happy-Go-Lucky Morgans*, 1913.

[2] See Letter 125, note 1, and *JM*, p. 184 ff. Locke Ellis's conventional sonnet
sequence in memory of ET is in R. P. Eckert, *These Things the Poets Said* and in
In Memoriam: Edward Thomas, No. 2, *Green Pasture Series*, 1919.

[3] See Clifford Bax, *Some I Knew Well*, 1951, pp. 177–89.

planted ourselves from the end of October 1912 until April 1913.
While there ET visited us at intervals; and my wife went to the
Petersfield house, while I was never able to undertake the journey. GB

*   *   *

127

November 1912   *Wick Green*

My dear Emily,

Thank you. At any rate it is fixed that I come to you on
Wednesday next week. Probably Helen can't but if she can she
will. If it is fine I shall ride, but in case it is not I shall be glad
of the lift up as Mrs. Trevelyan will have the cart down at
Gomshall. On Thursday, however, I ought to leave soon after
breakfast, as I must arrange to see somebody or another that
day in London. If the car does come—you will let me know the
chances—I shall be glad. I hope Gordon will fall in love with the
Liphook country on his way & become inseparable. It would
please us very much. Till next Wednesday I have to write about
poetry & colonial poetry: also Harold Monro is coming down
for the weekend, who although he sells poets is really no better
than a poet himself.[1] I rather envy you Sturge Moore.[2]—I hope
Gordon isn't become too classic to like Lawrence.[3] Still, in any
case, my love to him & to you & Helen's also.

Yours ever Edward Thomas

128

5 December 1912   *At Selfsfield House, East Grinstead*

My dear Gordon,

Are you at the Shiffolds now? I have thought many times of

[1] A reference to Monro's Poetry Bookshop. Like Vivian Locke Ellis, Monro was a
member of the group of literary friends of ET and Garnett who met at St. George's
Restaurant in St. Martin's Lane. See *Georgian Poetry, 1911–12*, reviewed *DC*, 14
January 1913.

[2] T. Sturge Moore was GB's neighbour while the latter stayed in Surrey at The
Shiffolds, R. C. Trevelyan's house on Leith Hill.

[3] D. H. Lawrence, *Love Poems and Others*, reviewed *DC*, February 1913, and *B*,
April 1913.

you in these 2 months since I came here to live with Vivian Locke Ellis. And I should have written except that my letters have been getting worse & worse. In fact for 3 months I have been advertising my sorrows & decimating my friends. Briefly this year has been a bad one. I have gone down. I have had less & less work. My habit of introspection & self contempt has at last broken my spirit. Intense irritability made life intolerable in a cottage where I could not suffer without making 4 others suffer with me.[1] So I left home in October & came here as a boarder at Ellis's house for a start, & have worked moderately well & had cloistered days. A couple of days at home were enough to tumble me down again to an abject state from which I am now getting up. Helen & the children come here for Christmas. Tell me when if at all you can see me, supposing you are at the Shiffolds. I am not so bad to meet as to have letters from, as a rule. The thing is to avoid self discussion. In any case forgive what there was to forgive in my last letter & tell me how you & Emily are & believe that such of me as remains is

Ever yours ET

129

Christmas-time 1912   *Wick Green*
Friday

My dear Gordon,

 Thank you. I shall gladly carry the 100 Best Latin poems from Gordon Bottomley about with me until they or I get worn out.[2] I hope my parcel didn't bring pure gloom to you.[3] If not I will send another soon. And I will come myself before very long: I can't quite say when. I hope you are out of bed. Yet what could you do if you were? The rain up here is incredible. It is like living before the creation, like the Niflheim[4] that men ultimately

---

[1] For this sudden return of ET's melancholia, and his recovery, see *JM*, pp. 196–7, 202–4, 319–23.

[2] No such anthology by GB was ever published.

[3] An omitted note (dated November 1912) refers to his sending a volume by Robert Bridges and 'this *Swinburne*'.

[4] The underworld and abode of the dead in Scandinavian mythology. ET's interest in Old Icelandic poetry and saga was fed by his personal attachment to F. York Powell (at Oxford), by his own special study of William Morris, and by the interest shared in these topics with GB and E. Garnett.

emerged from:—when will they come? —We expect Davies today some time from Wales unless Swansea's defeat of the South Africans has been too much for him.[1] —I wish I could have your hunting *Pleur du cerf* out of the woods below us. Goodbye —a great while ago the world began & still the rain it raineth every day. With our love to Emily & yourself.

Ever yours Edward Thomas

130

26 February 1913   *c/o Clifford Bax*
but just going home

My dear Gordon,

Shall I be able to see you next week, on Thursday for example?

I have been away nearly 3 weeks bicycling & walking over Wiltshire & Somersetshire as far as Glastonbury, & taking copious medicine. I had a foggy week & a frosty week & now the rain's back & I may have to take a train home. Probably I shall not have my bicycle with me on Thursday if I come to you. I hope you have been able to enjoy some things. We hope Emily will come before March is over. April most of us expect to spend at a Norfolk cottage we have been invited to. We have not arranged to do anything with our house for that month & it occurs to me it might suit you to have it part of the time: I think the servant too would be at your disposal.[2]

With love to Emily

Yours ever Edward Thomas

131

7 May 1913   *Wick Green*

My dear Gordon,

I hope all is well with you & Emily.[3] I ought to have written

---

[1] At Rugby Football.

[2] Eventually Herbert and Eleanor Farjeon stayed at Wick Green and gave a typically extended Georgian house-party to their friends. See *EF*, p. 7 ff.

[3] The Bottomleys had now returned to the north of England. An omitted note

before but have filled my days with writing & much seeing of people & exhaustion etc. Now I am just going home to finish the book. Everyone has been away at the seaside & we shall like seeing one another again. My visit to London has brought no work. But I have some to go on with—another booklet for Batsford on *Ecstasy*.[1] Now that is why I write to you this moment,—to ask you to put me on to some books or poems or stories throwing light on rapture & man's belief at various times that something can clear things up for him without the immediate help of the intellect. The subject is endless but any references will be valuable.

The book (on the journey) will not be finished much before the end of June. After that I shall try to come to you, & I hope you will be able to have me if I can.

Goodbye.

Yours & Emily's ever Edward Thomas

132

Wick Green

9 June 1913

My dear Gordon,

I am glad to hear from you. I was afraid of worse news as you didn't write. But I am so wretched both as letter writer & as cause of letter writing in others. Since I wrote last I haven't done anything to improve, because I have written and rewritten or typed all my book.[2] It isn't a book, but you know what I mean. And so I should like to come to you. BUT. This isn't rhetoric tho I haven't wrung the beast's neck yet. The fact is we may be moving rather soon.[3] Just at this moment I am not very full of

(dated 7 April 1913) states that ET had left Norfolk for London to continue his work and had stayed with A. M. Freeman while preparing *In Pursuit of Spring* for the press.

[1] Intended for Batsford's *Fellowship Series*. See *EF*, p. 43: 'Also I meant to type *Ecstasy*. I did a third, then soberly and finally decided it was mostly muck and so ill-arranged that it could not be rewritten.'

[2] *In Pursuit of Spring*, 1914.

[3] The move to a much smaller semi-detached house in the village, Yewtree Cottage, took place in August; it was close to Bedales where Merfyn and Bronwen were day scholars. See *WWE*, pp. 143–6 and *EF*, pp. 13–14. These notes cannot

work & I do want a change. Could I come, say, early next week? I am not sure that I can but if you can have me I may discover that I can. If you can & if you know any train I ought to take please tell me.

I don't know about Guthrie. But I should think he would just be back.

The other day I was asked to do *Homes & Haunts of Words-worth* for an atrocious price, suitable for a young lady author living with her family. That might draw me near the homes & haunts of my dear Gordon. But I shall not accept this atrocious [price], never, well hardly ever, perhaps not till next year, if Fate continues thus.

I'm selling books in order to fit into our little cottage &c. Do any of these appeal to you particularly? There is a good deal of French too, Gautier, Hugo, France, Daudet, Ronsard. Please return the list when you write.

I agree about Douglas & Ransome.[1] Douglas must be ¾ mad & ought not to have been allowed to victimize Ransome— They say he was really aiming at Ross.

Shall I come? Give my love to Emily please

Yours ever Edward Thomas

133

Mid-June 1913   *Wick Green*
Sunday

My dear Gordon,
    I am sorry.[2] Yesterday I started on a long bicycle ride to a friend but gave it up exhausted & dispirited a third of the way &

---

include all the cross-references to ET's letters printed in *EF* which contains a minute account of ET's movements until his death in so far as they affect Eleanor Farjeon.

[1] Arthur M. Ransome, *Oscar Wilde, A Critical Study*, 1912, occasioned a legal action by Lord Alfred Douglas against the book. However, Methuen reprinted the book in their Shilling Library in 1913. I have been unable to trace a review by ET.
[2] An omitted note and a telegram (both dated 13 June) refer to this unsuccessful attempt to visit Cartmel. See *EF*, p. 13, for ET's acute state of indecision and self-consciousness at this time.

sent that telegram to you among other things. It was the beginning of a period when I can't make up my mind to be away from
home although for many reasons it is then the worst place for
me. However I need not explain this but only tell you I am very
sorry to have involved you as well as others in what should
concern only myself. I will try to come in July instead. When I
hear that you would like *Ancient Irish Poetry*[1] I will send it with
Aglavaine & Séleysette. No hurry, & if I don't hear before I will
bring them down with me.—My telegram at any rate arrived
before my letter I hope.

Yours & Emily's abjectly ET

134

2 August 1913   *Steep, Petersfield*

My dear Gordon,

I am only very sorry you weren't able to write.[2] Even had you
been well my letters invited a return but didn't exactly provoke
or inspire or facilitate one. I will not be such a nuisance again
just yet, as I am at last realizing I had better fight my battles
instead of sending out lists of the opposing forces &c. Things
have gone ill & better again—no work, no unusual strength, but
a better equilibrium & a certain amount of gain from various
studies in Mysticism & Mental Science—browsings, not studies.
We have moved & are now fairly fitted into our narrow quarters
to everyone's satisfaction.[3] The children are home for 8 weeks
holiday & we have begun with bicycle rides, an excursion to
Goodwood Races & so on.[4] I go away tomorrow for a few days
riding west. Then from 16th to 23rd Mervyn & I are guests at a
houseboat on the Broads.[5] The end of the month the two elder
children & I will be near Guthrie probably, the cottage shut up
& Helen in Switzerland with Irene.[6] I was to have done a book on

---

[1] The omitted note contains the offer of Kuno Meyer, *Selections from Ancient Irish Poetry*, reviewed *DC*, 4 August 1911, and, presumably, Alfred Sutro's translation of Maeterlinck's *Aglavaine and Sélysette*.

[2] An omitted note (dated 27 June) to Emily Bottomley refers to GB's illness.

[3] Yewtree Cottage in the village of Steep.

[4] 'In The Crowd At Goodwood', *The Last Sheaf*, pp. 173–84.

[5] With Gertrude and Stacy Aumonier and Eleanor Farjeon. See *EF*, pp. 155 ff.

[6] Helen's sister, Irene MacArthur.

Homes & Haunts of writers but didn't want to & the terms were atrocious & I refused: it could hardly be well done. My fiction appears early in Autumn & might help me. . . .[1]

I don't want you to *buy Aglavaine* but to keep it. And I am pleased to have given you Kuno Meyer.

Perhaps September will see us together. If not I shall ride up to the Shiffolds gladly some Autumn day.

I sent on the letter to de la Mare. He was very much run down & fine drawn when I last saw him a fortnight ago & will have been glad of a greeting from you. Helen & I send our love to you both & hope you can enjoy the sun.

Yours ever Edward Thomas

*   *   *

Our wintering in Surrey in 1912–1913 was so successful that our friends there suggested we should return to them for the worst months of the following Winter. We were at their house on Leith Hill again from November 1913 to early February 1914—returning North then to arrange for our removal from Cartmel to our present residence at Silverdale at the head of Morecambe Bay.

ET visited us again on Leith Hill while we were with Mr. and Mrs. Trevelyan. Our nearness and meetings (we met in London, too, during our journeys) account in some degree for the absence of letters about this time: but I suspect that letters of his during that time were mislaid and lost, on account of my being away from home and unable to add them to the main store as they arrived and were answered. And others may have been mislaid during our removal.

Our last days that we spent with Edward in Surrey were untroubled by any suspicion of what 1914 was to come to mean: as indeed the particularly riant and happy visit which he paid to us in our new house in July was.

After Edward went, Paul Nash arrived:[2] and he too left us without any of us realizing what the threats were which were darkening the horizon.

After Edward moved into the small cottage near Bedales he was always restless and off on new journeys, and his letters were irregular, spasmodic, and unsettled: while I, on my side, was oftener ill and

---

[1] *The Happy-Go-Lucky Morgans.*

[2] See *Poet and Painter. Being the correspondence between Gordon Bottomley and Paul Nash 1910–1946*, edited by C. C. Abbott and Anthony Bertram, 1953.

unable to write. These things explain our correspondence reflecting more the doings and moods of the moment, and rarely settling down to its earlier adventures among ideas and authors.[1] *The coming of the War intensified this, until Edward had made his final choice and enlisted: then his new power to write brought back days that were among the happiest for both of us, and this fruitful tranquillity was unbroken until the shell broke it. GB*

*   *   *

135

22 May 1914   *Steep*

My dear Gordon,

This is chiefly to ask you if you will be free early in July because Helen & I may very likely take a week's holiday then & come to you for part of the time—if you are free.

I hope you are liking the new house, but I haven't heard.[2] I meant to have written 2 months ago. But I returned home before the end of February & worked hard.[3] Then all April I was away chiefly with Mervyn & Bronwen in Wales & near Robert Frost in Herefordshire—also near Abercrombie & Gibson by the way.[4] And now I am again working hard, mostly at uncalled for little Welsh pictures, of a plain perhaps lucid kind, in my later manner, if it is a manner.[5] So I have my usual excuses for not writing anything but a request for news of you & Emily. At least I hope you will be well enough to write but too busy enjoying the sun to do more than say so. Let it be done quickly.

[1] For this gap in the letters to GB, when ET first read Robert Frost's poetry and then met the American (in February 1914 at the Locke Ellises), see *JM*, pp. 199–206, *EF*, pp. 18–141, and Robert P. Eckert, *Edward Thomas* (hereafter referred to as *RPE*) pp. 128–48.

[2] The Sheiling, Silverdale.

[3] ET had been staying at Selsfield House, East Grinstead, with Vivian Locke Ellis. Helen and the children joined him there for Christmas 1913 and then, in the New Year, moved on to stay with Helen's sister at Chiswick. ET spent part of February at the Hammersmith town house of Clifford Bax. See *EF*, pp. 55–60.

[4] Frost had left America for England in September 1913 and stayed at The Bungalow, Reynolds Road, Beaconsfield, until 25 March 1914 when he moved to Ledington where his neighbours were Lascelles Abercrombie and Wilfrid Gibson.

[5] Some of the 'little Welsh pictures' are included in the posthumous *The Last Sheaf* and *Cloud Castle and other Papers*.

At this moment I am expecting a telegram from Guthrie to say he is at home, & if so I shall cycle over. I don't want to waste every one of these glorious days in writing. He is busy, I believe. He meant to go to town to seek work but seems to have put it off.

I found Abercrombie curiously like Ransome in some ways—I liked him. But he doesn't look well & I should say takes no care of himself & is not quite the kind of man that needn't & will get along somehow without. Gibson & I are too conscious of what we used to think of one another.[1] I like his later work, but temperately. What imbeciles the Imagistes are.[2] I think Frost will do something. In fact he has done already. One or two things in his first book were very good.[3] I have seen a lot of him. But I can't gossip on paper. So goodbye—forgive this unseemly ending at the bottom of a page. With love to Emily

Yours ever ET

136

24 May 1914   *Steep*

My dear Gordon,

The letter came a little after you were receiving mine & I was glad. I noticed R. H. Law's book being acknowledged & will cock the right sort of eye at it if it comes to Steep.[4] The difficulty of Davies is greater. I have said the true thing perhaps twice in print—he thought it meant hostility tho I personally thought it would do him & me good that our position was not the blind adorer & the blind adored. You can't talk to Davies except personal talk. He pretends to understand but doesn't & goes on his way.[5]

[1] See W. W. Gibson, *Akra, the slave*, reviewed *DC*, 9 August 1911 and especially Gibson, *Fires, Book I*, reviewed *DC*, 9 March 1912: 'At the end of the book we have the feeling that after all, he has merely been embellishing what would have been more effective as pieces of rough prose, extracts from a diary, or even a newspaper. The verse has added nothing except unreality, perhaps, not even brevity.'

[2] *Des Imagistes: An anthology*, reviewed *DN*, July 1914.

[3] Robert Frost, *North of Boston*, reviewed *DN*, July 1914, and *ER*, August 1914. 'First book' probably refers to *A Boy's Will*, reviewed *The New Weekly* (date uncertain) and, possibly, in *A*, 20 September 1913.

[4] R. H. Law, *Moorland Sanctuary and other Poems*, 1914.

[5] For a just appraisal of ET and W. H. Davies see R. J. Stonesifer, *W. H. Davies: A Critical Biography*, 1963.

I have been reconsidering & it seems to me the best thing would be for me to come about June 13 for a week, or perhaps a little earlier, the 10th. Helen & I are to have such a little time together that we couldn't manage more than such a few days North that I thought this plan better, tho it robs her of a very long desired pleasure. Now if I may come on the 10th or 13th may I do a morning's work? I get about so much now that if I don't work a little and everywhere I get behind.[1]

Well I saw Guthrie. He did complain a lot. It is partly habit, for I gather that he can still enjoy idle days with the boys which is a very good sign indeed, I think—if he could not I don't see how he would survive that household long.

Ever yours & Emily's Edward Thomas

137

29 May 1914   *Steep*

My dear Gordon,

Then I shall most likely come on the 13th & hope to find you recovered from Whitsun. But Helen can't come then & later on when we are together we shall have too little time, or that is what we should have done. She is sorry & I expect will write to Emily. Frost's book is out & some things I have read in it are excellent.[2] His getting back to pure speech rhythms is going to do good & to provoke the Noyeses among bards & critics.[3] I hope you will see the book—& if you approve could you issue an order to Marsh?[3]

Yours & Emily's ever Edward Thomas

[1] For ET's movements see *RPE* and *EF*. His principal work at this time was the preparation of 'Homes and Haunts of English Writers' which was later published as *A Literary Pilgrim in England*. Certainly his anthology *This England* benefited from this intensive preparation. During this period, too, ET's significant and little-known reviews of modern poetry were appearing in *SR*, *B*, *DN* and, I think, *ER*.

[2] *North of Boston*. The beginning and end of ET's *DN* review is quoted in *EF*, pp. 77–8: the valuable central comment on specific lines is omitted.

[3] Alfred Noyes and Edward Marsh.

138

27 June 1914   *Coventry*

My dear Gordon,

We are just leaving Frost's & on way round towards home again.[1] Just the same weather has pursued me here, as I had with you. I did enjoy those few long days. I carried your message to de la Mare & some of your criticism to Frost, which did not prevent him from saying how much he admired *Mrs Lear*.[2] He has been reading or seeing it somewhere. He puts it above Abercrombie's *End of the World* for example. By the way, if this does not make you too vain, don't forget to send me those poems typed to *Steep*. I will try & remember to get an opinion about 'copyright by T. Mosher' when I get home.

I won't send you my *T.P.'s Weekly* article,[3] but the badness of it proves how much I enjoyed my time with you because when I am really enjoying friends I never can write. However, I do not make you responsible.

On Tuesday we went to the Russian ballet & heard Strauss's *Joseph*. I suspect the music was not good. Anyhow I did not like it, & the ballet itself was a failure. The story outline was not simple & significant enough for the dancers to do much with it. *Papillons*, founded on Schumann, was very charming—a Pierrot story of 1830. *Thamar* I expect you know—an Eastern Carpet set to music. We hope to go again next Tuesday.

We saw Rupert Brooke at Gibson's on Wednesday, browner & older & better looking after his tour.[4] Yesterday we saw the 4 Abercrombies! Ezra Pound has tried to honour himself by challenging Abercrombie to a duel. He tries to make believe he is in Provence, I suppose. Won't you make the epigram founded on the fact that his father was Homer Pound & his wife a Miss Shakespeare? With our love to you & Emily

Yours ever Edward Thomas

1 Helen and ET had spent a few days walking in Ledington—via an evening at the ballet in London—finding holiday accommodation for the summer. They went on to Coventry where their ex-Bedales friends, C. and F. Hodson, lived.

2 GB's play, *King Lear's Wife*, first published in *Georgian Poetry 1913–15*, which also included Lascelles Abercrombie's play, *The End of the World*.

3 'How I Began', reprinted in *The Last Sheaf*, pp. 15–20.

4 Wilfrid Gibson's house at Greenway in Herefordshire. See Christopher Hassall, *Rupert Brooke/A Biography*, 1964.

139

7 July 1914   *Steep*

My dear Gordon,

I thank you & am very sorry for Emily. I thought you had a typewriter & foreseeing the hurry which is now in progress (so to speak) I presumed to suggest a copy from you. Please tell her how sorry I am. I will write to Mathews. At present I think of using all three poems.[1] I just remembered about *The Riding to Lithend* & have seen that my copy has some colour on the title page & I think that is all. Is that as it should be? And looking on my shelves I came upon *Chamber of Imagery II*[2] which makes me want 'Eager Spring' & 'When Robert put the seed in', or at least the first. May I? Don't hurry to answer unless it is No.

Pound merely said something like 'Your stupidity now amounts to a public insult' & 'My seconds will wait on you'. Whether Abercrombie had trounced the Imagists I don't know, but I fancy not. Ezra has long been antipathetic to his betters.

Yes I told Frost both sides of your view. For my part he does so much that I have perhaps overlooked what he doesn't do. And I like him more & more. Which is as it should be if I am to till New Hampshire at his side which appears more & more likely.[3] I wish it didn't: I mean I wish I wasn't being driven. But if I could hit off some sort of a life out there it would be better than running a losing race with Haldane Macfall.[4] As a matter of fact a safe £100 a year wouldn't quite solve my difficulty I think.[5]

But the 'Midsummer' was dreadful.[6] Tracts of headily insincere words among better things & quite nice little islands ruined by their surroundings. I hope I shall come again. But

[1] This projected anthology was never published, although some of the material went into *This England*.

[2] See Letter 124, note 2. 'Eager Spring' was included in *This England*.

[3] See a letter (dated 17 July 1914) in *EF*, p. 79.

[4] A prolific writer of books. See his *A History of Painting* in 8 vols., reviewed *N*, 13 May 1911, and *The Splendid Wayfarer*, reviewed *ER*, January 1914.

[5] ET was thinking of the possibility of applying for a Civil List pension. See a letter from W. H. Hudson to E. Garnett (dated 10 December 1915): 'I had a letter from Thomas a day or two ago after a very long interval, in which he asks me if you spoke to me about something being done to get him on the Civil List. I believe you did speak about it, but I can't remember just what you said.' *Letters from W. H. Hudson to Edward Garnett*, 1925, p. 150.

[6] 'Midsummer', reprinted in *The Last Sheaf*, pp. 21–5.

just now I feel I ought to be a lot alone for some time & I know I am not going to be in August & tho I shall like it well enough I know I shall feel the need of being alone afterwards. I will however try to come up to you in October. If only I could pay my way by an account of a cycle journey up, for example, it would be simpler.

Now I am typewriting all day & ruining such lovely weather —wet nights, glorious early mornings, some later showers & fine days after.[1] Ellis motored over & tried to take me to Lulworth but luckily rain drove us back at Bournemouth & I could work again.[2] It would be so easy for me to cease pretending to be a working man.

Now I should like a letter from you on one of the days when I have finished the anthology, about the 12th. Tell me did Browning really expect to meet Evelyn Hope again & do you suppose he has done?

My love to Emily & you

Yours ever Edward Thomas

140

25 August 1914   *c/o M*[r]*. Chandler,*[3]
Ledington, Ledbury, Herefordshire

My dear Gordon,

How are you & Emily? You gave an illusory (but not binding) promise to write when you last wrote. I should have written but I was doing an anthology[4] & finishing the vile *Homes & Haunts* book & really doing nothing. We have been here since early August enjoying fine weather & stupidly wondering about the War, not writing poems like all those London bards. What

---

[1] 'Homes and Haunts' was sent to the publishers on 1 August. See a letter (dated 2 August) in *EF*, p. 85: 'I am a little at a loose end after sending off Homes and Haunts yesterday. Who will want the thing now? I may as well write poetry. Did anyone ever begin at 36 in the shade? . . . Meantime apples and walks and (I trust) some reviews to write.'

[2] Vivian Locke Ellis.

[3] ET and Merfyn had cycled to Ledington via Basingstoke and Kingsclere on 3 August; Helen and the two daughters followed the next day on a delayed journey after war was declared. See *EF*, pp. 82–94.

[4] *This England.*

makes me write this moment is the chance of being near you about September 10th. I have promised to write an article for the *English Review* after going round Birmingham, Bradford, Newcastle & other towns & hearing what people say about the War.[1] Now I might—if I knew you were free—come on to you for a few days & write the article at your house & then have still a day or two when it was finished. Will you tell me if this is possible? Meantime, any northern newspapers might be useful to me that may reach you, so that if you have more than you need for fire-lighting will you put them aside, supposing I am to come? I have no other work.

Yours ever Edward Thomas

141

3 September 1914   *Coventry*

My dear Gordon,

I am very sorry to hear your bad news & hope I shall not hear worse. So far as it concerns me immediately never mind. I will come if I can when you are better placed. But my plans are uncertain. I have of course no prospect of earning any sort of living while the war lasts, thought I don't know what may turn up. It would be a good time for trying America if I could leave Helen & the children with a conscience, but I can't. I should join the Territorials if it didn't mean asking others to keep my family. I don't know what I shall do. For a week or so I am travelling here & there with no address or certain movements.[2] Any papers you send to Steep will be welcome though. I left Ledbury on Wednesday & Helen & the children went home. I shall be glad to be back with them. I saw too little of Abercrombie, too much of Gibson, & Frost daily—our families interwove all day long & we enjoyed many days but with all sorts of mixed feelings.[3]

---

[1] 'Tipperary', *ER*, October 1914, pp. 349–60. Reprinted in *The Last Sheaf*.
[2] He was collecting material for two more *ER* articles—'It's a long long way', December 1914, pp. 82–92, and 'England (In time of peace)' April 1915, pp. 88–99. (Both in *The Last Sheaf*.)
[3] See *WWE*, pp. 158–9.

Excuse these generalities—I write after 2 days in pubs talking to workmen & eavesdropping them. My love to you both

Yours ever Edward Thomas

142

21 September 1914   *Steep*

My dear Gordon,

I got the papers last week. Most neat & complete, but there was a pang in my gratitude, because in fact they were too late. Forgive my not being plain enough & so giving you & your father such unnecessary trouble. The M.S. had to be in on Sept. 15 to appear on Oct. 1.[1] I was sorry to go thro Leeds & not to Carnforth. But it was better not, because the job was a dirty one & would have spoilt a visit perhaps. And you were not well either. There were so many fine warm days & I thought you would be enjoying them on your little crag. They lasted on to my tour northwards & heated the pavements of Coventry Birmingham Sheffield Manchester & Newcastle. I liked Newcastle best for its bridges & its riverside. In fact I never enjoyed a night in any city so much, just for the city's sake & nothing but the city. I shall send Frost's book on condition that I hear the unvarnished judgment of the great man.[2] Don't forget that. I should like to see as many reviews as possible, views but not reviews.

I haven't received *New Numbers* yet.[3] If Abercrombie's contribution is on the 'Massacre of Innocents', I don't think much of it. I saw it in proof. It seemed to me not much more than A. hastily turning on to the theme in an almost journalistic effort. Drinkwater must be hopeless in this incarnation & I haven't heard of another. Gibson I gather is likely to be just sending suitable things to the market he has discovered. But I don't see that Abercrombie can hurt him. Brooke was going to war when I last heard.

Now God bless you & Emily. We send our loves to you.

Ever yours Edward Thomas

[1] See page 238, note 1.
[2] *North of Boston*. The 'great man' is T. Sturge Moore.
[3] W. W. Gibson, Rupert Brooke, Lascelles Abercrombie, and John Drinkwater, *New Numbers*, Part I, reviewed *DC*, 29 April. This query probably refers to Part II which never appeared.

143

19 December 1914   *Steep*

My dear Gordon,

You wouldn't promise to give me Sturge Moore's pronounce-
ment so I am punishing you by giving you the book. But that
needn't disarm Moore. Also I send for inspection a volume of
Morris containing some things I think you wanted to see.[1] Will
you forward it, as if from me, to

> Thomas Thorp
> Bookseller
> 93 St. Martin's Lane
> London WC.

I thought you might like to see this book of Burton's but if not
enclose it to Thorp.

How are you both? I can't remember when I last heard. But it
was a long time. Since then I think, unless it was after the end of
October, I cycled to Wales & back by Abercrombie's to see Frost
who is using part of the house, or all while A. is away.[2] I wish
you could sit up & talk for hours & that I was near. Tell me
when you can have me & I will try to come.

There is little work that has to be done, so I do the other kind.[3]
Some day you may see it. I kept making excuses for not trying to join the army & know I am made to believe I should
probably be refused, but am none the easier for it.

Now you certainly owe me a letter. This however ought to
have waited a few days but I have to be in town almost up to
Christmas.

Ever yours & Emily's Edward Thomas

[1] *The Collected Works of William Morris*, vol. XXIII, contained *Signs of Change.
Lectures on Socialism*. This and the Burton (specific reference untraced) were
review copies.

[2] Frost spent the winter of 1914–15 at Lascelles Abercrombie's house in Ryton. Cf.
EF, p. 99.

[3] The first reference to his poetry in this correspondence. Cf. *EF*, pp. 103–4 who
states that the 'first positive reference to his poems' occurs in a 'letter written
shortly before Christmas. "I hope it won't seem unkind to send you some poetry
in return. As for my own it isn't running just now. I sent what I had to Monro
asking for secrecy." '

144

28 December 1914   *Steep*

My dear Gordon,

I am so glad you were glad to have the Morris. I don't think Thorp will suffer if you keep it a week after the New Year, but if you send it earlier all the better. Don't talk of paying for the Burton if you really want to keep it. You shall have *Morris XXIV* when it comes.[1] Your letter came the evening of the day mine (which wasn't a letter) went. And the photograph, too, which is quite keepable. It helps the memory. I don't blame at all when I don't hear from you. I only wish I did hear. But my own letters, I always feel, are rather perfunctory & usually only replies when they are not groans. I've given up groaning since the war began, I believe, & have been mainly the better for it. But that is the one good effect of the war. It leaves me otherwise rather stranded, tho habits of work keep me up at my study for almost the usual hours. I travel a little more may be. I am travelling this moment or my handwriting should be better & this letter longer. But it's quite a short journey. We are all at home now, including Bronwen who has been away 2 terms at school in London but is now back for good, I hope. Mervyn will be leaving in a year or so—he is just on 15—& going (we fancy) to some engineering school or works. Then we may move to a less uncongenial neighbourhood. I don't like Bedales folk.[2] All I like is the hills & my study. I don't know where we shall go. But the American plan is by no means off yet.

I haven't seen Trevelyan[3] again yet I am going to be near him tonight but shall hardly venture there as Mrs. Abercrombie is a little hostile because I sometimes criticize Lascelles.[4]

Goodbye to you & Emily

Yours ever ET

---

[1] *Collected Works*, containing *Scenes from the Fall of Troy and other Poems*.
[2] See *WWE*, pp. 163–4.
[3] R. C. Trevelyan.
[4] See L. Abercrombie, *Mary and the Bramble*, reviewed *DC*, 9 August 1911: 'The versification is vigorous and gives a lively impression of the wild purity of early morning and solitude. But to philosophise the crude original is perhaps impossible and certainly Mr. Abercrombie's attempt has few charms except an evident delight in naiveté.'

145

30 January 1915   *Steep*

My dear Gordon,

I am sorry to get this news of your mother & all I can hope is that it will be something that her illness brings you so near to one another. Incidentally I hope I may see her when I come down to you again. But it will be strange to see her so when I recall her most plainly coming towards me over the meadows (which I think you used to call the Hollow Land: hadn't it a rocky islet or two with beeches on them?).

We are going to have some changes. It is being arranged that Mervyn goes over to New Hampshire with the Frosts when they go next month. He is to join an old schoolmaster friend of ours there for at any rate 6 months. Perhaps he has seen the last of his schooldays. He didn't do much good but just kept in the middle of his form. This may mean we shall leave the neighbourhood of Bedales & seek the neighbourhood of more real friends than we have there, perhaps the Ellises in Sussex, which is also much nearer London yet just as far from its influence. But we haven't begun to talk of this yet. I may still go to New Hampshire myself if the war ends and leaves things not too troubled here for me to be free.

Guthrie talks of having to move before very long. I haven't seen him since he got back from Cornwall. I was laid up 3 weeks with a sprained ankle & am still a cripple. He has been a good deal relieved since the war I fancy, & no wonder he feels so easy about his little pretty schemes. They are so fantastic to me that I can't begin to criticize them as I could if I saw their roots. It would be like saying to a man Why have you got such a funny face?

You shall have the other Morris when it comes of course, of course.[1]

I keep getting little scraps of work that prevent me from quite seriously facing questions, though I have been interviewing army people this week to see if there is something like a niche for me to crawl into excepting a trench. It doesn't look as if there is. My latest job is to be an English anthology of prose & verse to give as various an impression as possible of English life, landscape,

[1] See Letter 144, note 1.

thought, ambition & glory.[1] The thing is to arrange it so that it will be as simple & rich as a plum pudding. Can you suggest any plums or sixpenny bits to be found in it? I am not going mainly for the explicitly patriotic. It is for the Oxford Press & is to be done quickly of course. It is to cover the whole of time from the landing of Brutus to the Zeppelins.

Your house must be like our old one in the wind & rain, but with the advantage that it is very distinctly divided into an inside & an outside, whereas ours was like one of those carpets that can be used either side. So with your cushions & wallpapers & books & gramophone I hope you keep the weather out better.

Is there any news of the new Georgian poetry book, or is it indefinitely postponed?[2] You saw that Hodgson got the *Polignac* £100, I expect.[3] He & I are not meeting till the war is over. I am not patriotic enough for his exuberant taste.

My love to Emily & you.

Yours ever Edward Thomas

146

13 February 1915   *Steep*

My dear Gordon,
   Here is *Morris XXIV* & will you do the same as before with it to Thomas Thorp, 93 St. Martin's Lane, W.C.? If you can read 'The Wanderer' & 'Aristomenes' & 'Orpheus' I shall believe you sham when you say you are not a strong man.[4]

I will get it off at once & it may reach you on Monday.

Mervyn is sailing to America today with the Frosts.[5] I don't pretend to expect this or that of it but I believe the time had come to let him see what people were who couldn't make him do

---

[1] *This England.*

[2] *Georgian Poetry 1913–15* appeared in November 1915 and contained Ralph Hodgson's 'The Bull' and 'The Song of Honour'. See Letter 138, note 2, and R. J. Stonesifer, *W. H. Davies*, pp. 96–107.

[3] A literary award. Hodgson had been one of ET's companions at the St. George's Restaurant meetings and was a close friend of W. H. Davies.

[4] 'Poems of the Earthly Paradise' in *Collected Works*, vol. XXIV, pp. 87–316, viz. 'The Wanderers', 'The Story of Aristomenes', and 'The Story of Orpheus and Eurydice'.

[5] ET was laid up with a sprained ankle. Helen had gone to Liverpool to see Merfyn off to America with the Frosts.

things as I can or a schoolmaster can but who nevertheless will
expect him to give as well as take. However, as I say, I don't
know except that he could not be worse off, even if the Germans
torpedo the *St. Paul* (an american ship).

I am still a cripple. My ankle mends slowly if at all: & I'm
stupid, I haven't got the doctor to say whether I am overdoing it
if I tire it at all. I haven't walked strong now for just 6 weeks.
Can't even go up to my study more than once a week.

What are the most English things you know in English? I am
making an anthology of them.[1] They needn't be explicitly about
England but must be rich in English landscape or character or
thought. Do tell me one thing, preferably not by a living author.

Frost has almost bound me to go out in the summer when he
has got a farm working. But I must see you before then.

My love to Emily

Yours ever Edward Thomas

147

2 March 1915   *Steep*

My dear Gordon,

Your card this morning wasn't the first reminder that I owed
you a letter. But I have been very uncommonly driven—finishing
that anthology, reading & reviewing (imagine it!) a book on
Babylonian mythology[2] & (worst of all) making an index to a
book I finished in the summer for Methuen:[3] & all done down here
because the ankle I sprained on New Year's day, wouldn't let
me up to my study. However, it is all done now, & the ankle is
beginning to mend. The Morris was no doubt in time. I expect
they have a purchaser who takes the volumes as they come, & he
simply had to wait.

We have only heard so far that Mervyn's *ship* arrived. I
expect his being there will make it easier for me to go in the
Summer, if I decide there is anything in it. I now gather that

---

[1] *This England.*

[2] R. Koldeway, *The Excavations at Babylon*, translated by A. S. Johns, reviewed
DN, 10 December 1914.

[3] '*Homes and Haunts*', eventually published as *A Literary Pilgrim in England*,
1917.

Frost's idea is that helping him on the farm will set me up & set me free from English journalism, & that I might find a market out there for what I really want to do. What that is I am not perfectly sure yet. But I have begun to write in verse & am impatient of anything else. Don't mention it. I am trying to test the unsympathetic world first by using a pseudonym.[1] Someday I will show you what I am doing. Perhaps it is only like doing the best parts of my prose in verse & leaving out the connecting futile parts. That would be something if it were self contained & better than the best of my prose as I imagine it is. But it doesn't simplify the problem of a living.

I shall surely come up & see you before long. Let me know when a time seems possible & I will try to bring it about. We always have gaps to close up: but fewer than anyone would think likely considering our long absences.

Helen has just been staying a bit (with Baby)[2] at the Ransome's. A. is away. She likes Mrs. R. very much indeed & consequently thinks even less of A. than before.[3] He has turned Superman.

This is a poor letter for yours. But I am not up to much after my indexing, which is the vilest work I know. I love emptying slops by comparison.

Guthrie is down in his beamends rather more than usual, but I suspect him of being a foulweather seaman by this time. Like everyone else, he wants it all his own way, & I hope he will get it.

Yours ever Edward Thomas

148

6 May 1915   *Steep*

My dear Gordon,

Your card is a great relief. I was afraid someone was very ill or I would have asked before. For I sent the M.S. & letter on April 12 in an envelope much like this.[4] The M.S. was about the

---

[1] 'Edward Eastaway'. For the evolution of the name, see *EF*, pp. 118–9.

[2] His younger daughter, Myfanwy.

[3] Arthur Ransome.

[4] Manuscript of his verse. See GB, 'A note on Edward Thomas', *The Welsh Review*, IV, no. 3, September 1945, pp. 166–78.

same in bulk as this. Fortunately I believe I had duplicates of them all. If you can recover them I shall be pleased. And I was picturing you for a time as possibly floored with embarrassment though I am sure after what I used to say of your diction you won't easily be beaten. Which is a silly remark & just means I am shy about it. By the way the M.S. was really typescript.

Now I am glad to hear things grow better. I have been wondering many times about you all, your Mother, Aunt Sarah, Mrs. Burton & You & Emily with those four points to her compass. I hope she isn't tired out.

Here my only news is I am buried under a book on the Duke of Marlborough.[1] It is the only chance of earning anything. It is by far the worst job I ever undertook. I can't get out in less than 2 months if I ever do.

Guthrie has had more trouble—his wife very ill again—but also some relief. I haven't seen him though for a couple of months almost.

I had almost forgotten. May I use your 'Eager Spring' in my English anthology?[2] I thought of it at the last moment, slipped it in, & forgot to ask your leave. There are very few living people—Hardy, Doughty, de la Mare, & you; I think that is all.[2] I think it may please you. It is prose & verse in extreme variety, but I hope well mixed. The Oxford Press does it.

Yours ever Edward Thomas

149

17 May 1915   *Steep*

My dear Gordon,

Here they are & no mistake.[3] I hope they will not tire you.

[1] *The Life of The Duke of Marlborough, 1915.*

[2] *This England,* 1915. Besides the four 'living people' ET included something by W. H. Hudson and, on pp. 111 and 112, two poems ('Haymaking' and 'Manor Farm') by Edward Eastaway. ET wished to include A. E. Housman 'who always said No to anthologists—but atoned by praising my *Swinburne* which is the highest compliment I have yet had.' [*EF*, p. 118.] The Anthology has seven sections: This England, Merry England, Her Sweet Four Corners, London, Abroad and Home Again, Great Ones, The Vital Commoners.

[3] Mss. of his poems. According to the evidence in *EF*, pp. 107–44, the following poems had been written at this time: 'Haymaking', 'Manor Farm', 'After Rain', 'Old Dick', 'Tears', 'The Child on the Cliff', 'Lob', 'April', 'Pewits', 'March the

There are one or two I like that I haven't by me, but these are—practically all. It will interest me very much to see which you prefer. Do not let anything that occurs to you slip, unless there are so many things.

Now I am back & just about to begin to get rid of the effects of these 2 months of reading & note-taking.[1] I expect to be hard at work at least 2 months more. And the prospect stifles me.

I have just heard from Abercrombie that his wife has been very ill. He doesn't speak of his work, but I fancy he is being looked after.

With our love to Emily & you

Yours ever Edward Thomas

150

About 21 May 1915 [GB]   *13 Rusham Rd, Balham,*
London SW.

My dear Gordon,

Thank you. But it didn't actually find me out till yesterday morning & I have been too full of reading & odd company in the intervals to write, though not to turn over your passage about using words in the spirit of the prose writer & not freed from everyday syntax etc. I think that is quite an essential remark, & yet not one I can do anything with but remember.[2] I mean I can't *try* to get free & not to use words so, but only hope that practice &, far more, good fortune in not writing till I really ought to (with some impetus beyond habit & pleasure), will ultimately set me freer if not free. You please me by preferring 'Old Man'. It was one of the first. But I wonder if I can touch 'Swedes'. It is one of the least like myself I fancy. It is the only

___

3rd'. In a letter to Eleanor Farjeon (dated 5 May) ET states that he had sent Monro a 'lot of verses' that he would not accept for publication and that 'Ellis doesn't like them'.

[1] For his *Duke of Marlborough* and *This England*.

[2] Cf. *EF*, p. 141, a letter (dated 25 May 1915): 'I don't know if I shall be able to send any more [i.e. verse] out. I hadn't meant to, except to one or two people like Gordon Bottomley, who tells me I am still too much bound [by] my prose methods of statement. I suspect he is right, but of course I can't do anything but hope that experience and honesty will lead me to a better way if there is one (for me).'

one that an editor nearly took—I have tried some everywhere with an impenetrable pseudonym & address.[1] I am sure the one thing is to try & keep myself for the moods most likely to crystallize all my various familiar & unfamiliar material. Well, before long, if you really are not going to be tired with it, I shall try you with a large batch. You will then see that I duplicate rather & *I* see that this means I am sometimes not on the right level. But I will not instruct you further. I am keen to know just how they come to you. One spare copy of a recent thing I have by me & enclose.

Forgive me writing more out of this crush of work. My head is full of foreign matter. But I must say I am glad to hear good news of everyone, though sorry that in Emily's case it just cancels out bad.

Ever yours Edward Thomas

I return early next week to Steep.

151

16 June 1915   *Steep*

My dear Gordon,

Thank you. The MS & your letter came safe today forwarded to town where I am getting some scraps for *Marlborough*. It is practically finished & I am off for a few days' cycling if the weather holds.[2] No work to do. I think probably I shall go to the United States in September.

I am glad you found things to like. I hope you are right about 'Lob'. I incline to like it best, but about the other things I don't know. What you say is very interesting & likely to be right, but unless it happens to coincide with feelings I have about those particular poems all I can do is to try to discover reasons for

---

[1] Edward Eastaway, c/o Mrs. Farjeon, Fellows Road. Edward Garnett had also seen some of the poems; a few had been sent to *Blackwood's Magazine* and one to *The Times*.

[2] His cycling companion was to be his old friend Jesse Berridge, to whom he wrote on 25 May 1915: 'I tried to get a job at the historical section of the War Office, but only had my name put down on possibly a very long list.' According to letters in *EF*, pp. 142–8, ET was still thinking of going to the U.S.A. as late as 29 June.

agreeing.[1] Fancy your liking the child crying in the snow. It is interesting. I must go through them again when I get home on Friday & really have time to read your letter. This is only to thank you & acknowledge the M.S. I quite feel though that I may have been in a hurry often & that delight in the new freedom—I hope to God it is freedom—has made me too ready to accept intimations merely. Also there is the writing habit. 75,000 words on the Duke in 26 days. But of course I can't be somebody else.

I beg leave to be certain Moore is wrong.[2] He heard Frost was a theorist & thinks Frost wrote in accordance with a theory & so of course knew he must expect something moderate & of course found it, tho it isn't there.

God bless us all, what a thing it is to be nearing 40 & to know what one likes & know one makes mistakes & yet is right for oneself. How many things I have thought I ought to like & found reasons for liking. But now it is almost like eating apples. I don't pretend to know about pineapples & persimmons, but I know an apple when I smell it, when it makes me swallow my saliva before biting it. Then there are pears, too, & people who prefer pears. It is a fine world & I wish I knew how to make £200 a year in it without sucking James Milne's ————.

Give my love to Guthrie[3] as well as Emily. I was going over to him this week when I had to go to town instead.

Yours ever Edward Thomas

152

18 June 1915   *Steep*

My dear Gordon,
   I am afraid I let my irritation at Sturge Moore's criticism of

---

[1] See a letter (dated 18 June) in *EF*, p. 147: 'Bottomley sent me a letter about my verses the other day. He agrees with everyone about "Lob" and is decided about it, but speaks in a way I can't be sure of about the rest. I imagine however that I may have rushed along rather and taken very slight invitations sometimes when I could have resisted had I known. Well, I am not somebody else.'

[2] T. Sturge Moore.

[3] For Guthrie's life at Flansham at this time and later—and for evidence of Guthrie's artistic integrity—see *EF*, pp. 155–64, especially Guthrie's autobiographical letter on pp. 160–2. See, too, the typescript in the British Museum, 'James Guthrie: Biographical Notes', by Robin Guthrie, 1953.

Frost run over into what I said about your criticism of me. I mean I think it may have appeared so. But really it did not. I could not help, of course, some uncertainty as to the extent of your qualification when you advised me to 'stick to' my material. But I was pleased entirely with your liking of 'Lob' and everything you said was either pleasant or interesting. Not that what was interesting was unpleasant & what was pleasant uninteresting. No it was a letter I was altogether glad to have apart from the quotation from S.M.[1] & even that gave me the satisfaction of knowing that if a man like S.M. misses Frost so completely I can stand being missed myself in turn. There. I do hope I have undone anything I did that I ought not to have done in my letter on Wednesday.

Now I am going to cycle & think of man & nature & human life & decide between enlisting or going to America before I enlist.[2] Those are the alternatives unless something turns up out of the dark.

Yours ever Edward Thomas

153

30 June 1915   *Coventry (till tomorrow then home)*

My dear Gordon,

Your letter followed me about on a cycling journey up thro Gloster here—a premature holiday to get rid of the effect of *Marlborough*, for they now tell me the beastly thing is not up to length. However.

I was glad to have the letter. I never have found you ready to misunderstand. But I knew I had been in a hurry & a whirl. So I am glad to know I didn't make a mess.

Moore was excellent in principle. But in condemning Frost I think still that he had been misled into supposing that Frost

[1] Sturge Moore.

[2] See *EF*, pp. 147–8, where enlisting is not mentioned as an alternative to America. While arranging this cycling trip with Jesse Berridge, ET wrote in a letter (dated 25 May 1915): 'I am still suffering from my ankle or perhaps I should regard some military service as the thing for me especially if ordinary work fails. Nobody that I know well has enlisted so I am at sea as to how men really feel about it and if my own hesitations are at all common.'

wanted poetry to be colloquial. All he insists on is what he believes he finds in all poets—absolute fidelity to the postures which the voice assumes in the most expressive intimate speech.[1] So long as these tones & postures are there he has not the least objection to any vocabulary whatever or any inversion or variation from the customary grammatical forms of talk. In fact I think he would agree that if these tones & postures survive in a complicated & learned or subtle vocabulary & structure the result is likely to be better than if they survive in the easiest form, that is in the very words & structures of common speech, though that is not easy or prose would be better than it is & survive more often. I feel sure that no one who knows as much as Moore would dispute this, tho I admit I may not have put it in an intelligible & unquestionable form.

Frost's vocabulary & structure deceive the eye sometimes into thinking it is just statement more or less easily put into easy verse forms. But it is not.

His theory is only an attempt to explain & justify observed facts in Shakespeare for example & in his own earliest efforts.

As to my own method I expect it to change if there is anything more than a doting replica of youthful eagerness in this unexpected ebullition. But although it has a plain look it does so far, I think, represent a culmination as a rule, & does not ask or get much correction on paper.

We shall certainly not all go to America. I should go alone if other things fail, & stay perhaps some time looking about. But I am told I shall have to change my spots if I am to get on there—English people say so—& I do not really know of a method of doing so. I do not know what I shall do before going. I shall have to let you know later whether I can come to you & when. I hope if I can you will be free. But it is not certain I can afford it.

By the way my travelling companion as far as Stroud (Jesse Berridge)[2] and I stopped one night at Ransome's—with *Mrs*

---

[1] See Letter 137, note 2, ET's review of *North of Boston* : 'These poems are revolutionary because they lack the exaggeration of rhetoric, and even at first sight appear to lack the poetic intensity of which rhetoric is an imitation. Their language is free from the poetical words and forms that are the chief material of secondary poets. . . . In fact the medium is common speech and common decasyllables, and Mr Frost is at no pains to exclude blank verse lines resembling those employed, I think, by Andrew Lang in a leading article printed in prose.'
[2] See Letter 152, note 2.

Ransome—& had a most pleasant time. I must say I like her very much & can't think why she married such a great man. She still has an irreducible maximum of admiration & affection for him. . . .[1] The place is however very full of him, his pipes & books, photographs of him, certificates of prizes which his white mice have won &c. You know it is close to another great home, Beckford's Fonthill.

> Yours ever with love to Emily
>
> Edward Thomas[2]

154

14 July 1915   *Steep*

My dear Gordon,

I have just knocked my American plans on the head but without making a visit to you possible, I am enlisting in the Artists Rifles, a territorial corps which trains men to be officers. Yesterday I passed the doctor. Now I am returning home to put my papers in order & get a walk with Helen. I am to be attested on Monday. Don't I wish our camp were near you. But it will be in Richmond Park or Epping Forest, after a week or two in London. Then in a few months I expect to go to France to finish my training. Here then ends reviewing & I suppose verses, for a time.[3]

> With love to you & Emily
>
> Yours ever Edward Thomas

155

21 July 1915   *13 Rusham Rd*

My dear Gordon,

I was almost coming down to you today. For I am ashamed to say the new boots I wore on my first day's drill so pressed the big

[1] 10 words omitted.
[2] A typescript of the 'Words' poem was enclosed in this letter. [*GB*]
[3] See *EF*, pp. 151–3, for more detailed letters (dated 10 and 21 July) about his change of plan. He was attested on Monday 19 July and did six hours drill on that day.

tendon at the back of my right foot that I have been given leave
for the rest of the week.[1] But I was not sure if my pass would
take me really, & on the whole I thought I would rest my foot
here. It is a great nuisance & it may recur. Suppose it did &
suppose I could get a pass up to you[.] What times should I
avoid? I would then wire to you with a reply form & come down
if you were free. Otherwise, normally, I should not have more
than a short weekend except one I expect. But I don't like to talk
about the possibility. I want to mend & get on with this. It was
not at all a desperate nor yet a purposed resolution but the
natural culmination of a long series of moods & thoughts. I went
suddenly off at a tangent from the American scheme. I was very
happy about it & so was Helen, though she was happy perhaps
chiefly to see me so clearly resolved & satisfied at once. And now
I dread its being upset. But don't mention this to any one. And I
didn't really mean anyone to know about my verses. I have
shown them to a few only. But I was keeping them rather secret.
However I am so pleased at having Abercrombie's liking that I
should not dream of complaining. In fact when I can get at them
I will sort some out for you, 'Lob' & a few more & some recent
ones.

I can't say how pleased I was by your letter & your good
wishes. My pleasure is only modified by the feeling that perhaps
I shall never get out & need them. Please remember me to
Abercrombie & Trevelyan.

                                  Yours ever Edward Thomas

*   *   *

*It was at this moment and in this connection that I had shown a
sheaf of ET's first poems to Lascelles Abercrombie and R. C.
Trevelyan. They were here to discuss the issue of* An Annual of New
Poetry, *which came out with Constable in 1917 a few weeks before
ET's death: and, having his poems in the house, I brought them out
and urged that some of them should be included in our* Annual. *The
other two were deeply interested and agreed at once: and ET let
them go in under the Eastaway pseudonym. I look back on this with
gratification, for these were the only poems that he saw come to
publication.   G B*

*   *   *

[1] During this initial training period ET was billeted at his parents' home.

156

23 July 1915   *13 Rusham Rd*

My dear Gordon,

I think most of those you liked are here & a few later ones. Will you return them to me here unless you know I have gone away? I am busy with my *Marlborough* proofs now.

Yours ever Edward Thomas

P.S. Your letter came after I had sealed this. How quick you were. It was quite all right. I only thought perhaps I had forgotten to say I was keeping these things a sort of a secret.[1] So I shall keep your address by me & telegraph if I am free. The foot seems all right now, but then I have not brought it near the boot again. I am sorry I shan't see Trevelyan if I come next week, nor Abercrombie. But they would want to walk & so should I & I couldn't. Goodbye. My love to Emily.

157

Post Mark: Battersea. S.W. 12.15 a.m. Aug. 3rd. 1915[2]
1 August 1915   *Steep*

My dear Gordon,

No luck. I am afraid now that however my tendon behaves I can't get a pass up to you. The pass I had merely gave me freedom to leave my quarters. The only chance is that I shall get a long leave after a series of short ones at home: then I could come to you & would let you know at once. So far my foot is really not right & I have not become a normal soldier yet.

I am sending you a few more verses. If Marsh likes any of them well & good.[3] But I should not be vastly interested in his adverse opinion. The Mrs Greenland's Hawthorn Bush lines[4]

---

[1] See Letter 155. It was ET's father who revealed the identity of Edward Eastaway after the poet's death. See Letter 184.
[2] GB's insertion.
[3] Edward Marsh. None of ET's poems appeared in *Georgian Poetry*.
[4] The lines are in 'A Private' (*CP*, p. 183) which was one of the *Six Poems*, by Edward Eastaway printed by Guthrie.

I can't lay my hands on, but I think I can copy them out &
include them. I have done as you see.[1]

Don't trouble to answer this but when you write I shall be
glad. I am at home for a day & Helen sends her love with mine to
you & Emily.

Yours ever Edward Thomas

158

B. Company, Artists Rifles, High Beech, Loughton, Essex.[2]

I am now *Pte P. E. Thomas, 4229,* & not able to write many
letters. We moved to camp last week & your letter came soon
after. Thank you for reporting what Trevelyan & Abercrombie
liked. Trevelyan is wrong if he thinks I have consciously obeyed
some principle or fad. It is very easy to explain what he finds
difficult, I suppose through a classical point of view. But I can't
now. When I shall really get any time to spare, beyond a 24
hour week end I can't guess. It won't be soon. I wish it could. So
now I could only wish *Mrs Lear* the kind of success you would
like. Goodbye.[3] E.T.

159

6 November 1915   *Steep*

My dear Gordon,

I don't know how long your letter had been waiting for me.
The battalion left High Beech a fortnight ago[4] & I with it &
your letter was sent on to Headquarters in London where it lay
some time. Now in a week or so we are off to another camp,
probably at Romford. Nobody wants to go, least of all I, as I can
see people I want to in London. Still, in camp I found I could get
on with people I had nothing in common with & almost get fond
of them. As soon as we were in London the bond was dissolved

---

1 The poem was enclosed. [GB]
2 ET moved to camp at High Beech, Loughton, on 23 September.
3 Written during the production (the first production) of *King Lear's Wife* at the
   Birmingham Repertory Theatre. [GB]
4 For extra details see *EF*, p. 169.

& we had blank looks for one another. The weather was mostly fine & there was really a great deal to enjoy & what I couldn't enjoy I am glad to have been through. Things have changed a little. I am now a lance corporal (L. Cpl. P. E. Thomas, 4229) & an assistant instructor in mapreading. I help to look over men's work & take a squad of 20 or so out on Hampstead Heath to take bearings & sketch a map on the spot etc. The experience is very useful whether I am to stay on as an instructor or to take a commission later. I don't know yet which I shall choose, supposing I am free to choose.

I am now at home for a weekend gardening, lighting a fire in my study up on the hill, seeing Muirhead Bone & Maitland Radford & a few others.[1] I can't write. Once when I had a bad knee[2] I got 20 lines written & felt just as I used to, which is more than I dare do as a rule, It is curious how the mind steadily refuses to hanker after what it knows is absolutely forbidden for (it believes) a comparatively short time. So far I don't think I have resented or regretted anything or longed for the impossible.

My books come streaming out.[3] One or two you might like to see & I will try & manage to send them.

I am not grumbling about Trevelyan's criticism, but quite doubtful still whether he was trusting to ear & not a theory as to my theory (when I had none). Guthrie is going to print some things in his rummy magazine over an assumed name.[4] It will be my first appearance as bard.

I heard nothing about *Mrs Lear* till your letters.[5] The paper I never look at except for headings and casualties & now a little for reviews of my 5 works (as Davies calls them). But I am glad you saw the thing well done. I had always heard ill of Drinkwater & rated him by his verses which was pretty hard on him. Is

---

[1] See *EF*, pp. 111–3. Maitland Radford was a doctor who occasionally stayed at Steep with ET's neighbour, Montague Fordham. Muirhead Bone had moved to Steep that his children might go to Bedales. (According to an omitted note dated November 1912.)

[2] In a letter to Eleanor Farjeon (dated 17 October 1915) he states that he was 'lame with an injured knee'.

[3] Books or reprints that appeared in 1915 were *The Life of The Duke of Marlborough*, *Maurice Maeterlinck*, *Four-and-Twenty Blackbirds*.

[4] Guthrie's occasional magazine, *Root and Branch/A Seasonal of the Arts*, first appeared in Spring 1912. Number 4 (undated, but probably 1917) contained two poems by Edward Eastaway ('House and Man' and 'Interval'), pp. 59–60.

[5] See Letter 158. John Drinkwater was the producer.

the play to be in the new *Georgian Poetry*?[1] I forgot to ask Monro.
I think he said the volume was ready. I shall try to see it, tho I
simply read nothing but service manuals & not much of them at a
time. *Cymbeline* I reread in August again, but nothing since in
verse. Still do not give me up. Write when you can & give me
news. Steep is the best way to find me. Helen's love & mine to
you two.

ET

160

20 December 1915   *Hare Hall Camp*[2]

My dear Gordon,
    I am very glad you are sitting out in the air & suffering less.
In case you can attend to an anthology I am sending mine, with
your thrush in it.[3] It comes with love to you & Emily. But I wish
you wouldn't ask me such difficult questions about Guthrie. I
never do understand him except when he says he likes or dislikes
something or has done something, or the like. He seems to me to
talk & write almost always with a squint, as it were.
    Will you or can you invite me to see *Mrs Lear*? I am very
glad to hear the news. I have seen the 2nd Georgian Anthology
& didn't find much to like except yours & de la Mare's. Abercrombie's I didn't read again.[4] I wish he had succeeded in enlisting. He would be a great accession if he got here. We get on
well enough & have been busy these 3 weeks & are looking
forward actually to a whole week's holiday. Then we are to be
busy again. For all I know I can keep on at this job for a long
time yet. What is more, it seems unlikely I can afford to take a
commission, as the expenses would swallow all my pay, whereas
I must not do anything that robs Helen of her separation

---

1 GB's play was printed in *Georgian Poetry 1913–15*.
2 His full address, Hut 23, Hare Hall Camp, Gidea Park, Romford, Essex. His
friend Jesse Berridge had been preferred to a living at Brentwood in the summer of
1915. The majority of the manuscript poems preserved in the Bodleian were
written at Hare Hall.
3 'The Thrush', *CP*, p. 106. In the Bodley manuscript the poem is dated 'Hare Hall
XI.15—the day I was in as hut-orderly while the rest went to South Weald' and
entitled 'A Thrush'.
4 There were seven poems by de la Mare: 'Music', 'Wanderers', 'Melmillo',
'Alexander', 'The Mocking Fairy', 'Full Moon', and 'Off the Ground'. For LA's
play, *The End of the World*, see Letter 138, note 2.

allowance. So I may continue in this safe job, only too safe, with only too good company. I shouldn't mind being a great deal less comfortable. In fact I should be easier if I were less comfortable.

Did I tell you that three of the men I am working with are Maresco Pearce, W. P. Robins & Cole?[1] We get some good walks & talks. Also Edna Clarke Hall lives near & Pearce & I go in to lunch: & Jesse Berridge is at Brentwood 5 miles off.

Goodbye now. Write soon & cover your big pages as I do my little ones.

Yours ever Edward Thomas

161

from P. E. Thomas 4229, D. Coy. Artists Rifles,
11 February 1916   *Hut 15, Hare Hall Camp, Romford*

My dear Gordon,

I have suffered various fortunes of war since your letter reached me here. But for one I might have delayed writing still longer. I have had a bad chill & consequently a week or more extra leave, spent indoors at my Mother's till today. (This afternoon I trust I shall get to Petersfield.) The other may prove the more lasting. I was to have been made a corporal 3 weeks ago, but I had got into trouble for reporting a man present whom I expected in 'every minute'. The sergeant major wouldn't hear of my promotion after that, so it may be an age, it may be only in the next war, before I wear 3 stripes & a bayonet which were naturally my one ambition.

Otherwise all has gone well enough. Slowly I learn my job & the impossibility of doing it in the allotted time. I delivered a lecture on scales the other day & no doubt shall do again & again. Thence I shall rise to contours & so on. All which I value chiefly as a preparation for civil life. If I have to lecture or help Frost at a school in America I shall be so much the better trained.

At weekends especially on my way home I sometimes find I

---

[1] I have been unable to trace the connection between ET and Robins & Cole (? G.D.H.). Maresco Pearce had illustrated a few books and would have been known to GB.

can make verses. I enclose one of the last.[1] I have yet to expose myself to the cross-eyed gents still serving their country on the 'best papers'; for presumably those not cross-eyed are serving it elsewhere. But why worry what they say when the innocent public buys & goes on buying?[2] You really want to lie down with Squire & Brock & the other Landseer lions & Queen Mary, all in a gilt state bed with *Honi soit* on the quilt. I too shall come tumbling in one day to see what it is like after a single camp bed. The company in *Form* will be nigh as rum.[3] Spare I think doesn't know Eastaway. Please preserve his secret if you have a chance. As long as they don't misprint me I shan't mind my company or care if it minds me.

Among the men in my hut is one from Grange named Borwick, a very loud-voiced aggressive youth whose bite is much nicer than his bark. I forgave him all when he talked about Cartmel & said he had heard of Abercrombie & Rathbone.[4] I should think he was a bank clerk. I furbish up my knowledge of England by finding some place that each man knows & I know & getting him to talk. There isn't a man I don't share some part with.

I haven't seen anybody from outside this year, except John Freeman.[5] He is expecting another book of verses. De la Mare continues to wear himself out at reviewing & making more money than he really needs, except that he is committed like everyone else to some accidental standard of living. Guthrie remains a little silent. He talks of making a little volume of Eastaway but E. does not expect it to happen.

Now goodbye & my love to you & Emily & Abercrombie &

---

[1] There is a typescript of 'Roads' with this letter. [*GB*]

[2] ET's first poem in 1916 was 'This is no case of petty right and wrong'. [*EF*, pp. 179–80.] The poem's mood is reflected in the above paragraph.

[3] The magazine *Form* appeared in April 1916. Intended as 'a Quarterly of the Arts', it was edited by Austin O. Spare and Francis Marsden. (The second, and last, number appeared in April 1917.) Number 1 contained 'Lob' and 'Words' by Edward Eastaway.

[4] See Letter 50.

[5] John Freeman (1880–1929), poet, critic, novelist, and businessman was a friend of Roger Ingpen and de la Mare and a member of the Poetry Bookshop group. His first critical recognition came with *Stone Trees*, 1916, and was consolidated by *Poems New and Old*, 1920. See *John Freeman's Letters*, edited by Gertrude Freeman and Sir John Squire, 1936; especially his letters to John W. Haines (the young solicitor who met ET on his visits to Frost), which are responsible for the genesis of the often-quoted opinion that ET's letters are not 'particularly good or self-expressive. And where they are self-expressive they are inevitably melancholy.' Freeman first came to know ET in 1914.

Mrs. Abercrombie (if she really forgives me for sometimes saying uncomfortable things about Lascelles).

Yours ever Edward Thomas

P.S. I am expecting to make an anthology of English narrative poems.[1] When you write next do send me a list of suggestions. I need such a list to set me going. I have waited 4 months & done nothing.

162

18 February 1916   *Hut 15, Hare Hall Camp*

My dear Gordon,

Thank you for your quick reply. I wish you had liked 'Roads' more. I thought the particular ghosts came in comfortably enough after the ghosts in general.[2] For myself I didn't know whether it came off as a whole or not.—I hope I can find enough suitable things for the anthology.[3] It is very hospitable of Abercrombie & Trevelyan to ask me in, & when I go home in a fortnight's time I will send you a big dose. Will you tell me meantime whether you would rather not have the 2 poems appearing in *Form*? They are 2 you liked most, 'Lob' & 'Words'. If I can find your letter I will see which the poems were that you liked. As a matter of fact one at least occurs in a half dozen that Guthrie is using. 20 pages will give me a chance.

I don't know what exact arrangement you will make with Constable,[4] but I should say that royalties ought to begin to come in after the sales have reached a certain fixed figure, not after expenses have been paid, which leaves the publisher too free to decide when he begins to pay out. It is extremely rum that Waugh & Tynan should administer the laurels to Mrs Lear, unless it is that they respect the amount of water that has run under London Bridge since you began to publish. I think I heard

---

[1] Probably intended as a companion volume to *This England*. Many of ET's letters written at this time refer to 'two books' he has on hand.
[2] See *CP*, p. 164.
[3] A reference to *An Annual of New Poetry*.
[4] See Letter 163, note 3.

too that Courtney decided not to admit he wasn't convinced. He is afraid of not going to Heaven with you (or anybody else who may be going).

About the matinée, Romford is only 12 miles from Liverpool St, but the difficulty is I can never get away except on a Saturday morning, so that I couldn't see the play unless it was on a Saturday.[1]

I got back here on Wednesday half-mended, & have had a fairly easy time to get quite well in. Tomorrow I hope I may go to Coventry & see Mervyn at his new last school there.[2]

I had 4 days convalescence at home which I enjoyed, except that I wasn't fit for much except strolling in the sun & sitting down for a half an hour to do a panorama. This is one of the gentlest of military arts. One gradually learns to do something quite like a landscape. I do one or two every week for practice. I can imagine becoming almost good enough to illustrate a travel book with sketches—except that I can't imagine ever doing a travel book or any writing I don't entirely like.

By the way I prefer to remain Eastaway for the time being. People are too likely to be prejudiced for or against E.T.

Yours ever Edward Thomas

163

24 February 1916   *Hut 15, Hare Hall Camp*

My dear Gordon,

Thank you for being so quick. I am afraid *Form* must have 'Lob' & 'Words' (the one you spoke of, including the Welsh nightingales) as they are in type & as far as I know going in in March, if *'Form'* is born in March. One or two of the best are going into a booklet by Guthrie. It won't circulate more than

---

[1] *King Lear's Wife* was to run at His Majesty's Theatre, Haymarket, after its Birmingham premiere. The references in the previous paragraph are to notices of the premiere by London critics.

[2] Merfyn had returned from America at Christmas 1915. He then went to school at Coventry (under ET's friend, Hodson) from January 1916 until he was apprenticed to an engineering works at Blackhorn Lane, Walthamstow, in September 1916.

261

Root & Branch, but it will [be] a book in a sense.[1] However I
think you will find enough to please you out of the remainder. I
have written more than a dozen things since I joined in July.[2]
Well, as soon as I get home, & I hope that will be at the end of
next week, I will make a big selection for you to choose from.

Mervyn returned just before Christmas & then in mid-
January went to Coventry to School. He is living in the house of
the headmaster who was a master at Bedales some years back.
He is very well & not very American. He is brighter & more
cheerful & seems to be looking ahead a little & inclined to work.
I made sure I told you he was due back before Christmas. We
were very glad to see him safe at home.

I should think it worthwhile to let Constable hear the opinion
that royalties should begin when the sales reach a certain figure.[3]
Otherwise it means the old style of agreement which *The Author*
pillories every month. But I should not like to suggest holding
out against the present arrangement if it might mean not finding
a publisher. As to the reissue, too, of separate parts of the collection, there should be a condition that this would take place
only after an agreement with the publisher, unless they will make
an agreement now that the author is to draw royalties after a
certain number of copies are sold, certainly not more than 500—I
should say 250.

I heard a great deal from Guthrie about *Form* but did not at all
understand the reasons for the change, though he invited me to
support him.[4] Of course I couldn't in my ignorance.

The list is quite what I hoped for & if you add to it so much
the better. I can get to work now on the anthology. But there can
be no translations, I think not even Dryden's, nothing nearer to a
translation than Marlowe's *Hero & Leander*. I mean to include
his part, rather than *Venus & Adonis*. There can hardly be room
for both.

I wonder what Frost is sending. It is an age since I heard

---

[1] *Six Poems*, by Edward Eastaway, 1916. See page 256, note 4.

[2] The poems in the Bodley manuscript with dates between 20 July 1915 and 24
February 1916 are 'October', 'Liberty', 'Rain', 'There's Nothing Like the Sun',
'Cock-Crow', 'The Ash Grove', 'The Thrush', 'February Afternoon', 'Two
Houses', 'The Unknown', 'Song', 'These Things that Poets Said', 'Roads', 'This
is No case of petty Right or Wrong', 'No One So Much As You'.

[3] Constable later became GB's publisher, but this is a reference to *An Annual of
New Poetry*.

[4] Guthrie had resigned from the literary editorship of *Form*.

from him. Yet I expect I shall go out there when the war is over,
bar accidents & goodness knows how many accidents there are
certain to be. Goodbye. My love to Emily & you & all.

Yours ever Edward Thomas

164

11 March 1916   *Hut 15, Hare Hall Camp*

My dear Gordon,

Here are 40 to select from.[1] Most of those I remember your
liking are here. I hope you will include 'Old Man' though I don't
want too much blank verse in. A good many of these you haven't
seen, & I shall be most curious to hear which you choose. Will
you let me have the others back?

I promised to send them a week ago, but I didn't get my leave
till this weekend I hope the delay doesn't matter.

What is happening to *Form*? I thought it was to be out in
March: yet I haven't had a final proof I was promised.[2] Of course
if it should be postponed indefinitely or dropped I would rescue
'Lob' & 'Words'.

I can't write a letter now. We are in a great state of uncertainty & change still. When I get back tomorrow night, goodness knows what change will have taken place, may be for better,
may be for worse. This is the 3rd or 4th week of this state of
things & we are sick of it. When it clears up I shall try to write
at once.

Yours & Emily's ever Edward Thomas[3]

165

7 April 1916   *Hut 3, Hare Hall Camp*

My dear Gordon,

Thank you for your packet. I think the selection very just.
I only wish you had taken some more of those written since

[1] These were poems from which 18 were selected for inclusion in *An Annual of New Poetry*.
[2] *Form* eventually appeared in July 1916. See *EF*, pp. 200 and 205.
[3] A M.S. of 'Snow' with this letter. [*GB*]

263

August.[1] But that is mere tenderness for the younger. You need not have worried a moment about the duplicates. As a matter of fact I had forgotten you had them & they are a pure windfall to me. I shall be looking forward to proofs & print. 'Lob' & 'Words' I suppose are *Form's*, though Spare hasn't answered my card inquiring.[2]

May 19 is too far ahead for me to think of it.[3] I don't like trying. Can you remind me later. But a Friday is not very likely, unless I am a sergeant by then, which I shall hardly be, as I have only just been made a full corporal. Nor do I know where I shall be. We may go under canvas before then in some remote part, impossible for a London visit. We have had no leave for 4 weeks & no promise of any. Luckily, Helen was in town lately & came over for a few hours. She stayed some time, helping Irene to nurse her husband till he died a week ago.[4] I want to go home badly. But especially in this fine weather I enjoy a great part of this life. I have quite got used to lecturing, by having to do it twice a day.

This is my news. It is no news that I can't write a letter, nor that I like having one from you. This address should last some weeks at least, possibly for the duration of the war, unless a Zeppelin hits us. We see them, but so far they hit ploughed fields chiefly about 7 miles off.

My love to Emily

Yours ever Edward Thomas

166

from Cpl P E Thomas 4229, D Coy. Artists Rifles
16 April 1916   *Hut 3, Hare Hall Camp*

My dear Gordon,

Is it too late for you to reconsider one of the pieces you included in your selection? 'Wind & Mist' is perhaps a little too like 'The New House' to be put with it in such a small number, &

---

[1] See Letter 163, note 2. Only three of these later poems were included in *An Annual of New Poetry*: 'The Unknown', 'Song', and 'Roads'.

[2] Austin Spare of *Form*.

[3] For a visit to London to see *King Lear's Wife*.

[4] Irene MacArthur, Helen's sister.

I thought you might take 'Aspens' & 'After Rain' in its place. I
am sending them for you to look again. 'Aspens', I have thought,
was decidedly one of the better pieces. At the same time I am
sending a set of 4 I did lately,[1] not because I think you will want
to use them but because they are rather different in kind.

I hear Paul Nash has left the Tower & joined the map readers,
but in London, not here. I hope I shall meet him, & think very
likely I shall, as it is not likely they will continue to teach map
reading in town.

I came across the author of *A Flute of Sardonyx* here the other
day—Edmund John.[2] Do you remember his amorous censored
note, with an introduction by Phillips? Not good except in a kind
where it is impossible to be very good & easy not to be bad. He
wears several rings & looks as if his past did not agree with him.

We have no leave nowadays & I am wondering if I shall have
any before my 1st year's service is up. We get a week then. It
should be near the end of July & Helen is already thinking of it.
We might reach you.

Have you been wishing you were one of Elizabeth Asquith's
great bards who performed to a guinea audience?[3] The *Observer*
says nothing about them & a lot about Lady So & So, ————
& Mrs What d'jecall. Serves them right.

When is the *Annual* to be expected? Also, are you coming to
town for your play, because if so I will make every effort to see you.

My love to Emily

Yours ever Edward Thomas

167

24 April 1916   *Hut 3*

My dear Gordon,

You shall have 'Wind & Mist'. But what about 'The Glory'?
Could 'After Rain' take its place? However, if you would rather
not, leave the selection as it is: for after all I have only fondness

[1] The Bodley manuscript dating indicates that these four were the family poems
('If I Should Ever by Chance', 'What Shall I Give?', 'If I Were to Own' and 'And
You, Helen')—all dated between 6 and 9 April 1916. Two of them were com-
pleted before 2 April. See *EF*, p. 193.

[2] *The Flute of Sardonyx/Poems*, introduced by Stephen Phillips, 1913.

[3] For an account of these public poetry readings, see R. J. Stonesifer, *W. H. Davies*,
pp. 119–21, and W. H. Davies, *Later Days*, 1925.

to go by. 'Aspens' anyhow will have to stay out. The household poems ought perhaps to appear as a bunch.[1] John Wheatley here is talking of doing some etchings to illustrate these & one or two other Essex things. Do you know Wheatley's work.[2] Paul Nash I am not likely to meet unless he comes to camp here. He is with our old Sergeant Maresco Pearce in town, I gather.[3] We shall not come to town; that is fairly certain: nor to Hampstead. We might go anywhere under canvas, & I should not mind a change, though I have got to like this part very much. Soon it may be quite changed by spring excursions. Up to now it has been purely rustic, except for decrepit boards with 'teas' painted on them. Wherever we move I ought to be able to see you on one of your days. When you know (more or less) exactly which they are, will you let me know, so that I can be prepared. Perhaps I could see you at the Shiffolds. I want to see Trevelyan again, too.

I wonder what will happen to Edmund John. He has a new book coming & has been photographed in khaki.[4] I suppose he too is a Welshman like Davies. Davies, it appears, succeeded in looking natural. I believe he wore a new velvet jacket, which apparently is what a bard naturally wears. The poor men in black clothes were accused of dressing up, by one paper. I have not heard a word about it from de la Mare.[5]

I will certainly not give up the idea of coming to you in July & if it seems possible later I will let you know in time. At last we have had 2 days leave without asking for it & we all hope it means a return to the old state of things—fortnightly leave.

My love to your amanuensis

Yours ever Edward Thomas

168

13 May 1916   *Hut 14,[6] Hare Hall Camp*

My dear Gordon,

Now I have two letters to thank you for. And first about seeing

[1] See Letters 165, note 1, and 166, note 1.
[2] See Wheatley's unfinished sketch, facing p. 138
[3] See page 258, note 1.
[4] Edmund John, *Symphonie Symbolique*, 1919.
[5] See Letter 166, note 3.
[6] ET was made a full Corporal between 20 March and 2 April.

you in town. I am trying to arrange to be in London on Friday
the 19th. It will be easy to see the play but how about seeing you
sometime after?[1] I should have to be back at Liverpool St at
7.30 & so could you be seen before then somewhere near the
Theatre. Nothing is certain, but if you care to be at any place on
Friday after the play (before, I shall not be free, because my
excuse for being in town will be a dentist) I will do my best to
be there. Let me know if & as soon as you can because letters
are so likely to travel slowly. The chances of seeing you at any
other time are very slight. —Well, I know you are not free either
to make or to keep engagements. I leave it to you to suggest &
I feel pretty sure of being able to see you any time between 2.45
and 7 on Friday. One other chance—I may be having a day &
a night on the 27th. If you were in town on that Saturday
we might meet. I hope all will go well & you have an easy
time.

Thank you for the verses & for arranging the substitution,
which was what I wanted.[2] When you write again tell me
who really is coming in, & if Frost is. De la Mare came down
for a Sunday a fortnight ago, & spoke tentatively. He
mostly does now. He isn't well & might be perplexed in the
extreme. He doesn't always write as well as he used to. But
his verses I hardly ever see. John Freeman's weren't a bit in my
line,[3] but the angel (he is one) didn't mind my not concealing
it.

I congratulate you on refusing to indulge the editor of *The
Weekly Despatch*. I am sure he deserved it (i.e. to be refused).
Also I withdraw whatever I seemed to mean against the bards
who indulged Miss Asquith & performed round Davies.[4] He
alone could have refused, I suppose.

It is a horrible war but we have had some fine days for men
and vegetables lately. We have nightingales everywhere about
us. There is no vexation we do not fairly often forget. My love
to you two.

Ever yours Edward Thomas

[1] *King Lear's Wife* at His Majesty's Theatre, Haymarket. [*GB*]
[2] A reference to poems selected for *An Anthology of New Poetry*. See *EF*, pp. 191–2
and 197.
[3] See Letter 161, note 5.
[4] See Letter 166, note 3.

169

June or early July, 1916 [GB][1]
Sunday   *Hare Hall Camp*

My dear Gordon,
I have just heard that I have to report at my new unit (which is to be St John's Wood) on Friday next. Now if I could leave here at once all would be well: I could see something of you. But I can't leave today & probably not tomorrow. Also I shall probably have to return here on Thursday in order to proceed with the others as a party on Friday. Therefore unless something unexpected happens I shall not be able to reach you this time. There is still another chance, about a month later. I am very sorry about it. Still, there should be more chances. I don't know what my address will be, but you can always reach me at

13 Rusham Rd, Balham, London SW

Yes, I was rather hustled out of my study 2 months ago.[2] My landlord was at the front. His wife did what he never would have done. Still, we should have had to leave Steep for Mervyn's sake. We expect to move next month, probably I told you, to somewhere beyond Walthamstow: very likely at High Beech, right in Epping Forest, a most pleasant place 5 days in the week.
So I can't bring that picture, unless after all they do treat me better, in which case I shall wire. Well, writing's all over now. I may perhaps get a book of verses out.[3] The *Annual* will be something to look out for. Thank you for saying you will correct my proofs if necessary. My love to you & Emily.
Yours ever Edward Thomas

[1] Early in June ET was given a grant of £300 from the Royal Literary Fund and not a Civil List Pension. (See *EF*, pp. 194–8.) In July the Civil Liability Commission awarded him £1 a week 'so long as I am disabled from earning a living. This would cease if I became an officer.' See *EF*, p. 204. He had put his name down for a commission in 'R.G.A. or Anti-Aircraft' in June. The move to St. John's Wood eventually took place in late August. GB's dating is surely wrong and this letter was probably written in late August and is out of sequence here. It should follow Letter 171.

[2] Mrs. Geoffrey Lupton wished to let ET's study at the top of the hill. See *WWE*, pp. 166–8 and *EF*, p. 200 (which gives 24 June 1916 as the date of leaving the study).

[3] Arranged by de la Mare's brother-in-law, Roger Ingpen of Selwyn and Blount, whom ET met on 15 August 1916. See *EF*, pp. 208–9, and Letter 67.

170

30 July 1916   *Steep*

My dear Gordon,

Your 2nd letter arrived this morning when I was on leave for 24 hours. Probably my last leave from the Artists. I am going to the Artillery if I get through the tests. In a few days probably I shall be at an Artillery school.—I could not write. Things were too damnably confused & uncertain. Now I feel at ease again. I wanted a change. In the Siege artillery I shall get it. Nobody perhaps is quite as pleased as I am myself & shall be when I am gazetted.

Scott-James is in camp now—a recruit, 3 weeks old.[1] So is Blanco-White. Another discovery is an old college acquaintance just back from 10 years in California.

Of course writing is at an end for a time, has been impossible for a month. But I am pleased with the news of the anthology. I have looked at *Form*. It seems an ugly tasteless mess. If I can think of it, I will send you my copy. I wish I could bring it. But by September I might be preparing for France. It is possible! I dare not *expect* to see you. If I have leave now it will be short & I shall have to work through it. My mathematics are far short of what I shall need for the big guns. I believe they are the biggest.

Nash had to go after all.[2] He is packed off to a Cadet school at Denham near his father's house, where he will be turned into an infantry officer. Nothing disturbs him, but I am afraid he must have been annoyed. You are quite right about him. He is most uncommonly charming but he carries it to excess with friends who occasionally deserve better. I shall miss him & John Wheatley & one or two others, but I would not be the last to go. I might have stayed on with the permanent staff but I have had first too comfortable, & then too uncomfortable a job. I can't imagine regretting the change whatever the end is.

I saw Guthrie for a night a month ago. He was the same as ever, with an inclination to take an art mastership at Cheltenham.

[1] ET was a regular contributor to *The New Weekly*, edited by R. A. Scott-James (March–August, 1914). Blanco-White is G. R. Blanco-White, Q.C.
[2] Paul Nash. See two letters from Nash to GB in *Poet and Painter*, edited by C. C. Abbott and Anthony Bertram, 1953, pp. 82 and 88.

I wish I could see Frost's poems. Were you reminding me of my inspiration when you said *he* showed the influence of *my* things?[1] I couldn't help thinking it possible.

If I am not available, will you correct my proofs for me when the time comes?

Goodbye. My love to Emily.

Yours ever Edward Thomas

171

14 August 1916   *Steep*

My dear Gordon,

I have been upset by vaccination & came here till tomorrow. May be I shall have a few days at the month's end before going to my new unit—which has been put off, you see. I am still at Hut 3, Hare Hall Camp, till then. But I might go any time. Suppose I should be free in a week or in a fortnight would a wire to you be warning enough? I should so like it. But you must tell me if it is impossible. You will have seen *Form* by now, I hope. At least I posted it. We are preparing for our move. I am burning & selling more books.[2] I thought I should be accused of making a beacon for Zeppelins last night, I had such a huge bonfire at 10. We are thinking of a cottage at High Beech, very close to my old Autumn camp. It is a restless time. I was cleared out of my study on the hill 2 months ago. All anchors will be up soon, & I don't know where to look for good days beyond tomorrow. Goodbye to you & Emily, with love from all of us.

Yours ever Edward Thomas

172

2 October 1916   Royal Artillery Barracks, Trowbridge, Wiltshire

My dear Gordon,

I am very much behind with you now, & I am very sorry, but I

---

[1] No: I was not. [*GB*]

[2] Prior to the family's move to High Beech, Essex. At the same time ET burned most of the letters from his friends including those from GB, de la Mare, and E. Garnett.

have no time at all now.[1] From 6 a.m. to 7.30 p.m. except for meals, I am being lectured to about levers & pulleys & fuses etc. Then after the last meal I have a hopeless amount to read up on the subjects of the day. We practically can't leave barracks except on Saturday afternoon & Sunday, because we have to change from our working uniform to our cadet uniform before we go out. It is school again & I am far from the top of the class, which of course I don't like any the more for knowing that I really can't work wholeheartedly at such subjects. Incidentally the teaching is improvised & atrocious. We have therefore to teach ourselves bits of hydraulics etc.

In a fortnight I shall have to pass a test & if I get through, my commission will come along a month later: if I don't I have to fall back into another class & have another shot later. I don't see how I can pass: at the same time very few do fail & I feel I oughtn't to be amongst them.

Well, now, I may get some leave after I am gazetted: I may get some more before going out. All I can say is I will try to come to you in one of these periods if I get them. But there is my new cottage to see (they move in next week) at High Beech & my Mother in London I must see as often as possible. She has had an operation for cataract & I don't think it was successful. She is very lonely, with all of us away. Not that she complains.

I have just seen Steep for the last time. I had 15 hours there, & having to leave in the middle of the morning to catch the only Sunday train, & finding myself with time in hand I have been walking for a few hours & am now at an inn resting. This is the county where I stayed when I was writing *Swinburne* & I am going to call at the farmhouse on my way back to barracks.

So the *Annual* is beginning to be. I really believe I shall have to ask you to see the proofs. I will look at them but I can't be careful over them as I should wish. The question is whether you or I should see them first. Perhaps you should—if you would. Have you by any chance a list of my pieces? Because there may be a volume published[2] some time & I don't want to use any from the *Annual*, of course, before the year is up. If you see

[1] For some details of ET's life in August and September, see *EF*, pp. 207–14. He spent the period 21 August–21 September as a cadet at the Royal Artillery School, Handel St., W.C., and moved to Trowbridge for artillery practice on 22 September.

[2] Edward Eastaway, *Poems*, 1917. See *REP*, pp. 241–5, and Letter 169, note 3.

Trevelyan would you ask him for a list? He said he was going to see you soon. My safest address is

13 Rusham Rd, Balham SW.

Goodbye My love to you & Emily
                                    Yours ever Edward Thomas

173

Post mark: Trowbridge. 9 p.m. 27 Oct. 1916 [1]

Friday   *Royal Artillery Barracks, Trowbridge*

My dear Gordon,
    I thought it was I that owed you a letter. You sent me another card suggesting a time again for coming to you. I couldn't come. Later on I did have some days & I actually got a pass to Carnforth, but Helen had just moved & I went to the new house to help her settle in. [2] The address now is

High Beech, nr Loughton, Essex.

Here I have been 5 weeks & here I expect to be another 3 weeks. Then I may be an officer & from all accounts I may be going out soon after. I can't promise to come to you before, because I must spend any leave I do get before going out, in buying things & seeing the last of my family & my people.
    Thank you very much for promising to help me with my proofs. [3] I ought to be in England till well into December. By that time I may know about the proposed book of my verses [4]— thank you for telling me what those are which are to come into the *Annual*.
    This is country I know & I have seen something of it, but the work is very hard & long & the conditions uncomfortable & I can only look forward to a change of some sort. There is some company here, but almost no leisure, & at last I can't write any

[1] GB's insertion.
[2] See *WWE*, pp. 170–1 and 176–7.
[3] Of his poems in *An Annual of New Poetry*.
[4] Edward Eastaway, *Poems*, 1917.

more than I can read. Scott James is here, & one or two others.[1]
But away from here I can only see my family or anyone who
comes down to High Beech, which is in a beautiful part of
Epping Forest—you can't believe how perfect the illusion is
except on a fine Saturday or Sunday when the crowd comes out.
  Goodbye. My love to Emily
                              Yours ever Edward Thomas

174

TABERNACLE MEN'S INSTITUTE

6 November 1916   *Royal Artillery Barracks, Trowbridge*

My dear Gordon,
  If I get leave, as I hope, on Saturday week, I will come to you
on Monday though I must leave on Wednesday. I haven't a
timetable but any good train after 2 I would take. If you know
for certain & are writing please mention it. This will be my
address till Friday. After that for a week from the 13th it will be

        R.G.A., Wanstrow, Somerset.

Or High Beech.
  My love to Emily,
                              Yours ever Edward Thomas[2]

175

POSTCARD

Wanstrow Somerset,[3]

As far as I can see I shall come by the 2 if it runs, on Monday.

[1] See Letter 170, note 1, and a letter (dated 12 November 1916) in *EF*, pp. 219–22:
'Oh, Granville Barker is in my room now, but is just being shunted off to a school
for Coast Defence. I suppose his friends have urged his country not to risk his
life. I hope I shall always be as eager to risk mine as I have these last few months.'
[2] A typescript of 'The Child in the Orchard' with this. [*GB*] ET also wrote
'Lights Out', 'The Trumpet', and 'The Long Small Room' in the first half of
December. See *EF*, pp. 217–22.
[3] Postmark is 15 November. His leave began on the following Saturday and 'may
last anything from a week to a month. After Sunday with my mother I am going
up to see Gordon Bottomley. I shall be at home probably from the Thursday
(23rd) onwards.' See *EF*, p. 221.

I shall know for certain on Saturday & I will then send you another card if I make sure of the train. Otherwise, expect me if you do not hear again.

E.T.

This weekend I shall be at
13 Rusham R^d, Balham SW.

176

POSTCARD

Sunday[1]   *13 Rusham R^d, Balham SW.*

It is all right. I intend to catch the 2 tomorrow. I think I can stay till Thursday morning, though unfortunately my leave is indefinite & I might be wired for at any time. Thank you for your card here.

E.T.

*   *   *

ET came for his last days with us here on 20 November 1916, and stayed until the 23rd.

I have no written record of that time, but the memory of them is still vivid and new. There was talk and music, and he sang (he always sang when he came to us): beside his folk-songs he had acquired a riotous collection of army-songs, which he sang with a mischievous quietness that made the rowdy ones much funnier even than they were meant to be. He went one or two long walks with my wife; at other times he sat with me in my open garden-house. One afternoon we spent a long time indoors watching a marvellous storm gather about Ill Bell and High Street and come sweeping down Kentmere and the estuary: the cross-lights among the dark veils were unearthly: he said reflectively 'You are lucky.' I replied 'What, with my health?' He was silent for an appreciable time, then said still more quietly. 'Yes.'

When he had gone some days he sent us his poem 'The Sheiling' a quintessence of all his days here (including that unearthly storm).

While he was here I asked him why he had chosen to ask for a commission in the artillery, when that might be thought to be the professional soldier's particular province, with its special training and special risks. He replied 'To get a larger pension for Helen.'

[1] Postmark is 19 November 1916.

He left us by the early train, so that I could not be up to see him off and we all breakfasted in my room. My wife went to the station with him: the last I knew of him was his voice and the sound of his feet under my window. 'Good-bye—Good-bye, Gordon.'

He would reach London about tea-time. He slept that night at John Freeman's,[1] *who said that he arrived at his door with a copy of* Cymbeline *in his hand. Freeman understood that he had set out with it from here and had carried it all day, but had never begun to read it.*[2]

25 March 1936   **GB**

*   *   *

177

About December 1st 1916[3]   *High Beech, Loughton*

My dear Gordon,

Thank you for everything. I shall be glad if you will do as you suggest. I had no red ink so I have left *my* corrections in pencil in the hope that you had some.[4] I will send them with the booklet on Keats under another cover.[5] With that I send my very latest verses in which I suspect you will more readily detect heart than art, to speak Wilcoxically.[6]

I am still at liberty, but spending it at present in preparing my book of verses for 'Selwyn & Blount'—64 pp., but I find I can get a lot into 64 pp.[7] We have fine days at last. But I shall always remember those 2 days with you that weren't particularly fine

---

[1] See Letter 161, note 5.

[2] See letter (dated 23 November 1916) to Eleanor Farjeon: 'I enjoyed every hour at Silverdale and then went and wrote something about the house there, which I will try to copy tomorrow morning before we go over to see my mother and the John Freemans (till Saturday morning).' *EF*, p. 223.

[3] GB's insertion.

[4] Presumably, these are corrections to the proofs of his poems in *An Annual of New Poetry*.

[5] *Keats*, 1916.

[6] With this came his poem 'The Sheiling'—the very essence of his days with us referred to above, and his last days here. [*GB.*] The reference is to Ella Wheeler Wilcox whose poetry he had placed ironically on a level with Shakespeare in a famous review. See *EF*, p. 46.

[7] First printed October 1917, reprinted November and December 1917. The volume contained 64 poems which are the first 64 poems in *CP*. See Letter 172, note 2.

275

& couldn't have been better however fine. When I have something to tell you I will, & I hope some day to come & tell you more than I may write. Goodbye. My love to you both.

Yours ever Edward Thomas

178

11 December 1916   *R.A. Mess, Tin Town, Lydd, Kent*

My dear Gordon,

I am so glad you liked the verses. I shall include them in the book.[1] It will probably be published while I am out. At least it seems likely I shall go out very soon, possibly before Xmas. But till Saturday I shall not know anything for certain. I am not yet allotted to a battery. I might stay on here with a battery in training or I might go home for my last leave. So High Beech will be the safest address after Saturday. I will tell you my news when I have any.

All your queries were sound. 'Mabinogion' it should be—just the substantive used adjectivally.[2] I sent the changes in to Constable & I hope they will make them.

Yes I am commissioned now. In fact I am in every way ready to go. I wonder will it be Salonica. But it is a worse gamble than ever now everywhere. My love to Emily & please thank her for her letter.

Yours ever Edward Thomas

179

5 January 1917   *244 Siege Battery, Tin Town, Lydd, Kent*

My dear Gordon,

I haven't long to wait. We go out at the end of the month with six-inch howitzers & I am just going home for my last leave. Then tomorrow week we leave here for Codford on Salisbury Plain to get our guns & stores. Well, there is not much to say except that I hope we shall often meet again & after a not very

[1] See Letter 177, notes 6 and 7. 'The Sheiling' was included in *Poems*, 1917.
[2] See stanza 9 in 'Roads', *CP*, p. 164.

long interval. We have done our shooting & except for the critical audience I did not mind it at all. It is amusing to be a 'Young Officer' hauled over the coals by the Commandant for a quite imaginary offence. It will be a change to be in France & be judged simply by what one does or doesn't do. I have a good pair of fieldglasses & my ears can stand the racket, so I can only fail because I couldn't succeed. I have practically no chance of promotion. I shall first handle a Section of two guns & take it in turns to go to the trenches to observe. Give my love to Emily.

Yours ever Edward Thomas 2nd Lieut.

180

26 February 1917 [1]   *Arras* ? [1]

My dear Gordon,
   The gramophone here was playing 'Anitra's Dance' & other things from Grieg yesterday—& in the evening one Officer (named Berrington) was talking about Georgian Poets. So at last I will write a little. It isn't all Grieg & Poetry here. The old city I am in was shelled today. The village I went to for some map work was under shell & machine gun fire, & returning I was within 3 yards of being shot by one of our own guns. Worst of all was the din between 8.15 & 9.30 this morning when our Artillery was covering a raid—the prisoners arrived by 10. I can't pretend to enjoy it, but it does not interfere with the use of fieldglasses & compass though it stops conversation!
   It was not our Corps that was doing it so we felt no special interest.
   My address is 244 Siege Battery but for the present I am 3 miles away at the headquarters of a Heavy Artillery Group to which I have been lent. Before coming here I did a little firing & more observing & plenty of supervision of digging in & other preparations. [2] Observing is what I like & I am very anxious to

---

[1] Date and address added by GB. ET sailed to France on 29 January and arrived at his battery's position in the front line at Dainville, close to Arras, on 5 February. For other details, see *JM*, pp. 252–5, *EF*, pp. 246–52, and Mark Severn, *The Gambardier*, 1930.

[2] His battery fired for the first time on 14 February. By 21 February he had been transferred to Group HQ (in Arras); he rejoined his battery, a few hundred

get back to a more physically active life than I lead here as a sort of Adjutant.

We have been out a month but it took us over a week to crawl up to the front on snowy roads & sleeping in trains & tents & other cold places. But I enjoyed most of it. I like the country we are in. It is open hilly chalk country with great ploughed fields & a few copses on the hilltops. The ruined villages of brick & thatch & soft white stone have been beautiful. Of course one does not stroll about here, but the incidental walks to Observation Posts or up to see my battery are often very pleasant, both in the frost & in the sunny weather which has begun at last.

It is hard to keep warm—we are in a big modern house with only one shell hole in it & a few bullet holes in the windows—but we have only the fuel that can be stolen from the ruins & with arctic clothing on we are seldom warm indoors. Still, I get used to this & I don't read or write. I hear my proofs are going through.[1] I hope the *Annual* will come along to me. I shall read that.

One gets—I mean I get—along moderately well, or even more, with all sorts of uncongenial people, & I have nothing to complain of except lack of letters & parcels. They take a week to come out, & we had none for 3 weeks. So far I have not met anyone I know among all the officers I say good morning to in these streets or out in the country. In a month or so we shall be too busy to think about anything else, but at present we are comparatively quiet just here.[2]

Give my love to Emily & to Lascelles when you see him

Yours ever Edward Thomas

181

23 March ⌈*GB*⌉   *Péronne*?[3]

My dear Gordon,

I will write again while I can a little. Things are moving now

---

yards south of the village of Achicourt, on 9 March. See *JM*, pp. 256–7, *EF*, pp. 250–5, and *The Gambardier*, p. 127.

[1] The proofs of *Poems*, 1917, were read by John Freeman and Eleanor Farjeon.
[2] The next full-scale 'attack' began on 4 April.
[3] GB's guess; probably Achicourt.

& we move too. I have not long come back from 24 hours in our new front line. It was dirty wet & cold & I could only stand & mark the flashes of enemy guns at night, which was my business. Afterwards I slept 16 hours for the first time in my life. It taught me several things that others knew before. It made me cease to be alarmed by shells that could not harm me, for example, though they came over 20 or 30 a minute all night. They were flying home to a village that we used to fire at till this last move, a fascinating ghostly village of stark trees & ruins which I shall probably soon be sleeping in.[1] It was beautiful coming down to the city in sunshine & seeing the old ruined Town Hall like a thick white smoke just *beginning* to curl. Crossing the old No Man's Land crowded like a race course after a race, I couldn't take seriously the few small shells thrown at the working parties. Oh, I did eat & rest & sleep. Firing at night is a thing I still find not easy, counting the rounds & keeping the guns right every now & then. We seem to do little but are responsible for all.

Yesterday it was sunny & mild. Today it is cold & snows at times. I have forgotten what it is to have a window open except in my bedroom—I still have a bedroom in a house that has escaped. We never have enough fuel. We are not like the infantry who can find fuel in the barest trench & dig a hole in an hour & snore in it in an hour & a quarter. I never knew discomfort before or cold. Still I survive it. I left that chateau in the city 2 weeks ago, thank goodness.[2] The Sergeant Major was killed in his office next day. I am glad the battle is not to be fought mainly in the city, though it is being to some extent.

Fear too, I have discovered—to that point where the worst moment is when you find you have survived & that all your fear was useless. You screw yourself up for a second to bear anything & nothing comes—except a curious disappointment which I suppose is also relief. Sometimes at night I have been in this state a hundred times, but partly through inexperience, not knowing what might mean harm. Still, I shall never like the shell that flaps as it falls, or the one that suddenly bounces into hearing & in a second is bursting far off—no sooner does it open the

[1] Beauraims, near Arras, according to *JM*, p. 266.
[2] See Letter 180, note 2.

gate than it is right in the door, or even the small one that complains & whimpers & is called a 'pipsqueak' or a 'whizzbang', & flies into that ghastly village all night long like flights of humming birds.

I drew a good deal last week, but the ground I drew is ours now, so that it will merely be a memento, if it does survive.

I wish I could have some good things on the gramophone, but the best the Mess will tolerate are Ambrose Thomas's 'Gavotte' from *Mignon* played by the Philarmonic Quartette (which includes my Welsh viola-player[1]), and *John Peel*, and Chopin's *Berceuse*. Most of the rest is awful stuff that needs a lot of whisky to match, & I don't drink whisky—or anything else now but tea & coffee. We are a rum crowd of Eton, Scotland (Stranraer), Jew, Cockney & rich Glasgow, & me. So I don't think I dare suggest any revolution on the gramophone. It was at Headquarters they had a good deal of *Peer Gynt*.—I conclude I don't quite want *friends* here. I should be too introspective or too happy to meet the circumstance. And yet all sorts of things do make me happy—villages, the city in ruins, the larks in the bloody dirty dawn, the partridges, the magpies floating about among shellfire & once a bat, & a hundred different houses, in city, suburb, & village.

I hear now that America wants my verses & *Poetry* has taken some. Frost wants me to surrender my pseudonymity but I am not doing so. Of course I can't think of writing here & only keep the briefest of diaries. But I want to see the *Annual*. I hear Hodgson's poems are to come out.[2] I should like to see them. I should also like to hear that Abercrombie had either begun writing or had got over his impatience at not being able to. Why should he write now? Not because Gibson does, I suppose. I haven't met anybody out here yet who connected me with home. I don't think of home. I never did have pictures on the wall since I was 1.

Goodbye. My love to Emily. Yours ever

Edward Thomas

---

[1] Raymond Jeremy, later a member of the Music Department at Aberystwyth University College of Wales, with whose family ET had stayed at Laugharne. See Letter 182.

[2] Ralph Hodgson, *Poems*, 1917.

182

4 April 1917[1]

My dear Gordon,
    Your letter of the 28th of March has just come.[2] Letters are always a week old by the time they reach me. I think I had better

---

[1] GB's insertion.
[2] This letter, the only surviving letter from GB to ET, was discovered in May 1967 among some personal effects belonging to ET, which had been returned to Helen Thomas in April 1917, and is here printed in full:

28 March 1917   *The Shieling, Silverdale, near Carnforth, England.*

My dear Edward,
    We were happy with your letter last night. There is no afternoon post now, but just before supper the maid came in from the village with some letters which had come in a belated bag. So we had a pretty surprise, and we read it in the corner where you sat when you were here, in the small bright light of a lamp shaded so as to leave all the hinterland of our lighthouse-room in darkness.
    We too were glad you did not stay at the chateau.
    You made us see inconceivable things vividly. I need not tell you how keenly we look for your letters, which we devour and praise for being all that the usual photographies of the war-correspondents are not.
    I have nothing worth while to write you in reply. I still live the life of a vegetable, and I have not the vegetable's one virtue of being edible. Estimated as calories I am negligible. This is only a note in haste to tell you that the *Annual* is out. I asked Trevelyan to send your copy direct to France, but he had just sent it to Loughton. So I hope you have received it ere now. Trevelyan said he would write and tell you himself.
    The *Annual* seems to be selling. Lady A. Egerton likes Eastaway and wants to know who he is: but I won't tell her unless you say I may.
    There are no reviews yet, but I enclose the *Times Lit. Suppl.* 'Books Received' notice.
    I am glad to hear about 'Poetry'. Harriet is worth while for she promptly hands out drafts on Lloyd's Bank Ltd., regardless of expense.
    I often meditate as to what unknown process of nature and machination of Providence has ordained that the founders of poetry magazines should be called Monro(e). This is probably what the Americans mean by the Monroe Doctrine.
    Tell me if you haven't got the *Annual* and I'll ask somebody about it.
    I can't remember the name of your viola-player, though I feel I know it quite well, and I know the Philharmonic Quartette records too. They are very well performed, and there is one of Boccherini's *Minuet* which you would like better than the *Mignon*, and which at the same time your companions might tolerate. They seem to choose all their records from the 'Master's Voice' lists; if they could get hold of the Columbia lists too, you would find more interest and variety, beside getting a record on each side of the disc.
    Mrs. Gibson and her baby are staying at The Shiffolds while Wilfrid is in America, so I hear a good deal of news of him. He seems to be having a good deal of success with his readings of his own poems.

write back now just a word as this is the eve,[1] & I can't help realizing that I may not have another opportunity. It is the end of a beautiful sunny day that began cold with snow. The air has been full of aeroplanes & shells & yet there have been clothes hanging up to dry in the sun outside my window which has glass in it, though whether it will tomorrow not even the Hun knows. The servants are chatting outside in their shirtsleeves & war is not for the moment dirty or ugly—as it was this morning, when I was well in front & the shining sun made ruins & rusty barbed wire & dead horses & deep filthy mud uglier than they are in the stormy weather or in the pale cold dawn. I am muddy to the waist now, but not going to change till I go to bed, for we have a big woodfire supplied by the ruins of the neighbouring houses, & today is not a busy one.

I have not seen the *Annual* yet but by the same post as your letter came *The Times* review which I was quite pleased with.[2] I don't mind now being called inhuman & being told by a reviewer now that April's here—in England now—that I am blind to the 'tremendous life of these 3 years'. It would be the one

---

I don't wonder at Abercrombie feeling as he does: it would be one of the few things that I should find definitely unendurable. When he was rejected for the Army, his great desire was to take some other kind of adventurous service, and for a long time he had a definite intention of joining George Trevelyan in Italy and working in a mountain ambulance. But all the time there was the cruel and uncertain threat of disease hanging over his wife, and I suppose he felt he couldn't go until he knew that she was safe. In the meantime the War Office was worrying him to take some form of National Work; so they left their home and came to Liverpool, and he went to work in a shell shop. The weary round of ugliness and repetition in an engineer's shop or any kind of works or office is worse to bear than anything else for someone with such creative energy and vision as his, and (at a guess) I fancy he felt it a hateful and hope-destroying slavery. (I know I would rather die than work in an office again as my Father does; and I am pretty sure, too, that I should feel happier helping to serve a gun than helping to make it.) And it must be beastly to have to return to the provincial town from which one emerged.

I shall try to write again soon, and we shall be more than grateful if we may soon hear again from you. With great love from us both I am

always your Gordon Bottomley.

[1] Of the Battle of Arras. For the entire campaign see *The Times*, Monday 19 March to Tuesday 10 April 1917.

[2] *The Times Literary Supplement*, 29 March 1917, p. 151. 'He is a real poet, with the truth in him. At present, like most of his contemporaries, he has too little control over his eyes. . . . Or is the new method an unconscious survival of a materialism and naturalism which the tremendous life of the last three years has made an absurdity.'

consolation in finishing up out here to provide such reviewers with a conundrum, except that I know they would invent an answer if they saw that it was a conundrum. Why do the idiots accuse me of using my eyes? Must I only use them with field-glasses & must I see only Huns in these beautiful hills eastwards & only hostile flashes in the night skies when I am at the Observation Post?

I think I understand Abercrombie's care & it was silly to expect him to see it as I do as inevitable & right. I hope very much to see him & new work of his some day. I do not know his equal for keenness & warmth. Our ASC driver knows the part of Herefordshire where I saw Frost & Abercrombie & it was a pleasure to talk about those villages though he had only played cricket in them. The fire does not give much light.

But now I can go on a little.

No don't tell anybody about Eastaway tho naturally I want people to want to know who he is.

My Welsh viola-player who played to me all one Easter just 3 years ago was Raymond Jeremy. He was a most charming person with & without his viola. But he had an injury to the drum of his ear which has luckily kept him out of the army.

Goodbye. Yours ever & Emily's

Edward Thomas[1]

183

From Helen Thomas

Post Mark: Battersea S.W. 11.15 p.m. 12 April 1917[2]
High Beech, nr. Loughton, Essex

My dear Emily & Gordon,

I wanted to be the one to tell you that Edward was killed on Easter Monday.

You will know how desolate I feel, in spite of the perfect union of our souls which death only completes. He lives on.

Helen

[1] This was the last letter to GB. ET was killed at his Observation Post on the morning of Easter Monday, 9 April, by a direct hit from a shell. See *EF*, pp. 263–4, for a copy of his Commanding Officer's letter of condolence to Helen Thomas.
[2] GB's insertion.

184

From Eleanor Farjeon

18 April 1917   *C/o Mrs. Edward Thomas,*
            High Beech, Loughton, Essex

Dear Mr. Bottomley,

Helen wants me to write to you. Presently she will herself— she says she will always go on writing to you for Edward. But just now she can't write, and while I am with her I am sending word of and from her to the friends who want to know. Don't think of her as quite prostrate. Often her strength and courage are wonderful, and she is quite resolute against despair, even in the moments when she breaks down. She couldn't sleep at first, but has rested these last two nights. In a couple of weeks she is coming with Baba to our little cottage in Sussex.

She wants me to tell you about our dear Edward. Three days ago she had a letter from the Major of the Battery. He said Edward was killed instantaneously by a fragment of shell while he was in the Observation Post. 'It was in a moment of victory', he said. And Edward could have realized nothing. His body was recovered, and he was buried on the 11th. It is a great peace to Helen to know all this. She is glad to know there's a definite place she can one day sow with the flowers he loved. They will be able to tell her exactly where, and the Major wants to see her when he comes back & tell her anything she wants to know. He spoke much of Edward, very feelingly. He said that in the Battery they looked on him as a sort of Father, because he was the oldest of them, and was always doing all kinds of jobs—anything there was to do—for them, quietly & unassumingly and cheerfully. He spoke too of Edward's old clay pipes, as though that picture of him smoking his old clay had become an indelible one to them out there as it is to us here always. I won't try to write any more about Edward now.—I can't anyhow, I can only give you these details.

There are some things you ask about Helen wants me to write of. She would be so glad if you can write something about Edward. What his friends desire to write of him will mean a lot to her. I will tell you what we know of so far. John Freeman had a beautiful paragraph in last Saturday's *Times*, but that would not clash with the *Literary Supplement*, would it? I believe Squire is doing something for the *New Statesman*, & E. S. P. Haynes an article for *The English Review*. That's all. So far as I know there's nothing done in *The Nation* yet.

As regards the secret of Edward Eastaway, Helen has been thinking deeply. We all know how much he wanted it a secret—from the general public at least, for to all his literary friends it had become such a very open secret—and yet Helen & I feel pretty certain that he did not especially wish it to be a secret always. He wanted the poems to have a chance on their own, unallied with anything people might associate with his name. But then he expected to be carrying on the work of Edward Eastaway until it had—or hadn't—proved itself. After which the name wouldn't matter. Now that work can't be carried on, and if there is any moment at which Edward may own those poems for his own, Helen thinks it is this. And I agree with her, though we are all pulled by that knowledge of his desire for anonymity. But I think you're right in suggesting that that does not apply now, & that Edward should come into his own.[1] You know since he began to write poetry I have typed it nearly all for him, & with John Freeman have revised the proofs of this book.—It was good of you to offer to help Helen with the proofs. There's much unpublished work still that may presently be collected. And Helen will be glad of advice & help, and is so grateful for your offer, and for your letter & your wife's.

Sincerely yours, Eleanor Farjeon[2]

[1] And in fact we find that Edward's father announced his identity with Edward Eastaway in *The Times* Obituary notice. The secret is hardly possible to preserve now. (EF's note.)

[2] This letter from Eleanor Farjeon was included in the bundle of letters from ET given by GB to the Cardiff University College and is reprinted here by kind permission of her literary executor.

APPENDIX

Books by ET, Including Posthumous Publications

THE following list contains all the works by ET published in book form in Great Britain; it is essentially a booklist and not a complete bibliographical study. Unless otherwise stated, the place of publication was London; for American editions the reader is referred to *RPE*, Part II, pp. 185–277. The question of reprints and further editions of ET's books is extremely complicated and I have merely attempted to indicate significant reprints, the inclusion of some books in new series, and any change of publishers.

1 *The Woodland Life*, William Blackwood and Sons, Edinburgh and London, two editions, 1897.

2 *Horae Solitariae*, Duckworth and Co., 1902.

3 *The Poems of John Dyer* (Number 4 of *The Welsh Library*, edited by Owen M. Edwards), edited by ET, T. Fisher Unwin, 1903.

4 *Oxford* (*Black's Colour Book Series*), painted by John Fulleylove, R.I., described by ET, with 60 illustrations, A. and C. Black, 1903. Reprinted, 1911; revised, with 32 illustrations, 1922.

5 *Rose Acre Papers* (Number 2, *The Lanthorn Series*), S. C. Brown, Langham and Co. Ltd., 1904.

6 *Beautiful Wales* (*Black's Colour Book Series*), painted by Robert Fowler, R.I., described by ET, with a Note on Mr. Fowler's Land-scapes by Alex J. Finberg, and with 74 illustrations, A. and C. Black, 1905. Second edition, entitled *Wales* and with 32 illustra-tions, 1924.

7 *The Heart of England*, with 48 coloured illustrations by H. L. Richardson, J. M. Dent and Co., 1906. Second edition (in *The Heart of England Series*), 1909; third edition (in *The Open Air Library*), with a Foreword and 10 wood-engravings by Eric Fitch Daglish 1932 and 1934.

8 George Borrow (Number 151 of *Everyman's Library*), *The Bible in Spain*, with an Introduction by ET, J. M. Dent and Co., 1906.

9 *The Pocket Book of Poems and Songs for the Open Air*, compiled by ET (with musical notes), E. Grant Richards, 1907. Second edition (Number 97 of *The Travellers' Library*), Jonathan Cape, 1928.

10 *The Book of the Open Air*, edited by ET, Hodder and Stoughton, 1907.

11 *British Country Life in Spring and Summer, The Book of the Open Air*, edited by ET, Hodder and Stoughton, 1907.

12 *British Country Life in Autumn and Winter, The Book of the Open Air*, edited by ET, Hodder and Stoughton, 1908.

13 *Some British Birds*, reprinted from *The Book of the Open Air*, edited by ET, Hodder and Stoughton, 1908.

14 *British Butterflies and other Insects*, reprinted from *The Book of the Open Air*, edited by ET, Hodder and Stoughton, 1908.

15 George Herbert, *The Temple* and *A Priest to The Temple* (Number 309 of *Everyman's Library*), with an Introduction by ET, J. M. Dent and Co., 1908.

16 *Richard Jefferies, His Life and Work*, Hutchinson and Co., 1909. Second edition. 1911.

17 *The Plays and Poems of Christopher Marlowe* (Number 383 of *Everyman's Library*), with an Introduction by ET, J. M. Dent and Co., 1909.

18 Richard Jefferies, *The Hills and the Vales*, with an Introduction by ET, Duckworth and Co., 1909.

19 *The South Country* (in *The Heart of England Series*), J. M. Dent and Co., 1909. Second edition (Number 12 of *The Aldine Library*), with an Introduction by Helen Thomas, J. M. Dent and Sons Ltd., 1932.

20 *Windsor Castle* (*Beautiful England Series*), described by ET, pictured by E. W. Haslehurst, Blackie and Son Ltd., 1910; as Volume One of *Our Beautiful Homeland Series*, 1919.

21 *Rest and Unrest* (*The Roadmender Series*), Duckworth and Co., 1910.

22 *Feminine Influence on the Poets*, Martin Secker, 1910.

23 *Rose Acre Papers, Including Essays from Horae Solitariae* (*The Roadmender Series*), Duckworth and Co., 1910.

24 *Light and Twilight*, Duckworth and Co., 1911.

25 Isaac Taylor, *Words and Places in Illustration of History, Ethnology and Geography* (Number 517 of *Everyman's Library*), with an Introduction by ET, J. M. Dent and Co., 1911.

26 *Maurice Maeterlinck*, Methuen, 1911. Second and third editions, 1912 and 1915.

27 *The Tenth Muse* (Number 2 of *The Coronal Series*), Martin Secker, 1911.

Reissued 1916 and, with a memoir of ET by John Freeman, 1917.

28 *Celtic Stories*, Oxford at the Clarendon Press, 1911. Second and third editions, 1913 and 1918.

29 *The Isle of Wight* (*Beautiful England Series*), pictured by Ernest Haslehurst, described by ET, Blackie & Son, 1911; as Volume Two in *Our Beautiful Homeland Series*, Blackie & Son, 1919.

30 *Lafcadio Hearn* (*Modern Biographies Series*), Constable and Co., 1912.

31 *Norse Tales*, Oxford at the Clarendon Press, 1912. Second edition, 1921.

32 William Cobbett, *Rural Rides*, 2 vols., (Numbers 638 and 639 of *Everyman's Library*), with an Introduction by ET, J. M. Dent and Co., 1912.

33 *The Pocket George Borrow* (*Authors for the Pocket Series*), passages chosen from the works of Borrow by ET, Chatto and Windus, 1912.

34 *Algernon Charles Swinburne, A Critical Study*, Martin Secker, 1912.

35 *George Borrow, The Man and his Books*, Chapman and Hall, 1912.

36 *The Country* (*Fellowship Books Series*), B. T. Batsford, 1913.

37 *The Icknield Way*, with illustrations by A. L. Collins, Constable and Co. Ltd., 1913. Second and third editions, 1916 and 1929.

38 *The Happy-Go-Lucky Morgans*, Duckworth and Co., 1913.

39 *Walter Pater, A Critical Study*, Martin Secker, 1913.

40 *In Pursuit of Spring*, with Illustrations from Drawings by Ernest Haslehurst, Thomas Nelson and Son, 1914.

41 George Borrow, *The Zincali, An Account of the Gipsies of Spain* (Number 697 of *Everyman's Library*), with an Introduction by ET, J. M. Dent and Co., 1914.

42 *Four-and-Twenty Blackbirds*, Duckworth and Co., 1915.

43 *The Life of The Duke of Marlborough*, Chapman and Hall, 1915.

44 *This England, An Anthology from her Writers*, compiled by ET, Oxford University Press, 1915.

45 *Keats* (Number 126 of *The People's Books*), T. C. and E. C. Jack, 1916. Second edition, 1926.

46 *The Flowers I Love*, a series of twenty-four drawings in colour by Katherine Cameron, with an anthology of Flower Poems selected by ET, T. C. and E. C. Jack, 1916.

47 *Six Poems*, by Edward Eastaway, The Pear Tree Press, Flansham, Sussex, 1916.

48 *An Annual of New Poetry*, Constable and Co. Ltd., 1917 (contains 18 poems by Edward Eastaway).

49 *A Literary Pilgrim in England*, Methuen and Co., 1917. Second edition (Number 95 of *The Travellers' Library*), Jonathan Cape, 1928.

50 *Poems*, by Edward Eastaway, Selwyn and Blount, 1917.

51 *Last Poems*, Selwyn and Blount, 1918.

52 *Collected Poems*, with a Foreword by Walter de la Mare, Selwyn and Blount Ltd., 1920. New Edition, Ingpen and Grant, 1928. Fourth Edition, Faber and Faber Ltd., 1936.

53 *Cloud Castle and other Papers*, with a Foreword by W. H. Hudson, Duckworth and Co., 1922.

54 *Two Poems*, Ingpen and Grant, 1927.

55 *The Last Sheaf, Essays by Edward Thomas*, with a Foreword by Thomas Seccombe, Jonathan Cape, 1928.

56 *The Childhood of Edward Thomas*, a fragment of autobiography with a Preface by Julian Thomas, Faber and Faber, 1938.

57 *The Friend of the Blackbird* [written by ET in October 1911], The Pear Tree Press, Flansham, Sussex, 1938.

INDEX

Abbott, Claude Colleer, 2, 198 n., 231 n.
Abercrombie, Lascelles (1881–1938), 4, 177, 232, 239 n., 259; ET and, 31, 235, 238, 241, 246, 253, 254, 257, 260; ET on, 157–8, 195, 233, 239, 280, 283; Dixon Scott and, 184 n.; *Mary and the Bramble*, 212; *Emblems of Love*, 214; *End of the World*, 235, 257; Pound and, 235, 236; and Frost, 240; and ET's poetry, 253; *An Annual of New Poetry*, 253, 260; GB on, 282
Abercrombie, Mrs. Lascelles, and ET, 241, 260; ill, 147, 282
Academy, The, 84, 95, 96, 97, 99, 101, 111, 116, 125
Allingham, William (1824–89), 120
An Annual of New Poetry, 271, 272 n., 275 n., 278, 280
Artists' Rifles, ET enlists in, 32, 252
Asquith, Elizabeth, her poetry readings, 265, 267
Asquith, Raymond (1878–1916), 54 n.
Aumonier, Gertrude, 230 n.
Aumonier, Stacey, 230 n.

Bailey, J. C., 103 n.
Bailey, L. W., 100 n.
Baillie, John, 53 n., 56, 58, 66
Balmer, Clinton, 58 n.; ET wants to meet, 68; ET and, 70, 71, 76, 90–1, 92, 99, 139; illustrates GB's books, 70 n.; Ransome and, 97
Baring-Gould, Sabine (1834–1924), *A Book of South Wales*, 84 n., 86; 'All round my hat', 127
Barker, Harley Granville, *see* Granville-Barker, Harley
Barmby, Beatrice, *Gísli Súrsson*, 43
Barnes, William (1800–86), 120, 179
Bax, Sir Arnold Trevor (1883–1953), 224
Bax, Clifford (1886–1962), ET and, 29, 30, 221, 232 n.; ET on, 224; *Some I Knew Well*, 224 n.
Baynes, Godwin, 29, 221
Beardsley, Aubrey (1872–98), 65; supposed resemblance between ET and, 66
Beaumont, Francis (*c.* 1584–1616), 43

Bedales, 25, 26, 132; Helen teaches at, 27; Mervyn at, 27, 130 n.; Thomases hope to live near, 109; Mervyn and Bronwen at, 228; Thomases to leave area, 242; Muirhead Bone's children at, 256 n.
Beddoes, Thomas Lovell (1803–49), 115, 147 n.
Begley, Walter, 42 n.
Belloc, Joseph Hilaire Pierre (1870–1953), 25, 53 n., 54 n., 135; and ET, 11, 27, 60, 106; ET on, 106 n.; and ET's anthology, 116; and *The Heart of England*, 117; literary editor of *Morning Post*, 131 n.; *The Historic Thames*, 140 n.; *Old Road*, 207
Berridge, Jesse, 94 n., 97 n., 135 n., 257 n.; ET and, 4, 11, 32, 89, 258; ET sends his sonnets to GB, 44; and *Feminine Influence on the Poets*, 202 n.; ET cycling with, 248 n., 250 n., 251
Bertram, Anthony, 2 n., 231 n.
Besant, Sir Walter (1836–1901), *The Eulogy of Richard Jefferies*, 137; ET on, 154
Bettany, W. A. Lewis, 88
Binyon, Robert Laurence (1869–1943), 128 n.; *London Visions*, 175
Birds: nightingales, 77, 80, 86, 108, 110, 111, 267; owls, 170; at twilight, 197; ET on pigeons, 193; the cuckoo, 212; ET on birds among shellfire, 280
Blake, William (1757–1827), 126; *The Lyrical Poems of Blake*, 104; de Selincourt and, 184; Sturge Moore's study of, 200 n.; ET on, 204
Bond, R. Warwick, 42
Bone, Sir Muirhead (1876–1953), 53 n.; ET and, 25, 143, 144, 204, 256; and illustrations for *South Country*, 175, 177; financial matters, 199
Bookman, The, Ransome's article on ET for, 131; ET reviews for, 147
Borrow, George Henry (1803–81), 215; and *The Heart of England*, 107; ET's proposed biography of, 146
Bottomley, Emily, 2; a devoted wife, 3; ET writes to thank, 105–6; ET and, 152

PRINTED IN GREAT BRITAIN BY
W. & J. MACKAY & CO LTD, CHATHAM